Contents

Reading: The General Training module — **Skills and strategies** — **IELTS test practice**

Writing

CAMBRIDGE

New Insight into IELTS

VANESSA JAKEMAN AND CLARE MCDOWELL

Student's Book

WITH ANSWERS

CAMBRIDGE
UNIVERSITY PRESS

CAMBRIDGE UNIVERSITY PRESS

Cambridge, New York, Melbourne, Madrid, Cap⌐ ⌐, Singapore, São Paulo, Delhi

Cambridge University Press
The Edinburgh Building, Cambridge CB2 8RU, UK

www.cambridge.org
Information on this title: www.cambridge.org/9780521680899

First published 1999
Updated edition 2001
Third edition 2008
Reprinted 2009

Printed in the United Kingdom at the University Press, Cambridge

A catalogue record for this publication is available from the British Library

ISBN 978-0-521-68089-9 Student's Book with answers
ISBN 978-0-521-68092-9 Student's Book Audio CD
ISBN 978-0-521-68095-0 Student's Book Pack
ISBN 978-0-521-68090-5 Workbook with answers
ISBN 978-0-521-68094-3 Workbook Audio CD
ISBN 978-0-521-68096-7 Workbook Pack

Cambridge University Press has no responsibility for the persistence or
accuracy of URLs for external or third-party Internet websites referred to in
this publication, and does not guarantee that any content on such websites is,
or will remain, accurate or appropriate. Information regarding prices, travel
timetables and other factual information given in this work are correct at
the time of first printing but Cambridge University Press does not guarantee
the accuracy of such information thereafter.

Cover design and graphic by Tim Elcock

Speaking

Introduction

Who is this book for?

New Insight into IELTS has been designed as a coursebook for an IELTS preparation course. However, it is equally appropriate as a self-study resource book for students wishing to improve their IELTS skills on their own as it contains helpful advice, sample IELTS material throughout the units and detailed answer keys.

The book is appropriate both for learners seeking to enter an English-speaking university, school or college, as well as for people who may need to provide an IELTS score for the purposes of employment or immigration to an English-speaking country. The book is targeted at students of approximately Band 6 level; however, the earlier units in each section are designed for lower-level learners or students not familiar with the IELTS test format, while later units are intended to stretch stronger candidates beyond their immediate IELTS needs and enhance their language skills overall. The book contains material relevant to both the Academic and General Training modules (see the IELTS test format on page 189).

The Student's Book contains ample classroom-based material for a preparation course of between 40 and 50 hours. When used with the Workbook, which has activities specially designed to supplement each unit in the coursebook, and also a complete Practice Test, the material will last much longer.

Content of the book

The main part of the book is divided into four sections: Listening, Reading, Writing and Speaking, to reflect the format of the test, and these are broken down into manageable units. Each section begins with an overview of the IELTS test and students who work their way through the book will become familiar with all question types and tasks that they are likely to meet in the test. The skills covered are not restricted to test-taking strategies alone but also reflect the broader range of language that students will encounter in an English-speaking environment, whether at university or in the wider community.

The units contain class and pair activities and the opportunity for individual practice. Teachers may choose to work systematically through each section, taking advantage of the graded approach, or, alternatively, select the material to suit their learners' needs as required.

Recording scripts for all the listening content on the *New Insight into IELTS* Student's Book Audio CD are provided. These scripts have been annotated to show where the answers are to be found in the recordings.

A thorough Answer key is provided for all sections of the book. The key provides a framework of support to ensure that students can receive feedback on all activities and exercises undertaken. It includes a selection of model Band 9 answers to a number of the Writing questions. We would like to stress that these model answers represent only a sample of the many possible ways of approaching the Writing tasks, but we hope that learners will find them a useful guide.

The Workbook can be used to expand the units as follow-up work in class or as homework exercises. For students working on their own, it provides further opportunity to practise and consolidate the material covered in each unit.

The Cambridge Learner Corpus provides examples of genuine student errors in the IELTS test and these have been used to build appropriate remedial tasks in *New Insight into IELTS*. The Workbook, in particular, includes exercises focusing on these errors.

The Listening module

When you go to university or move to an English-speaking country, you will have to interact with many different people in a number of situations. The IELTS Listening test is designed to reflect some of these real-world listening situations. The level of difficulty increases through the paper and there is a range of topics and tasks which test your comprehension skills, such as listening for specific information, listening for detail, understanding gist and understanding speaker opinion. As you work your way through the Listening units of this book, you will be introduced to a wide range of IELTS question types and additional exercises to help improve your overall listening strategies.

Listening for IELTS

Listening test format

Section 1	A conversation between two speakers in a social or semi-official context
Section 2	A talk by a single speaker based on a non-academic situation
Section 3	A conversation with up to four speakers based on academic topics or course-related situations
Section 4	A university-style lecture or talk

The Listening test is the first part of the IELTS examination and takes place at the beginning of the day. It consists of four recorded sections, each covering a different type of language and context. There are ten questions in each section and each question carries one mark.

As you hear each recording *once only* it is very important to understand exactly what you are being asked to do in each question. You are given time to read the questions in each part, before you listen. The question types vary; for example, some questions involve completing a form, chart or diagram, others may require you to complete some notes or match some things in a list to what you hear about them. In addition there may be note-taking exercises and multiple choice questions.

You write all your answers on the question paper as you listen. The Listening part of the test takes about 30 minutes. After the recording has finished, you have ten minutes to transfer your answers onto the answer sheet (see page 190).

All aspects of the Listening test, as well as additional skills, are covered in this book.

Listening

1 Orientating yourself to the text

- Who are the speakers?
- Where are they?
- Why are they speaking?

In order to understand what people are saying, it helps to know what their relationship is to each other and why they are speaking. The language they use will depend on this relationship and the situation. Knowing these helps us to anticipate what the speakers are going to talk about.

Predicting the situation

1 Look at pictures **a–d**. Try to work out who the people are, where they are and what they are doing.

2 Look at pictures **a–d** again. Try to imagine what the people are saying. Work with a partner and use some of the words and phrases in the vocabulary box to help you.

Vocabulary	
where?	live
when?	afford
how much?	wait
how long?	arrive
which?	watch
accommodation	time
flights	news
TV channel	suburb
programme	area
problem	bus

3 How did you decide what the people were saying? Compare your ideas with the rest of the class.

4 Look at pictures **a–f**, which show people in different situations. Try to imagine what they are saying.

5 (◌02) You will hear six short conversations. As you listen, complete the first part of the table by matching each conversation to a picture (**a–f**). Then say what the situation is and how many speakers there are.

6 Listen to the conversations again and write the key words that help you understand the situation. If there are two speakers, say whether they know each other or not. Write your answers in the final two columns of the table below.

	Picture	Situation	Number of speakers	Key words	Do the speakers know each other?
1	f	Talk on first day at a college	1	Welcome you ... Introducing the teaching staff	No
2					
3					
4					
5					
6					

7 Look at the set of notes below and say what the topic is.

8 On the right, write what type of words you need to complete the notes.

9 (◌03) Listen and answer questions **1–4**.

Drive from Melbourne to Phillip Island:
- approx **1** .... km
- takes about **2** ....

People go there to:
- observe the **3** .... returning home
- watch seals from **4** .... or through telescopes.

Type of words
1 a number
2 ....
3 ....
4 ....

IELTS Listening test practice | Form-filling

Form-filling is a common IELTS Listening task, particularly in **Section 1**. You often have to provide factual information, including numbers. Use the words on the form as a guide to the information you need to listen for.

10 Work with a partner. Together look at the form below and discuss the situation and the relationship of the speakers. Then discuss what type of answers you need to listen for.

11 ⊚ **04** Listen and answer questions **1–4**.

Complete the form below.
*Write **NO MORE THAN ONE WORD AND/OR A NUMBER** for each answer.*

Hotel Novena
Guest Registration Form

Example	*Answer*
Name of guest:	Matthews
Room:	1 ....
Wake-up call at:	2 ....
Type of breakfast:	3 ....
Payment by:	4 ....

IELTS Listening test practice | Note completion

You often have to complete some notes in the IELTS Listening test. You should read the notes carefully before you listen, to work out what type of words are missing. The vocabulary in the notes can also help you predict the situation.

12 Look at the set of notes below and say what the topic is.

13 On the right, write what type of words you need to complete the notes.

14 ⊚ **05** Listen and answer questions **1–3**.

Complete the notes below.
*Write **NO MORE THAN THREE WORDS AND/OR A NUMBER** for each answer.*

Train now arriving at
1 ....

Meet boys outside station
2 ....

Bring leather jacket.
Bring 3 .... to repay
Charlie.

Type of words
1 a time
2 ....
3 ....

Listening

2 Listening for specific information

- What are the missing words?

- How can we prepare before we listen?

Sometimes when we listen, we are only interested in finding out very specific information such as a date, a time, a name or other details.

We can try to work out what type of words we are listening for. This will help us find the answer.

Predicting what type of words you need

1 Find out information from two other students to complete this questionnaire. Use your own words to form questions (e.g. for *Date of birth* ask, *When were you born?*).

?	Questionnaire	Student 1	Student 2
How	Name		
When	Nationality		
What	Date of birth		
	Telephone number		
Where	Usual wake-up time		
Which	Means of travel to college		

2 You are going to hear five voicemail messages. Say what type of word(s) you need to listen for in each message and write it (them) in the table below.

3 **06** Listen and complete gaps **1–10**.

4 Listen to the recording again and make a note of the words each speaker said which helped you to answer the questions. The first one has been done for you.

Voicemail messages		Type of word	What the speaker said
A	Julia confirming dinner on **1** .... at **2**	day/date time/place	I'm coming for dinner on Friday night
B	**3** .... ready. Cost of repairs **4** $		
C	**5** .... called. Can't get textbook because it is **6**		
D	Dr Boyd is ill with **7** .... New appointment on **8**		
E	Sam rang. **9** .... for Prof. Hall on Saturday. Please ring this number: **10**		

> **Test tip**
> You need to be able to recognise paraphrases, i.e. words which have a similar meaning to those used in the question.

IELTS Listening test practice   **Table completion**

Before you listen

- Look at the words used in the task to help you guess the topic.
- Decide who the speakers are.
- Study the table carefully to work out what type of words are missing.
- Note whether the columns or rows have a heading.
- Note the order of the questions, i.e. do the numbers move across the rows or down the columns?

5 ⏱ Take 30 seconds to look at the table below and then discuss what type of information is missing.

6 🔊07 Listen to the first part of the conversation and answer questions **1–6**.

Test tip

Words included in the table are there to guide you.

Test tip

You must use correct spelling in the Listening test.

Complete the table below.
*Write **NO MORE THAN TWO WORDS AND/OR A NUMBER** for each answer.*

City Aquarium

Type of ticket	Cost	Advantage	Requirements
Adult	1	2	
3	$19	30% discount	must have a 4 ....
Group	$250 for ten people	price includes a 5	must pay 6 ....

IELTS Listening test practice   **Sentence completion**

If you have to complete some sentences, you need to work out what type of words are missing but also remember that the sentences need to be grammatically correct.

7 The sentences which follow are based on the second part of the conversation between the man and the receptionist at the City Aquarium.
⏱ Take 30 seconds to prepare before you listen.

8 🔊08 Listen to the second part of the conversation and answer questions **7–10**.

Test tip

Use the time given between the two parts of a recording to read the next set of questions carefully. They will always involve a different type of question.

Complete the sentences below.
*Write **NO MORE THAN THREE WORDS AND/OR A NUMBER** for each answer.*

7 You can buy a book that tells you about the .... in the aquarium.

8 The gift shop is situated next to the ....

9 The aquarium closes at .... today.

10 The tickets are cheaper when you buy them ....

9 How is the answer in sentence **9** different from the other answers?

IELTS Listening test practice　　　　　　　　　　　　　　　　**Section 1**

In **Section 1** of the IELTS Listening test, you will hear a conversation between two people. One of the speakers needs some specific factual information (e.g. names or dates) which you will have to write down. **Section 1** tasks are often *gapfill* (e.g. note, table or form completion). You will get an example at the beginning and the recording will be divided into two or three parts with some reading time before each part.

Before you listen

- Look at the task below, which consists of a form with some information missing. Try to work out the situation from the task. Who could the speakers be? Why are they speaking?
- Decide what role you will be playing when you complete the form. What type of information will you be listening for?
- Try to predict the language that you need to listen for.

10 (●**09**) Listen and answer questions **1–10**.

Questions 1–6
*Listen to the telephone conversation and complete the form below. Write **NO MORE THAN THREE WORDS AND/OR A NUMBER** for each answer.*

GOLDEN WHEELS CAR RENTALS

Customer request form

Example	*Answer*
Customer's name:	Frank Moorcroft

Address:	1　26, ..., Richmond
Telephone:	2　02 ....
Type of licence:	3　......................
Type of vehicle:	4　......................
Date for collection:	5　......................
Length of booking:	6　......................

Questions 7–10
Complete the sentences below.
*Write **NO MORE THAN TWO WORDS** for each answer.*

　7　The man will pick the car up from ....

　8　The car is required at ....

　9　A .... is also needed.

　10　The man decides to take the ....

11 What does the number in the address on the form tell you?

12 What do the words *type of vehicle* tell you?

Test tip
Section 1 always has an example question first to give you plenty of time to get started.

Listening

3 Identifying detail

- Why is detail important?

  We need to show that we can listen carefully to a description and understand it fully.

- When do we need to listen for detail?

  If someone is describing something, it is the detail in the description, such as the colour or a reference to the shape, which allows us to picture it accurately.

Understanding form, position, colour

1 Work with a partner. Look at pictures **a–h** and take turns to describe the objects. Try to say what material they are usually made of. Use some of the descriptive words and phrases in the vocabulary box below to help you.

Vocabulary	
Shape	round oval rectangular circular spherical cylindrical shaped like a … square/cube/sphere long thin flat curved pointed
Qualities	coloured striped spotted sharp
Parts	head face eye neck top main/outer/inner part side handle bottom end
Position	on one/both side(s) in the middle on/at the top above below around inside horizontal vertical
Material	wood(en) paper leather rubber metal glass plastic

2 Think of two more objects and describe them to your partner. Can he/she guess what they are?

14

| **IELTS Listening test practice** | **Labelling a diagram** |

You may have to label a diagram, map or plan. There are three types of diagram task in IELTS Listening.

Type 1   You complete the labels on a diagram with words from the recording.
Type 2   You match options in a box to points numbered on the diagram.
Type 3   You match points numbered on the diagram to items or descriptions.

3   You are going to hear a description of how a fire extinguisher works. Look at the diagram of the fire extinguisher below and discuss the parts you need to label. What do you think they might be? What sort of descriptive words and phrases might help you?

4   ⊙**10** Listen and answer questions **1–5**.

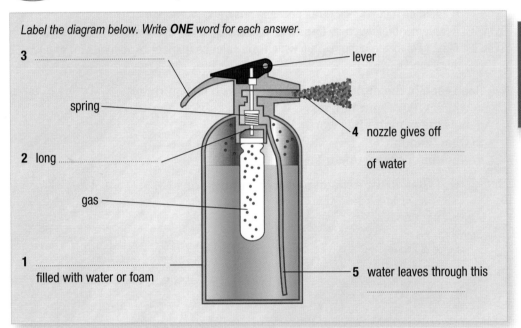

*Label the diagram below. Write **ONE** word for each answer.*

3 ....

spring

2 long ....

gas

1 ....
filled with water or foam

lever

4 nozzle gives off
....
of water

5 water leaves through this
....

Test tip
The answers will come in question order on the recording.

5   Listen to the recording again and complete the second column of the table with the words that are used to describe the parts of the fire extinguisher.

Part	Description	Position
container		
lever		
pin		
gas cartridge		
handle		
nozzle		
spring		
discharge tube		

6   Listen to the recording a third time and complete the third column of the table with the expressions of position that help you know where the parts are.

7 (●11) Listen and complete the notes using not more than three words in each gap.

In case of emergency

- Remove from case and withdraw **6** _____.
- **7** _____ extinguisher at burning object.
- **8** _____ top lever which **9** _____ gas.
- Point nozzle at **10** _____ to extinguish.

IELTS Listening test practice	**Multiple choice**

Multiple choice questions are common in the IELTS Listening test. They are used to test detailed understanding. There are three types:

Type 1 A question followed by **three** possible answers, worth one mark

Type 2 A statement followed by **three** possible endings, worth one mark

Type 3 A list of possible options from which you select a number of answers for one or more marks.

8 Read each of the multiple choice questions below and say
- which type of question it is
- how many marks it is worth
- what the topic is
- who the speakers might be.

Test tip

Always follow this procedure when you first read the questions.

9 (●12) Listen to the extracts and answer questions **1–7**.

Test tip

In the IELTS Listening test you will need to use the questions to help you follow the talk and find the answers but you also have some time before the talk begins to read through the questions.

1 Which lecture does the woman attend in the middle of the day?

- **A** Library skills
- **B** Technical design
- **C** History of architecture

2 *Circle **TWO** letters **A–G**.*
Which **TWO** things should they take on the walk?

- **A** large rucksack
- **B** drink container
- **C** soft drinks
- **D** cold food
- **E** insect repellent
- **F** camera
- **G** sunglasses

3 The speaker says sharks are unlike any other fish because they

- **A** cannot float in water.
- **B** are unable to swim backwards.
- **C** catch their prey in the air.

4 What is the Tjibaou building?

- **A** a home for the native people of New Caledonia
- **B** a unique example of Italian architecture
- **C** a place to learn about Kanak culture

5–7

Which **THREE** things does the woman like?
- **A** the appearance of the planes
- **B** the idea of working for an airline
- **C** travelling to unusual places
- **D** collecting airline equipment
- **E** watching the planes take off
- **F** the noise of the engines
- **G** being a passenger

10 Work with a partner. You are going to hear part of a radio programme. Together, read questions **1** and **2** below and discuss how you could rephrase each question and the three possible endings in your own words.

11 (🔊**13**) Listen to the introduction to the radio programme and choose the correct letter, **A**, **B** or **C**.

> **1** The announcer says that canoeing is
>   **A** safer than people think.
>   **B** enjoyable for most people.
>   **C** becoming more popular.
>
> **2** The speaker says that canoes may be hard to
>   **A** steer.
>   **B** balance.
>   **C** get going.

12 Listen to the recording again and note the exact words that helped you to answer questions **1** and **2**.

13 Repeat the process from exercise **8** (page 16) with questions **3–6**, below. Say what you think the answers might be to the questions before you listen.

14 (🔊**14**) Listen and answer questions **3–6**.

> **3** Where does the term *white-water canoeing* come from?
>   **A** the type of river that is chosen
>   **B** the effect of the paddles on the water
>   **C** the speed at which the boat travels
>
> **4–6** *Circle **THREE** letters **A–G**. Which **THREE** things does Cynthia recommend you buy to get started?*
>   **A** a low-budget canoe   **E** a long-sleeved sweater
>   **B** protective headgear   **F** rubber boots
>   **C** a waterproof jacket   **G** gloves
>   **D** a short-sleeved wetsuit

15 Listen to the recording again. Look at options **A–G** in questions **4–6** and say why some of these are incorrect.

16 Read question **7** below on your own and rephrase the question and the three possible answers in your own words.

> **7** According to Cynthia, serious canoeists
>   **A** take risks on purpose.
>   **B** prefer to teach people in the winter.
>   **C** avoid rivers that are too high.

17 (🔊**15**) Listen to the end of the programme and answer question **7**.

18 Listen to the recording again.
  a Which words helped you to answer the question?
  b Why are the other two possible answers attractive, but wrong?

Listening

4 Following a description: diagrams, maps and plans

■ What information are we listening for?

If we need to understand a diagram or follow a map, we are usually trying to find out where things are, what something is made of or how it works. We may be listening for places, buildings, names of parts or stages in a process.

■ What cues can we use to help get the right answers?

Certain words are included to guide you. These may be things like the compass points, left and right, expressions of position and place, verbs, and adjectives of size, shape, quality, et

Following directions on a map

1 Look at the street map and then use the compass points to help you find somewhere that is:
   a in the northwest corner of the map.
   b in the northeast corner of the map.
   c on the east side of the map.
   d south of Beach Road.

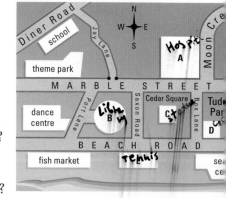

2 Look at the street map again and answer the questions.
   a Are there any streets that run parallel to each other?
   b What is at the south end of Jay Lane?
   c Which road crosses Marble Street?
   d Travelling north, which street does Jay Lane lead into?
   e Travelling north, which building is on the left-hand side of Port Lane?

3 Look at the five labels on the map, **A–E**.
   (●16) Listen and say which place each label represents.
   A is the ....
   B is the ....
   C is the ....
   D is the ....
   E is the ....

4 Look at the recording script on page 165 and underline the words which helped you.

5 Work with a partner. Ask each other some further directions. Use the expressions opposite to help you.

> Giving directions
> You go along ...
> Go to the end of the street / road ...
> Go round the corner/bend / up the hill/steps
> Walk past the ...
> Turn left / Turn right / Go straight ahead ...
> The place is opposite / next to / behind ...

> How do you get to the school from the dance centre?

> You go along Port Lane and ...

IELTS Listening test practice   Labelling a map or plan

You may have to listen to a description of where some places are located on a map or plan and match these to the correct point on the map.

6 🔊**17** Look carefully at the plan of an Australian airport, then listen and answer questions **1–4**.

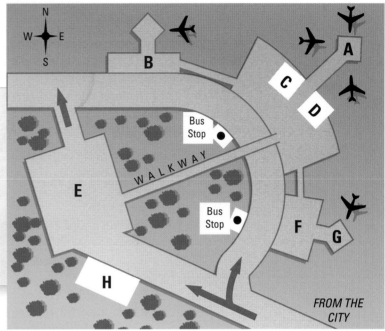

> *Label the plan.*
> *Write the correct letter A–H next to questions 1–4.*
>
> **1** Car park .... ~~B~~ E
>
> **2** Domestic Terminal .... F
>
> **3** Lifts .... D
>
> **4** Regional Terminal .... B

7 Listen to the recording again and note which words helped you to answer questions **1–4** above. Then check your answers with the script on pages 165–166.

IELTS Listening test practice   Summary completion

If you have a summary to complete, you need to work out the type of words that are missing and listen for these on the recording. As in sentence completion, your answers should make sense grammatically.

8 You are going to hear a local woman giving directions to a visitor from another country. Read the summary below and try to work out what type of words are missing.

9 🔊**18** Listen and complete the gaps (**1–5**) in the summary below.

> *Write **NO MORE THAN THREE WORDS AND/OR A NUMBER** for each answer.*
>
> ### How to get to the Peace Hotel
>
> You need to travel by **1** .... Get off after **2** .... at the People's Square and walk along Nan Jing Road East. There is no **3** .... on this road. Eventually you will get to the Bund and the Peace Hotel is on the **4** .... The entrance to the Tourist Tunnel is **5** .... the hotel and you can go through this if you want to visit the Oriental Pearl radio and TV tower.

> *Type of words*
> 1 ....
> 2 ....
> 3 ....
> 4 ....
> 5 ....

10 Look at the recording script on page 166 and underline the words which helped you to complete the summary.

In **Section 2** of the Listening test you will hear someone giving a talk on a topic of general interest.

Before you listen

- Use the reading time to decide who the speaker might be and what the topic is.
- Read through the summary and work out what type of information you need to listen for (e.g. *directions, places, position*).
- Note the words/features and also the order of the questions on the plan as these may help guide your listening.
- Note what the questions ask you to do (e.g. write words? choose letters from a box?).

11 ⊙**19** Listen and answer questions **1–10**.

Questions 1–5
Complete the summary below.
*Write **NO MORE THAN THREE WORDS AND/OR A NUMBER** for each answer.*

Getting to the Hillside Water Park

The water park is situated in the **1** .... area of the town.

You can get there on foot but this takes about **2** ....

There are regular buses from the **3** .... and the most direct is the

number **4** ....

Taxis are also available but they are not **5** ....

Questions 6–10
Label the plan.
*Choose **FIVE** answers from the box and write the letters **A–H** next to questions 6–10.*

HILLSIDE WATER PARK

A   lifeguard's hut
B   parent viewing area
C   first-aid centre
D   sunbathing area
E   poolside bar
F   coach park
G   pay kiosk
H   adult pool

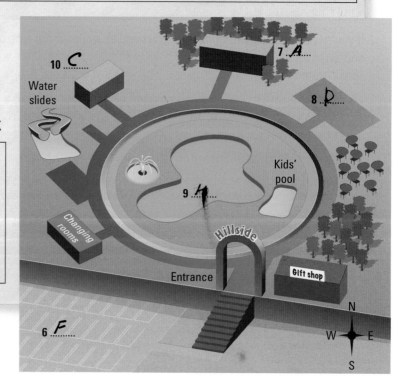

Listening

5 Identifying main ideas

- What are the speakers talking about?
- How do the ideas develop?

To follow what people are saying, you need to be able to identify the main ideas and separate these in your mind from the supporting detail. Understanding the main ideas helps us to follow the speakers' arguments.

Thinking around the topic

1 Work with a partner. Look at the statements, **A–F**, and say whether you agree or disagree with them. Together, make a list under the headings **For** and **Against** to show some different viewpoints. An example has been done for you.

A
University education should be free.

B
People should have to stay at school until the age of 18.

C
Newspapers are old-fashioned and serve no purpose in today's world of electronic media.

D
All members of a society should have the right to free health care.

E
Nuclear power stations provide a clean and efficient source of energy compared with burning coal or oil.

F
It makes good sense for private companies to fund the building of highways and then charge a fee for motorists to use them.

For ✓	Against ✗
Everyone has the right to a good education – not just wealthy people.	If universities are free, too many students are encouraged to go when other forms of training might suit them better.
The state has a duty to provide free university education by giving funding for fees.	Free education benefits wealthy students, while ordinary people end up subsidising them through their taxes.
Well-educated citizens make good citizens.	If you pay for something, you value it more highly.

> **Test tip**
> Sometimes it is useful to try to see both sides of an argument, even if you don't agree, as it helps you to predict what you may hear.

2 ⟨🔊20⟩ You are going to hear six short conversations based on the topics on the previous page. Listen and say

■ what the topic is
■ how many speakers there are in each conversation.

The first one has been done as an example.

Conversation	Topic	Number and type of speakers
1	The cost of university education	2 / one man, one woman
2		
3		
4		
5		
6		

IELTS Listening test practice   **Short-answer questions**

You may have to answer some of the questions with short answers. There are two types of short-answer question used in IELTS Listening:

Type 1   A question requiring an answer of no more than three words for one mark
Type 2   An instruction to make a list of things, each for one mark.

3 Read questions **1–6** below and underline the key words which tell you what type of answer you should write. Say what you expect to hear. The first one has been done as an example.

4 Now listen to the recording again and answer questions **1–6**.

Write *NO MORE THAN THREE WORDS* for each answer

1 According to the woman, what <u>type of education</u> should be <u>free</u> today?
Expect to hear something about funding for different types of education.

2 According to the man, who is working too hard in the National Health Service?

3 What form of energy does the woman recommend?

4 Name two trades mentioned by the man.

5 Name two countries where you pay to use the roads.

6 What has replaced newspapers for many young people?

Were your predictions correct about what you expected to hear for questions **1–6**?

IELTS Listening test practice   Multiple choice

5 (21) You are going to hear two more short conversations. Listen and answer questions **1** and **2**.

*Choose the correct letter, **A**, **B** or **C**.*

1 What pleased the tutor about Jamie's composition?
   A It was well researched.
   B It was neatly presented.
   C It included plenty of data.

2 How will the tutor make sure that the students work on relevant topics?
   A by asking them to get together to discuss their choices
   B by talking to each student individually
   C by handing out a list of topics to the class

6 Check your answers in the key. Were you tempted to choose any of the wrong options? If so, why?

7 Listen to the conversations again to see why the other options are not correct.

IELTS Listening test practice   Matching

In IELTS Listening, sometimes you have to match a list of options to a list of questions. There will always be more options than questions.

8 You are going to hear part of a conversation. Look at the words used in questions **1–3** and then the options in the box, including the heading. Say what you expect the situation to be.

9 Read the question and all the options (**A–F**) carefully before you listen to the recording. Make sure you understand what you have to do and then rephrase the advantages (**1–3**) in your own words.

10 (22) Listen and answer questions **1–3**.

Which course has the following advantages?
*Choose **THREE** answers from the box and write the correct letters **A–F** next to questions 1–3.*

Advantages

1 good work prospects   ....

2 plenty of work opportunities   ....

3 lower entry requirement   ....

Courses
A Arts
B Computing
C Dentistry
D Law
E Medicine
F Science

11 Read the questions below to decide what the topic is and note the layout of the questions, i.e. *Vehicle 1*, etc.

12 Rephrase the options in **A–G** in your own words.

13 ⊙**23** Listen and answer questions **1–4**.

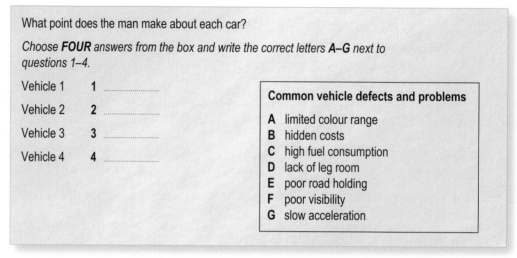

What point does the man make about each car?

Choose **FOUR** *answers from the box and write the correct letters* **A–G** *next to questions 1–4.*

Vehicle 1   **1** ....

Vehicle 2   **2** ....

Vehicle 3   **3** ....

Vehicle 4   **4** ....

Common vehicle defects and problems

A   limited colour range
B   hidden costs
C   high fuel consumption
D   lack of leg room
E   poor road holding
F   poor visibility
G   slow acceleration

> **Test tip**
> The vehicles are referred to as Vehicle 1, 2, 3 and 4, so use this to guide your listening.

14 Work with a partner. Find the difference(s) between the matching tasks in exercise **10** on page 23 and exercise **13** above.

15 Listen to the recording again and check your answers by making a note of the exact words which the speaker uses to describe the defects or problems on the four vehicles.

Defect or problem	Words speaker uses
A limited colour range	
B hidden costs	
C high fuel consumption	
D lack of leg room	
E poor road holding	
F poor visibility	
G slow acceleration	

16 Check your answers with the recording script on page 168.

Listening

6 Seeing beyond the surface meaning

- What does the speaker mean exactly?
- How can we interpret stress and intonation?

As listeners we must learn not only to interpret the words people use but also their word stress and intonation patterns.

In this unit, we will investigate some ways of seeing beyond the surface meaning of spoken language while following a conversation.

Understanding stress and intonation

1   Read the statement below and then practise stressing different words, to produce different meanings. The first one has been done as an example.

Example

I thought the assignment was due in on Thursday.

I thought the assignment was due in on Thursday.

2   Work with a partner. Say the sentence stressing *assignment* and then *Thursday* to create two other meanings. Together, discuss what questions you think they might answer.

3   Ask the question below by stressing *you*, *dictionary* or *elementary* to produce three different meanings.

Would you recommend this dictionary to an elementary student?

- At the beginning of each IELTS Listening section, there will be a brief introductory statement about what you are going to hear. It may mention where the speakers are or their relationship to one another. The speakers may also introduce the topic in the first few words of the recording. If you identify the topic early, it will help you to understand the conversation better.

4   (24) You are going to hear the beginning of four different conversations **A**, **B**, **C** and **D**. Listen, and for each conversation answer these questions.

	A	B	C	D
Where is the conversation taking place?	university library			
What is the main topic of the conversation?				
How many speakers are there?				

5 Listen to the recording again and say in which of the conversations **A–D** the following feelings are expressed:

- surprise ▪ satisfaction ▪ concern ▪ annoyance

6 Work with a partner. Read the posters advertising five student debates. Then together, say what you think each of the debates is about.

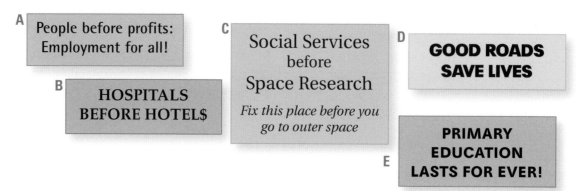

A People before profits: Employment for all!

B HOSPITALS BEFORE HOTEL$

C Social Services before Space Research
Fix this place before you go to outer space

D GOOD ROADS SAVE LIVES

E PRIMARY EDUCATION LASTS FOR EVER!

7 Make a short list of some points you could use which either support the argument in each poster or which give the opposite view. Compare your ideas with the rest of the class.

IELTS Listening test practice   **Classification**

In the IELTS Listening test, you sometimes have to classify a list of ideas or concepts into categories. There are always fewer categories (options) than ideas, so you may have to use some of the options more than once.

8 Read the main question below and look at options **A–C**, which are the possible answers to the categories in questions **1–5**.

9 Identify the topic and then say what the context is. Then look carefully at the numbered questions **1–5** and note the relationship to the options **A–C** to make sure you understand what you have to do. Find another way to express the three options **A–C** in your own words, e.g. **A** *spend more money.*

10 ⏹**25** Listen and answer questions **1–5**. For each question, write **A**, **B** or **C**.

> What does the politician say the government will do in the following areas?
>
> **1** hospitals
> **2** prescription drugs
> **3** schools
> **4** research and development
> **5** public works
>
> **A** increase expenditure
> **B** maintain the same level of expenditure
> **C** reduce expenditure

11 Listen again and note the key words which contained the answers to **1–5**. Then check your answers in the recording script on page 169.

IELTS Listening test practice   Section 3

In **Section 3** of the IELTS Listening test you will have to follow a discussion with up to four speakers talking about a study-related topic. You will have to listen for important facts, reasons or ideas, or be asked to identify views or opinions. There may be more than one task type in **Section 3**.

Before you listen

■ Decide what the topic is.
■ Read the summary and try to predict what is missing.
■ Note the words/features in the diagram that may help guide your listening.
■ Note how you should do the questions (do you have to write words or letters from a box or do you have to write the words that you hear in the recording?).
■ Note the order of the questions (i.e. how the numbers move around the diagram).

12 🔊 **26** Listen and answer questions **1–10**.

Questions 1–3
Complete the summary. Write **NO MORE THAN TWO WORDS AND/OR A NUMBER** *for each answer.*

ROVER ROBOT

The robot does the same work as a **1** .... Some people think it looks like a **2** .... on wheels. It is quite small, weighing only 16.5 kg and it moves relatively slowly, with a maximum speed of **3** .... km an hour.

Questions 4–7
Label the diagram of the rover robot.
Write **NO MORE THAN THREE WORDS** *for each answer.*

4 ....

6 ....

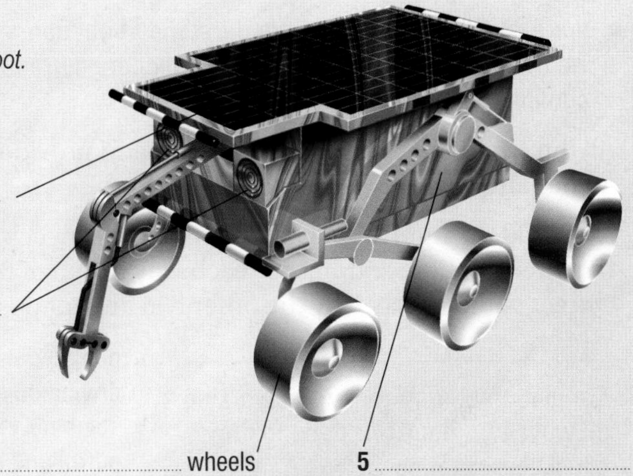

7 .... wheels   **5** ....

Questions 8–10
Answer the questions below.
Write **NO MORE THAN THREE WORDS AND/OR A NUMBER** *for each answer.*

8 How long does it take the radio signal to travel from Earth to Mars? ....

9 What stops the scientists from steering the rover in real time? ....

10 What do scientists believe Mars has, which is similar to Earth? ....

Listening

7 Following signpost words

- What are *signpost words* and how do they help us to understand?

Good public speakers and lecturers indicate the stages of their talk through the use of *signpost words*. These words direct our listening: they warn us that more information is coming and suggest what kind of information this may be. Being able to identify and follow the signpost words will help you make sense of what you hear and help you answer the questions.

Learning to direct your listening

1 Read the unfinished statement below and the three possible ways of completing the idea. What does the word *although* signal?

> **Although** a great deal has been achieved in the area of cancer research, …

    a there is still a lot we do not understand about cancer.
    b we need to get our governments to allocate more funding.
    c continued research is still essential.

All three possible endings make sense and provide a **contrast** to the idea that a lot has already been achieved.

2 Now read the unfinished statements in the speech balloons **1** and **2** below and the three possible endings for each. Say which of the endings (**a–c**) to **1** and **2** are correct and then say why the other two are not possible.

> 1 Car manufacturers today are working on ways to reduce our dependency on oil. **For instance …**

    a people can walk to work instead of driving, to save fuel.
    b some new cars run on a combination of petrol and electric power.
    c there has been no real economic incentive until recently.

> 2 Not only is Swahili spoken by the people of East Africa, it is **also** …

    a full of Portuguese and Arabic words.
    b quite difficult to learn.
    c used as a language of trade in many African countries.

3 Look at the list of 'directions' in Box **A** and then match them to the signpost words in Box **B** and Box **C**.

A Directions
1 Signalling a contrast or opposite
2 Introducing an example
3 Giving a reason (cause and effect)
4 Providing extra information
5 Setting out the stages of a talk / signalling a sequence
6 Signalling an explanation or result

B Signpost words within a sentence		
although	even though	despite
even if	also so	but while
because	as well as	unlike whereas

C Signpost words which link two sentences	
On the one hand …	Lastly
but on the other	Then
In addition	However
For instance	For example
Consequently	By contrast
First of all	In other words

4 Underline the signpost word in the following ideas, and complete the sentences in your own words. Say what direction the signpost words are signalling.

1 I'm interested in history <u>but</u> … I prefer science.
   (signalling a contrast)
2 Studying abroad is worthwhile, even though …
3 Working in the library is uncomfortable as well as …
4 The Internet has changed the way we all live because …
5 I never learned to play a musical instrument, so …
6 Learning a foreign language can be difficult and at times frustrating. However, …
7 The climate of South East Asia is tropical. By contrast, …
8 My brother never studied much at school and consequently, …
9 Rice is the staple diet in Asia, whereas …
10 The effects of global warming are evident everywhere. For example, …

■ Note how the words from Box **B** above join ideas and how the words from Box **C** always come either at the start of a new sentence or after *and* joining two main ideas.

5 ⑤**27** You are going to hear six unfinished statements, each ending with a signpost word, signalling further information. Listen to the unfinished statements and, for each one, note the signpost word you hear and say what direction it is signalling.

	Signpost word(s)	Direction
1		
2		
3		
4		
5		
6		

6 Listen to the recording again and try to complete the unfinished statements by creating an ending which makes sense in each case, following on from the signpost word.

7 ⑤**28** Now listen to the endings of the unfinished statements you heard. How similar are they to your endings?

IELTS Listening test practice	**Completing a flowchart**

There are two types of flowchart question used in the IELTS Listening test:

Type 1   A chart with gaps to complete from the recording

Type 2   A chart and a list of possible options from which you select answers.

8 Read the notes below to get an idea of the context and direction of the talk.

9 Decide what type of words are missing.

10 🔊 **29** Listen and complete the flowchart.

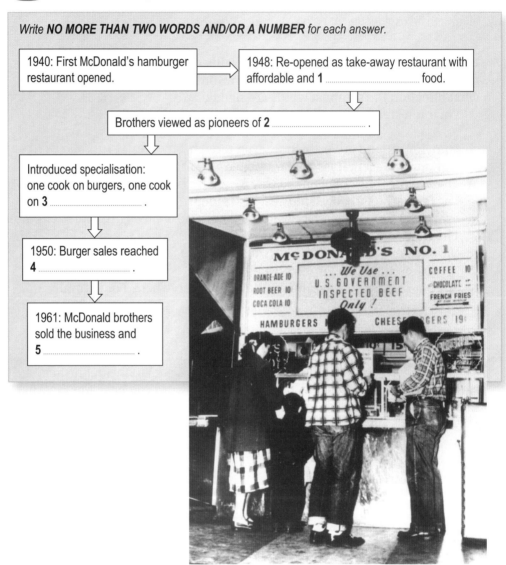

Test tip
There is no break in Section 4, so you need to read all the questions before you hear the recording.

Write **NO MORE THAN TWO WORDS AND/OR A NUMBER** *for each answer.*

1940: First McDonald's hamburger restaurant opened. → 1948: Re-opened as take-away restaurant with affordable and **1** .... food.

Brothers viewed as pioneers of **2** ....

Introduced specialisation: one cook on burgers, one cook on **3** ....

1950: Burger sales reached **4** ....

1961: McDonald brothers sold the business and **5** ....

11 Listen again and make a note of the different types of signpost words that you hear in the talk. Then check your answers in the recording script on page 171.

Listening

8 Following a talk

- How can I make sense of what I hear?

You should listen out for signpost words to follow the stages in the talk and take note of stress and intonation used to highlight important information.

Using your own knowledge of the topic

1 🔊**30** Read the introductory part to a **Section 4** lecture below, and underline the key words and phrases. Then listen and answer these questions to complete the first row of the table below.

a What is the broad topic?
b What, if anything, do you already know about this topic?
c How do you think the talk will develop after this introduction?

> *Have you ever wondered why you can recognise people's handwriting? The many styles of handwriting which exist have attracted a wide range of scientific studies, each with its own aims.*

Intro	Key words and phrases	Topic	Own knowledge	Possible development
A	recognise handwriting/ scientific studies			

Test tip

The speaker may introduce the topic at the start of the talk. Whenever you listen to a talk or lecture, you should draw on your own knowledge of the topic to help you make sense of what you hear.

2 🔊**31** Now listen and complete the table for Introductions **B**, **C** and **D**.

B				
C				
D				

3 Work with a partner. Together, discuss the questions below to find out what you already know about the topic.

a What do you know about the game of chess?
b Have you ever wondered where the game originated?
c Who are the most famous chess players and where are they from?

31

IELTS Listening test practice	**Note completion**

4 Look at **1–6** in the set of notes below and then say what the topic is.

5 Say what type of words you will need to listen for and then write them in the yellow box.

6 (32) Listen and complete the notes below.

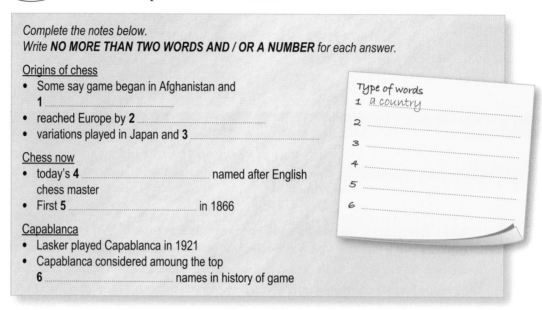

Complete the notes below.
*Write **NO MORE THAN TWO WORDS AND / OR A NUMBER** for each answer.*

Origins of chess
- Some say game began in Afghanistan and
  1 ....
- reached Europe by **2** ....
- variations played in Japan and **3** ....

Chess now
- today's **4** .... named after English
  chess master
- First **5** .... in 1866

Capablanca
- Lasker played Capablanca in 1921
- Capablanca considered amoung the top
  6 .... names in history of game

Type of words
1 *a country* ....
2 ....
3 ....
4 ....
5 ....
6 ....

7 Work with a partner. Together, discuss the questions below to find out what you already know about the topic.

a When do babies start to speak?

b Is it useful to study how we learn our first language? If so, why?

c How is learning to speak different from learning to read and write?

IELTS Listening test practice   Section 4

In **Section 4** of the IELTS Listening test you will always hear a lecture or a talk on a study-related topic. Because information is sometimes presented sequentially or chronologically in a talk, a flowchart may be used to test your understanding of the sequence of ideas.

Before you listen

- Look at all ten questions and decide what the topic is. Consider what you know about it.
- How many different sets of questions are there?
- What types of question are they and how are they arranged?
- From the questions, can you say what sub-topics will be discussed?
- Make sure you know what form of word you need for questions 1–6 (e.g. noun, adjective, verb).

8 (33) Listen and answer questions **1–10**.

Questions 1–3
*Complete the notes below. Write **NO MORE THAN ONE WORD** for each answer.*

The Study of Child Language Acquisition

| Fascinating | because people have an **1** .... in children's learning |

| **2** .... | because it leads to greater understanding of language |

| **3** .... | because of the difficulties encountered |

Questions 4–6
Complete the flowchart below.
*Write **NO MORE THAN TWO WORDS AND/OR A NUMBER** for each answer.*

Discussion of **4** .... includes the use of diaries, recordings and tests.

↓

Speech in infants' **5** .... of life   Children become aware that they can speak.

↓

Speech in children **6** .... years   Linguistic analysis becomes possible.

Questions 7–10
Complete the flowchart below.
*Choose four answers from the box and write the correct letters **A–G** next to questions 7–10.*

Educational approaches, i.e. ways of developing **7** .... in schoolchildren

↓

a) focus on **8** ....

↓

b) how to teach **9** ....

↓

c) review of contemporary ideas on development of **10** ....

A	language
B	listening
C	reading
D	speaking
E	spelling
F	thinking
G	writing

Test tip

A flowchart represents a sequence of events, so use this to help you anticipate what is coming. Use the words in the flowchart as anchors to guide you.

9 Listen to the lecture on child language again. Make a list of all the signpost words, especially those which came before the answers.

10 Check your list with the script on page 172. All the signpost words are printed in *italics*. Take note of those which come before the answers.

Extra test practice for Section 4	Mixed question types

11 (34) Listen and answer questions **1–10**.

Questions 1–3
Complete the table. Write **NO MORE THAN THREE WORDS AND/OR A NUMBER** for each answer.

Animal	Brought by	Reason
1	settlers	for food
fox	settlers	**2** ....
cane toad	**3**	to kill beetles

Questions 4 and 5
Complete the flowchart below.
Write **NO MORE THAN TWO WORDS AND/OR A NUMBER** for each answer.

Beetles' effect on sugar cane

Beetle lays eggs

Eggs become grubs

Grubs eat the **4** ....

Sugar cane **5** ....

Questions 6–10
Choose the correct letter, **A, B** or **C**.

6 The cane toad originated in
  A Central America.
  B Hawaii.
  C Australia.

7 In Australia, the toads
  A grew extremely large.
  B multiplied in number.
  C ate the cane beetles.

8 The farmers' plan failed because
  A there were too many beetles.
  B their own research was faulty.
  C they believed the reports
    they read.

9 The sugar cane industry
  A thrives today.
  B has died out in some areas.
  C survives alongside the beetle.

10 The second lesson to be
  learned from this story
  is that
  A the environment is
    constantly at risk.
  B first-hand research is
    not always necessary.
  C caution is necessary
    when dealing with nature.

Summary of IELTS Listening strategies

	Approach	Reason
	There are four sections, and you have time to read the questions thoroughly before you listen to each recording. Take the sections one at a time.	It is difficult to concentrate on making sense of what you hear if you are trying to read the questions and work out what is required at the same time.

	Approach	Reason
Before you hear the recording	Read through the tasks for each section and make sure you know what sort of answer you have to write (e.g. *words*, *a letter*, *an option from a box*, etc.).	If you need to write something, you must spell the words accurately. Sometimes you may hear a word spelled out so you need to know the sounds of the letters of the alphabet in English. For multiple choice questions or when you have to choose options from a box, you only need to write the correct letter(s) as your answer.
	Use this time to work out the topic, and decide what sort of information and answers you need to listen for.	This means you do not waste time doing this while the recording is playing.
	Use a pencil to underline key words in the question.	Key words usually carry meaning and help you make sense of the questions.

	Approach	Reason
During the recording	Use the words on the question paper to guide you through the listening.	They act as anchors throughout the recording and stop you from getting lost.
	Remember that Section 1 will have an example and Sections 1, 2 and 3 are divided into two parts.	This allows you to keep up and gives you time to complete your answers.
	You should write your answers on the question paper as you listen.	It is not possible to remember what you heard and complete the task from memory at the end.
	If you cannot answer a question, move on to the next one.	You do not want to risk missing the answer to the next question too.

	Approach	Reason
After the recording	Transfer your answers onto the answer sheet carefully. Make sure you put the right answers in the right place and check your spelling.	You have ten minutes to do this, but you need to get going on this straightaway. If you put your answers in the wrong place on the answer sheet you will lose marks.
	Go back to any questions you could not answer and try to guess the answer from the context.	You should attempt all the questions, as a blank space can only be marked wrong.
	Make the most of the questions in Sections 1 and 2 as they are often easier than Sections 3 and 4.	There is one mark for every question, making a total of 40 marks.

The Reading module

When you go to university or college you may be overwhelmed by the amount of reading you are expected to do. You will have to do a lot of this reading on your own and you will need to be able to read *discriminatingly*. This means you will need to have the skills required to *focus* in on the information that is important to you and to *skim through* the information that isn't.

The IELTS examination tests your ability to read approximately 2,750 words in a fairly short period of time in order to find out certain information. In both the Academic and the General Training modules, you are given 60 minutes to answer a total of 40 questions and each question is worth one mark. Within this time, you also have to transfer all your answers onto an answer sheet (see page 191).

Academic Reading module

The test has three reading passages and each of the passages is accompanied by a set of 13 or 14 questions. The passages will be written in a variety of different styles. Generally, **Passage 1** is a more descriptive text, while **Passages 2** and **3** are discursive and contain some argument.

Each passage may have more than one type of question. For example, you may be asked to find detailed information in a passage in order to complete sentences; you may have to identify views within a passage; you may have to understand how something works and complete a diagram or chart. If you can identify the reading skills being tested in each set of questions and if you have a strategy for doing each question type, you will have a better chance of completing the Reading test successfully.

General Training Reading module

The test has three sections. **Section 1** contains two or more texts which are based on social situations, **Section 2** contains two texts based on work- or course-related situations, and **Section 3** contains one text that tests general reading comprehension. The question types are similar to those in the Academic module. The texts in the first two sections are more likely to be descriptive and factual. The text in the third section may contain some argument.

If you are studying for the General Training module you will benefit from doing Reading Units **1–7** as well as Units **8–10**.

All aspects of the Reading test, as well as additional skills, are covered in this book.

Reading

■ How do I get started?

As a reader you need to have strategies to help you understand a text quickly. The first step is to predict what the text will be about by reading the title and subheading.

■ How can I form a quick overview of the text?

You can form a quick overview by asking yourself certain questions as you read. You need to pay attention to paragraph themes and key words.

1 Re-read the introduction to the Reading module on page 36 and answer the questions.
  a What is the introduction about?
  b Why was the text written?
  c Who was it written for?

■ These are critical questions that can help you **orientate** yourself to a text.

Using titles and subheadings

Nearly all articles that you read in journals, magazines and newspapers will have a title.
Many will also have a subheading.

2 Read the title and subheading of this magazine article and answer the questions:

  a What will the article be about (i.e. What is the topic)?
  b What kind of person would be interested in this article?
  c What would you expect to read in the first paragraph?

Air Heads

Pilots' judgement may be impaired by too many long-haul flights

3 Now read the first paragraph of *Air Heads* and answer the questions which follow.

Globetrotting across several time zones on long-haul flights impairs memory and reaction times by shrinking part of the brain. This might mean that airlines should allow their crews at least 10 days to recover from jet lag before they work on another long-haul flight, says the scientist who discovered the effect.

  a What is the writer's purpose in this first paragraph of *Air Heads*?
  b Is there a sentence that best summarises the main idea in this first paragraph?

■ These are the types of questions that you can ask yourself when you first read a text. They should form part of your reading strategies.

4 Work with a partner. Read this title and subheading and then discuss the questions **a–c** in exercise **2**.

Pearly Gems

Would women through history have been so keen on the pearls around their necks if they'd known what was inside? Robert Dunn peels back the layers of this eco-miracle

5 Now read the first two paragraphs of *Pearly Gems* and answer the questions which follow.

Test tip

Sometimes if a passage in the IELTS Reading does not have a title or a subheading, this is because one of the questions will test your understanding of the theme of the whole passage or the reason why the writer wrote the passage.

There is a mystery and preciousness that we attach to pearls, yet despite what some people believe, it has nothing to do with a grain of sand. Pearls, which have long been the treasures of the wealthy, are often the products of dead worms, which remain entombed at the centre of the jewels, minute, translucent and ethereal.

Larval tapeworms drill into the flesh of mussels to use them as intermediate hosts *en route* to their later hosts, which in most cases are ducks or fish. The mussels' immune systems battle the worms by encircling them in layer after layer of nacre, the same calcium-based material found in the mussels' shells. The invaders suffocate and then rest for eternity encased in these tiny chambers.

a What is the writer's purpose in the second paragraph?
b How would you expect the article to continue?
c Is *Pearly Gems* factual and descriptive or does it present opinions and argument?

■ If you begin your reading by asking the questions you have met so far in this unit, you will get off to a good start.

Using paragraphs and main ideas

As you read through each paragraph of a passage, you gradually build on your understanding of what the writer is trying to say.

6 Work with a partner and discuss these questions.

a How do paragraphs help the reader?
b When you first read a passage, what should you look for in each paragraph?

7 Read the title of the passage on the next page and discuss with a partner what you think it will be about.

8 Now read the whole passage and underline the main idea in each paragraph.

The Undersea World of Sound

*Snorts, clicks, groans –
tune in to the long-distance
language of the ocean*

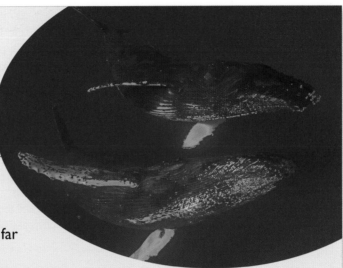

A The vast oceans of the world are dark, deep and mysterious places where eyesight counts for little as soon as you venture very far beneath the surface.

B For humans, who live in a world dominated by visual stimuli, to exist in such conditions would be impossible. But for whales and dolphins that live in the ocean or, in the case of a few species, muddy rivers and estuaries, the darkness is unimportant. What is crucial to them is sound.

C Sound is an efficient way to transmit and sense information, especially as it travels five times faster through water than through air. If humans shout to someone, it is unlikely that they will be heard a kilometre away. But if a whale 'shouts' in an ocean channel, another whale may hear it tens, if not hundreds, of kilometres away.

D Whales and dolphins use sound in two ways: for communication and for echolocation. Dolphins, porpoises and toothed whales communicate through a wide variety of high-frequency sounds – pure tone whistles, pulsed squeals, screams or barks – generally at frequencies of 500Hz to 20kHz (where a hertz is a cycle per second and a kilohertz a thousand).

E But as well as using sounds to communicate, toothed whales and dolphins also rely on echolocation to learn about their immediate environment, including prey that might be lurking nearby. They produce intense short broad-band pulses of sound in the ultrasonic range of between 0.25 and 220 kHz. These clicks are brief – typically less than one millisecond long – but they are repeated many times each second.

9 Discuss what you have underlined with a partner, then write two sentences that summarise the passage.

10 What is the writer's main purpose in this passage?
    A to explain the function of whale and dolphin sounds
    B to account for the development of underwater sounds
    C to compare the sounds made by whales and dolphins
    D to give the results of his studies on underwater sounds

Test tip
Underlining the main idea in each paragraph will help guide you to the information you need to find.

IELTS Reading test practice	Finding information in paragraphs

Some IELTS questions ask you to decide which paragraph contains certain information. It is best to start by reading the first paragraph and then deciding whether it contains the information in any of the statements. Note how the statements begin and note the key words.

11

The Undersea World of Sound passage has five paragraphs, **A–E**.
Which paragraph contains the following information?

1 **a contrast** between the speed of sound in and out of the ocean
2 **a reference to** how whale and dolphin noises can help them find food
3 **a description** of what it is like under the sea
4 **the names** of a range of noises whales and dolphins make underwater
5 **the various places** whales and dolphins can be found

Dealing with unfamiliar words

You are unlikely to understand all the words in the IELTS Reading passages, but often you can work out the meaning of difficult vocabulary.

- **Think about what part of speech it is**
  It helps to know what type of meaning the unknown word carries. For example, *minute, translucent* and *ethereal* in the *Pearly Gems* paragraph on page 38 are all adjectives. You do not need to understand these adjectives in order to understand the idea about the dead worms and where they are found. For this, you need to understand the verb *entombed*.

- **Look at how the word is formed**
  Sometimes it is possible to guess what a difficult word means. For example in *The Undersea World of Sound*, the word *echolocation* (paragraph **D**, page 39) is a noun formed using *echo* and *location*. The two parts of the word help you understand that it probably has something to do with echoes coming from a place. What do you think *entombed* means?

- **Read the word in context**
  You can also look at the text that comes before and after the word. For example in *The Undersea World of Sound*, the word *transmit* (paragraph **C**, page 39) is a verb that is followed by a rephrasing: *If humans shout* …This helps you understand that it is another word for sending out messages.

It is not necessary to understand all the words in a passage but you do need to recognise which words are important because they give you key information.

12 Which key word in *The Undersea World of Sound* helps you answer question **2** in exercise **11**?

- Now try and put everything you have learned so far in this unit into practice with the exercises on page 41.

IELTS Reading test practice	Choosing headings for paragraphs

13 Read the title and subheading of the passage below and decide what it is about.

14 Read the article and underline the sentence which contains the main idea(s) in each paragraph.

15

The reading passage below has seven paragraphs **A–G**.
Choose the correct heading for each paragraph from the list of headings below.

> **List of Headings**
>
> i   Increasing customer confidence
> ii   A benefit to retailers
> iii   The bigger picture of how Internet use changes consumer behaviour
> iv   Introducing a novel approach to purchasing
> v   The dangers for retailers
> vi   Retraining staff
> vii   Changing the face of the shop and the Internet site
> viii   A look at the sales figures
> ix   Encouraging online feedback from consumers

1 Paragraph **A** _iii_   5 Paragraph **E** _ii_
2 Paragraph **B** _vii_   6 Paragraph **F** _v_
3 Paragraph **C** _ii_   7 Paragraph **G** _vii_
4 Paragraph **D** _i_

> **Test tip**
> Match ideas not words. You may find words from the list of headings in the passage but they may be in a different paragraph from the one that is the answer.

Wily, wired consumers

The Internet has empowered shoppers both online and offline

A The amount of time people spend researching, checking prices, visiting stores and seeking advice from friends tends to rise in proportion to the value of the **product** they are thinking of buying. A new car is one of the biggest **purchases** people make, and buyers typically spend four to six weeks mulling over their choices. So why are some people now walking into car showrooms and ordering a vehicle without even asking for a test drive? Or turning up at an electrical store and pointing out the washing machine they want without seeking advice from a sales assistant? Welcome to a new style of shopping shaped by the Internet.

B More people are buying products online, especially at peak buying periods. The total value of **e-commerce** transactions in the United States in the fourth quarter of 2004 reached $18 billion, a 22% increase over the same period in 2003, according to the Department of Commerce in Washington DC. But that just represents 2% of America's total **retail** market and excludes **services,** such as online travel, the value of goods auctioned on the Internet, and the $34 billion-worth of goods that individuals trade on eBay.

C If you consider the Internet's wider influence over what people spend their money on, then the figures escalate out of sight. Some carmakers in America now find that eight out of ten of their buyers have logged on to the Internet to gather information about not just the exact vehicle they want, but also the price they are going to pay. Similarly with consumer electronics, nowadays if a customer wants to know which flat-screen TV they should buy, they are likely to start their shopping online – even though the vast majority will not complete the **transaction** there.

D The Internet is moving the world closer to perfect product and price information. The additional knowledge it can provide makes **consumers** more self-assured and bold enough to go into a car dealership and refuse **to bargain**. As a result, the process of shopping is increasingly being divorced from the transaction itself. Consumers might **surf the web** at night and hit the shops during the day. Visiting bricks-and-mortar stores can provide the final confirmation that the **item** or group of items that they are interested in is right for them.

E Far from losing **trade** to online **merchants**, stores that offer the sorts of **goods** people find out about online can gain from this new form of consumer behaviour. This is provided they offer attractive **facilities**, good **guarantees** and low prices.

F Merchants who charge too much and offer poor service, however, should beware. The same, too, for shaky **manufacturers**: smarter consumers know which products have a good **reputation** and which do not, because online they now read not only the **sales blurb** but also reviews from previous purchasers. And if customers are disappointed, a few **clicks of the mouse** will take them to places where they can let the world know.

G Some companies are already adjusting their business models to take account of these trends. The stores run by Sony and Apple, for instance, are more like brand showrooms than shops. They are there for people to try out devices and to ask questions of knowledgeable staff. Whether the products are ultimately bought online or offline is of secondary importance. Online traders must also adjust. Amazon, for one, is rapidly turning from being primarily a bookseller to becoming a mass retailer, by letting other companies sell products on its site, rather like a marketplace. Other transformations in the retail business are bound to follow.

Vocabulary builder

Test tip
Both technology and consumerism are popular IELTS topics.

16 Work with a partner. Together, look at the words in **bold** in the Reading passage to make sure you know what they mean. Try to guess if you do not know.

17 Find the following more general words and expressions in the Reading passage and use your strategies for guessing the meaning of words to work out what they mean.

		Meaning
Example	seeking advice	*getting advice / help (with a decision)*
a	in proportion to	
b	mulling over	
c	turning up	
d	peak periods	
e	influence over	
f	gain from	
g	take account of	
h	try out	

■ Try to use some of these expressions in your next piece of IELTS writing.

Reading

2 Scanning for a specific detail and skimming for general understanding

- What are skimming and scanning skills?

- How does IELTS test my ability to find specific information and detail?

In IELTS you need to be able to read faster than your normal pace. You also need to be able to quickly find particular words and phrases.

There are a variety of IELTS question types that test how well you can find facts in a text. Often they are completion tasks, where you have a gap to fill, or you may have to answer short questions.

Scanning

Scanning means running your eyes over a text to find something that stands out, like a name or date. In IELTS Reading questions, there are often words, names or numbers that you can scan for. This helps you know where to find the answer.

1 ⏱ Take two minutes to scan the Reading passage on the last two pages of Reading Unit **1** for the following details.

1 a large amount of money	**4** two brand-name stores
2 a US government department	**5** an Internet trading company
3 a percentage	

Skimming

Skimming means reading a text quickly to find the main ideas or information. You need to skim IELTS passages to get a general idea of the content. You also need to skim the questions and passage when you are looking for the answers.

2 ⏱ Take three or four minutes to:
- read the title and subheading of the article on the next page and predict the content
- skim the passage and say what it is about.

IELTS Reading test practice   Short-answer questions

Short-answer questions often begin with *wh*-words because they are designed to test whether you can find concrete facts/information in the Reading passage. You should read the questions carefully before you start so that you know what you are looking for and whether you need to scan (e.g. to find a word/name/number) or skim for the answer.

> **Test tip**
> In a block of short-answer questions you will find that the answers occur in the text in the same order as the questions; i.e. you will come across the answer to question 1 first, and so on. Remember that when you move on to another block of questions you may have to start reading from the beginning of the text again.

3 Read through questions **1–6**, on the following page. For each question, underline the key words that tell you what you need to find.

4 Compare what you have underlined with the rest of the class and then discuss these questions.
  a Which question do you think will be easiest to scan for? Why?
  b Which questions might be harder to answer?

5 🕐 Take ten minutes to answer questions **1–6**. As you answer each question, make a mental note of what you are looking for while you read the passage, e.g. for question **1**: *I'm looking for the name of two types of material that people make.*

Sifting through the sands of time

When you're on the beach, you're stepping on ancient mountains, skeletons of marine animals, even tiny diamonds. Sand provides a mineral treasure-trove, a record of geology's earth-changing processes.

Sand: as children we play on it and as adults we relax on it. It is something we complain about when it gets in our food, and praise when it's moulded into castles. But we don't often look at it. If we did, we would discover an account of a geological past and a history of marine life that goes back thousands and in some cases millions of years.

Sand covers not just sea-shores, but also ocean beds, deserts and mountains. It is one of the most common substances on earth. And it is a major element in man-made items too – concrete is largely sand, while glass is made of little else.

What exactly is sand? Well, it is larger than fine dust and smaller than shingle. In fact, according to the most generally accepted scheme of measurement, devised by the Massachusetts Institute of Technology, grains qualify if their diameter is greater than 0.06 of a millimetre and less than 0.6 of a millimetre.

Depending on its age and origin, a particular sand can consist of tiny pebbles or porous granules. Its grain may have the shape of stars or spirals, their edges jagged or smooth. They have come from the erosion of rocks, or from the skeletons of marine organisms which accumulate on the bottom of the oceans, or even from volcanic eruptions.

Colour is another clue to sand's origins. If it is a dazzling white, its grains may be derived from nearby coral outcrops, from crystalline quartz rocks or from gypsum, like the white sands of New Mexico. On Pacific islands jet black sands form from volcanic minerals. Other black beaches are magnetic. Some sand is very recent indeed, as is the case on the island of Kamoama in Hawaii, where a beach was created after a volcanic eruption in 1990. Molten lava spilled into the sea and exploded in glassy droplets.

Usually, the older the granules, the finer they are and the smoother the edges. The fine, white beaches of northern Scotland, for instance, are recycled from sandstone several hundred million years old. Perhaps they will be stone once more, in another few hundred million.

Sand is an irreplaceable industrial ingredient whose uses are legion: but it has one vital function you might never even notice. Sand cushions our land from the sea's impact, and geologists say it often does a better job of protecting our shores than the most advanced coastal technology.

Answer the questions below.
Choose **NO MORE THAN THREE WORDS** from the passage for each answer.

1 What <u>TWO materials made by humans</u> are mentioned in the passage? *CONCRETE + GLOSS*
2 Which part of a grain of sand have scientists measured? — *DIAMETRE*
3 What **TWO** factors determine the size and shape of a piece of sand? — *AHE + ORIGIN*
4 Which event produced the beach on Kamoama island? — *VOLCANIC ERUPTION*
5 Where, according to the passage, can beaches made of very ancient sand be found? *SCOTLON*
6 Who claims that sand can have a more efficient function than coastal technology? *GEOLOGISTS*

Test tip
Make sure you use the exact words that are in the passage and that you spell them correctly.

6 Compare your answers to the six questions with the rest of the class. What sort of answers would lose marks?

7 ⏱ Take five minutes to find out what the passage starting at the bottom of the page is about.

Vocabulary builder

8 Now scan *Effects on Salmon Biodiversity* for words **1–9** and then match them to definitions **A–I**.

Words		Definitions	
1	endangered	A	electricity produced from fast-flowing water
2	migrations	B	confuse someone or something about where it is going
3	mature	C	change the shape or appearance of something slightly
4	breeding	D	at risk of being harmed or destroyed
5	hydropower	E	continued existence of a species
6	survival	F	become adult
7	disorient	G	natural area in which an animal lives
8	modify	H	mass movement of a species
9	habitat	I	producing young

Test tip
Passages about the natural world are common in IELTS and this vocabulary relates closely to this topic.

Effects on Salmon Biodiversity

The number of Pacific salmon has declined dramatically but the loss of genetic diversity may be a bigger problem

Each year, countless salmon migrate from the rivers and streams along the western coasts of Canada and the US to the Pacific Ocean, while at the same time others leave the ocean and return to freshwater to spawn a new generation. This ritual has been going on for many millennia. But more than a century ago, the number of salmon returning from the sea began to fall dramatically in the Pacific Northwest. The decline accelerated in the 1970s and by the 1990s the US Endangered Species Act listed 26 kinds of salmon as endangered.

In North America, there are five species of Pacific salmon: pink salmon, chum, sockeye, coho and chinook. Most of these fish migrate to the sea and then return to freshwater to reproduce. They are also *semelparous* – they die after spawning once. The life cycle of a typical salmon begins with females depositing eggs in nests, or *redds*, on the gravel bottoms of rivers and lakes. There must be large quantities of gravel for this process to be successful. The young emerge from here and live in freshwater for periods ranging from a few days to several years. Then the juveniles undergo a physiological metamorphosis, called *smoltification*, and head towards the ocean. Once in the sea, the salmon often undertake extensive migrations of thousands of miles while they mature. After anywhere from a few months to a few years, adult salmon return – with high fidelity – to the river where they were born. There they spawn and the cycle begins again.

45

Stream-type chinook spend one or more years in freshwater before heading to sea; they also undertake extensive offshore voyages and return to their natal streams during the spring or summer, often holding in freshwater for several months before spawning. In contrast, ocean-type chinook move out very early in life, before they reach one year of age. But once these salmon reach open water, they do not travel far offshore. They usually spend their entire ocean residence on the continental shelf and return to their natal streams immediately before spawning.

Because salmon typically return to reproduce in the river where they were spawned, individual streams are home to local breeding populations that can have a unique genetic signature and the state of the oceans influences this. Also, salmon react in complex ways to human-induced changes to their environment.

The extensive development of hydropower on the major rivers of the western US has clearly disrupted populations of salmon. Other problems come from the very engineering fixes made to protect these fish from harm. Dams on some rivers are equipped with submersible screens designed to divert migrating juveniles away from turbines. Unfortunately, these measures do not benefit all fish. These screens steer as many as 95 percent of the stream-type chinook around the turbines, but because of idiosyncrasies in behaviour these measures redirect as few as 15 percent of ocean-type chinook. One thus expects to see genetic shifts in favour of the stream types.

Fish ladders too have drawbacks. Although these devices have helped to bring survival rates for mature fish closer to historic levels, dams have certainly altered their upstream journey. Rather than swimming against a flowing river, adults now pass through a series of reservoirs punctuated by dams, where discharge from the turbine can disorient the fish and make it hard for them to find ladders. Such impediments do not kill the fish, but they affect migration rates.

Dams may also modify salmon habitat in more subtle ways. An indirect effect of the 92-metre Brownlee Dam on the Snake River provides a dramatic example. Historically, the upper Snake River produced some 25,000 to 30,000 chinook salmon that spawned during the early fall. The completion of the dam in the late 1950s not only rendered the vast majority of their habitat inaccessible, but also led to more extreme water temperatures downstream from the dam. These changes, in turn, altered the life cycle of the small population of Snake River chinook that remained. Today young chinook emerge from the gravel later than they did before the dam was built, and thus they migrate downstream later, when temperatures are higher and water levels lower.

Following referencing

Writers avoid repetition by using reference words and phrases that refer back (or forwards) to a word or idea in the passage.

9 Scan the text for the following reference words or phrases and then say what they refer to.

this ritual (Para **1**)	these measures (Para **5**)
the decline (Para **1**)	these devices (Para **6**)
there they spawn (Para **2**)	such impediments (Para **6**)
influences this (Para **4**)	these changes (Para **7**)
other problems (Para **5**)	

IELTS Reading test practice	Completing a flowchart / diagram / table

The information you need to complete a flowchart, diagram or table is usually based on one part of the passage. Use the title of the chart to help you find the right part. Use the words provided to help you predict the type of answer you need.

NOTE: Unlike sentence completion tasks, in this type of task the answers are not always in passage order.

10 Take eight minutes to answer questions **1–5** and complete the flowchart.

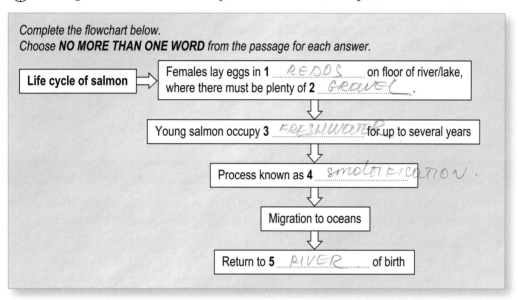

Complete the flowchart below.
*Choose **NO MORE THAN ONE WORD** from the passage for each answer.*

| Life cycle of salmon | → | Females lay eggs in **1** REDDS on floor of river/lake, where there must be plenty of **2** GRAVEL. |

Young salmon occupy **3** FRESHWATER for up to several years

Process known as **4** smoltification.

Migration to oceans

Return to **5** RIVER of birth

11 Take ten minutes to answer questions **6–12** and complete the table.

Complete the table below.
*Choose **NO MORE THAN TWO WORDS** from the passage for each answer.*

Effects of engineering projects on salmon

Engineering object	Purpose	Impact	Outcome
submersible screens	keep young migrating salmon clear of **6** TURBINES	mainly protect **7** STREAM chinook	one species will become more numerous
8 FISH LADDERS	to assist journey	fish can't locate them because of turbine discharge	negative impact on **9** MIGRATION LIFE CYCLE
Brownlee Dam		fish can't get to normal **10** access very great changes in **11** TEMPERATURE	**12** LIFE CYCLE of Snake River chinook changed

Reading

3 Identifying main and supporting ideas

- How are main and supporting ideas different?

- How does identifying main ideas and supporting points help me answer IELTS questions?

Most paragraphs in well-written, discursive or argumentative texts contain at least one main idea and very often these ideas are supported by examples or by further explanation.

Being able to separate main ideas from supporting points is a key reading skill. It helps you understand a text more quickly. It also helps you find the important information, which IELTS questions often test.

Understanding paragraph structure

In every paragraph, there are some parts that are more important than others. These are the main ideas and they are usually supported by other points of information and examples.

1   Work with a partner. Read this title and subheading and then together discuss what you think the text will be about.

> ## How to Win the Blame Game
>
> People are often more concerned about avoiding blame than achieving results. But blame can actually be a positive force in the workplace. The trick, says one former Major League baseball pitcher, is knowing how to use it.

2   Discuss these questions before you read on.

   a What is *blame* and what is the difference between *fault* and *blame*?
   b In what context is this passage going to discuss *blame*?

3   Read the first paragraph of the text and the labels which explain its structure.

Introduction to the topic

Main idea: two opposing attitudes to blame

Example that illustrates main idea

Topic

> When a new product **flops** in the marketplace or a new recruit turns out to be a poor worker, blaming somebody for the mistake seems a bit rude. So people talk politely around the **blunder**, saying things like 'sales targets were missed' or 'mistakes occurred', as if the error happened all by itself. Indeed, at many companies, blame is never even mentioned. At other organisations, people are all too quick to **point fingers**, leaving employees more concerned about avoiding blame than about achieving results. Such organisations have **given** blame **a bad name**.

New idea that may be developed in next paragraph

4 Try to guess the meanings of the words and phrases in **bold** in the first paragraph. Then check your answers in the key.

5 Take three minutes to complete the labels **a–c** for the second paragraph and answer the questions which follow.

a

b

The truth is, blame can also be a powerful constructive force. For starters, it can be an effective teaching tool, helping people to avoid repeating their mistakes. When used judiciously – and sparingly – blame can also prod people to put forth their best efforts, while maintaining both their confidence and their focus on goals. Indeed, blame can have a very helpful effect when it's used for the right reasons. The key, then, is the way in which blame is managed, which can influence how people make decisions and perform their jobs, and ultimately affect the culture and character of an organisation.

c

d Which words and phrases in this paragraph
did you have to guess the meaning of?
e Did you need to know these words to understand the main idea(s) of
the paragraph?
f What would you expect to read about in the third paragraph?

6 Take two minutes to read the third paragraph and then underline the main idea, two points which support the main idea (the *supporting points*) and any examples (use different coloured pens to do this).

Baseball managers spend most of their time and energy managing things that go wrong. Thus, baseball provides an excellent microcosm in which to study blame because mistakes and failures are a routine part of every game. In a typical game, managers, coaches and players can easily make more than 100 bad decisions – and still end up winning. Even very successful pitchers average more than two bad pitches per batter and if a batter bats well 40% of the time but badly the other 60% he is having a miraculous season. Thus, if managers and coaches got upset about every mistake, they would go mad by the end of the season.

IELTS Reading test practice	Multiple choice

Multiple choice questions often require detailed reading of paragraphs because the questions may be written to test your understanding of the main idea or supporting points. Also, the wrong options (called *distractors*) will come from the same part of the passage as the answer, and you need to eliminate these.

How to approach multiple choice questions

Underline the key words in the question and use these to quickly find the part of the passage that you need to read in more detail.

7 ⏱ Take five minutes to answer these questions, which are based on the three paragraphs in *How to Win the Blame Game*.

> **Test tip**
>
> In some multiple choice questions, the options complete a sentence (see questions 1 and 2) and in others, they answer a question (see question 3).

Choose the correct letter, A, B, C or D.

1 In the first paragraph, one of the writer's main points is that companies tend to
   A perform better when blame is avoided.
   B respond differently to errors in the workplace.
   C associate blame with poor sales figures.
   D blame employees rather than managers for things that go wrong.

2 In the second paragraph, the writer claims that one of the positive features of blame is that
   A everyone feels the same about it.
   B people can learn how to deal with it.
   C it can build confidence in less secure employees.
   D it can encourage employees to work hard.

3 Why does the writer choose to refer to baseball?
   A It is a well-known American sport.
   B The managers dislike blaming their players.
   C Error is an important aspect of the game.
   D Even good players have bad days.

Extracting key information

The *How to Win the Blame Game* passage shows how main ideas are expressed and supported in paragraphs and also how main ideas link paragraphs together into a text. In some passages, however, the same main idea may be developed across more than one paragraph.

8 Work with a partner. Read the passage on the next page and then discuss the questions.

   a What is the main idea in the first paragraph?
   b What is the structure of the passage overall?
   c Which words in the second paragraph help you identify the supporting points?
   d How easy would it be to make a mental summary of the passage? Why?

Going digital

Electronic libraries will make today's Internet pale by comparison. But building them will not be easy.

All over the world, libraries have begun the Herculean task of making faithful digital copies of the books, images and recordings that preserve the intellectual effort of humankind. For armchair scholars, the work promises to bring such a wealth of information to the desktop that the present Internet may seem amateurish in retrospect.

Librarians see three clear benefits to going digital. First, it helps them preserve rare and fragile objects without denying access to those who wish to study them. The British Library, for example, holds the only medieval manuscript of *Beowulf* in London. Only qualified scholars were allowed to see it until Kevin S. Kiernan of the University of Kentucky scanned the ancient manuscript with three different light sources (revealing details not normally apparent to the naked eye) and put the images up on the Internet for anyone to peruse. Tokyo's National Diet Library is similarly creating detailed digital photographs of 1,236 woodblock prints, scrolls and other materials it considers national treasures so that researchers can scrutinise them without handling the originals.

A second benefit is convenience. Once books are converted to digital form, patrons can retrieve them in seconds rather than minutes. Several people can simultaneously read the same book or view the same picture. Clerks are spared the chore of reshelving. And libraries could conceivably use the Internet to lend their virtual collections to those who are unable to visit in person.

The third advantage of electronic copies is that they occupy millimetres of space on a magnetic disk rather than metres on a shelf. Expanding library buildings is increasingly costly. The University of California at Berkeley recently spent $46 million on an underground addition to house 1.5 million books – an average cost of $30 per volume. The price of disk storage, in contrast, has fallen to about $2 per 300-page publication and continues to drop.

IELTS Reading test practice — *TRUE / FALSE / NOT GIVEN*

Take some time to read the instructions to this task carefully so that you understand the difference between a *FALSE* answer and a *NOT GIVEN* answer. If you write *FALSE* as your answer, you are saying that the information in the statement contradicts (is the opposite of) the information given in the passage. This is quite different from a *NOT GIVEN* answer, which says that you can find nothing in the passage about this information.

How to approach the task

- Underline the key words in the questions and use these to find the right part of the passage (even a **NOT GIVEN** statement will be based on something in the passage).
- For a **TRUE** answer, make sure that the information in the passage exactly matches the idea in the statement.
- For a **FALSE** answer, make sure that the statement contradicts the information in the passage.
- For a **NOT GIVEN** answer, you should be able to find the topic of the statement in the passage but nothing on what is said about this topic.

9 Take eight minutes to answer questions **1–7**.

Do the following statements agree with the information in the passage?

Write

TRUE	*if the statement agrees with the information*
FALSE	*if the statement contradicts the information*
NOT GIVEN	*if there is no information on this*

1 Digital libraries could have a more professional image than the Internet.
2 Only experts are permitted to view the scanned version of *Beowulf*.
3 The woodblock prints in Tokyo have been damaged by researchers.
4 Fewer staff will be required in digital libraries.
5 People may be able to borrow digital materials from the library.
6 Digital libraries will occupy more space than ordinary libraries.
7 The cost of newly published books will fall.

IELTS Reading test practice   **Note completion**

Taking notes from written sources is one of the main skills that you need when you study at university. Good note-taking depends on being able to identify the main idea(s) and supporting points. In the IELTS test, your ability to take good notes is tested in the note completion task in which you must select just the right information to fill the gaps.

10 Read the passage below and on the next page and underline what you think are the main ideas and supporting points.

The First Cyber Criminals

'Cyber crime' sounds like a very new type of crime. In fact, it has been around since the 1970s – before the personal computer was invented, when computers far less powerful than today's games consoles filled entire rooms and were monitored by technicians.

The first cyber crimes were carried out across telephone lines, by a group of electronic enthusiasts known as 'phone phreakers'. Having studied the US telephone system, they realised that it used a series of musical tones to connect calls. They found they could imitate those tones, and steal free phone calls, by creating small musical devices called 'blue boxes'. One famous 'phreaker', John Draper, even discovered that using a whistle given away inside a cereal box could do the same job as a blue box.

Cyber crime centred on the telephone for many years, until the first computer-to-computer cyber crime took place in the 1980s. 'Hacking', as it has since been referred to, gained new public visibility after the popular 1984 film *Wargames*, in which a hacker breaks into a US military computer and saves the world. Many hackers later said this was their inspiration.

It was the arrival of the Internet that was eventually to make cyber crime a big issue. When millions of home and business computer users began to visit the Internet in the early to mid 1990s, few were thinking about the dangers of cyber crime or about security and so it seemed only a matter of time before banks became the target for hackers.

In 1994 a group of hackers broke into US bank Citibank's computers and stole $10 million. This was later nearly all recovered. With the rise of the Internet, credit cards became the tools of cyber criminals: Kevin Mitnick was arrested for stealing 20,000 credit card numbers over the net in 1995. This and other credit card crime prompted credit card companies to consider ways they could make cards more secure.

11 ⏱ Take seven minutes to complete the notes **1–7** below.

Complete the notes below.

Choose **NO MORE THAN TWO WORDS AND/OR A NUMBER** *from the passage for each answer.*

Cyber Crime

First cyber criminals:	called **1** .... (1970s)
Nature of crime:	made free calls by copying **2** ....
Computer crime:	began in **3** ....
Crime known as:	**4** ....
Promoted by hit movie:	**5** .... (1984)
Internet crime:	initially unexpected, but quickly focused on **6** ....
Current concern:	**7** .... fraud

Test tip
The answers may not always come in passage order for note completion tasks.

Reading

4 Improving global reading skills

- What are global reading skills and how important are they for IELTS?

- How are these skills tested?

IELTS Academic Reading passages are long and reflect the type of reading you have to do on a course of academic study. You need to form a global idea of each passage: a mental summary of the content and overall structure.

Global multiple choice questions test how well you understand the purpose/theme of the whole passage. Paragraph headings test your understanding of the main themes of each paragraph.

Paraphrasing the main ideas

Texts are divided into paragraphs but these may have overlapping themes. Also, some paragraphs are longer than others, some are more important to the main message and some contain more detail/support.

1 Read the following text and then answer the questions.

  a Which paragraph contains the most detail?
  b Which three paragraphs cover one main theme?

Magazine circulations are in the millions and advertising revenue is rising, despite the growth of TV and electronic media, reports David Short

A Print is not dead yet – at least not when it comes to magazines. Despite ever-growing competition from television and electronic media, a new report shows that worldwide advertising expenditure in consumer magazines has doubled over the past decade.

B The report also shows that many magazines in Europe continue to enjoy circulations in the millions. Although there are more and more television channels, whether cable, satellite, terrestrial, analogue, or digital, and despite the incursion of the Internet, magazines are still a regular shopping or subscription item.

C Advertising expenditure worldwide was $225 billion last year, according to the report *World Magazine Trends*. $32 billion of this, or 14%, was taken by magazines. In Europe, the share of consumer magazine expenditure was $12 billion or 21% of an estimated overall spend of $57 billion. But the share had dropped in the past

15 years from 30%, with decline having been particularly severe in Belgium and Germany, where commercial television was introduced relatively late.

D However, the type of magazines which Europeans choose to flip through still varies dramatically according to country, with few signs that the European magazine with a common title is making inroads across nations. Interests which can create top-selling titles in one country are nowhere to be seen in the circulation lists of others.

E But whatever their relative importance across the world, magazines have one real advantage over broadcast media. For advertisers such as tobacco and alcohol producers, which are barred or severely restricted on television in some countries, magazines remain a safe haven for their messages. And new French research has revealed that magazines are still powerful tools for owners of brands.

2 Choose the sentence that best paraphrases the main idea in each paragraph of the text.

1 Paragraph A
  A The amount of money spent on magazine advertising is increasing.
  B The rivalry between magazines and other media is surprising.
  C Some magazines sell better than others.

2 Paragraph B
  A Magazines are more popular than they used to be.
  B A lot of people are still reading magazines.
  C TV is more available than ever.

3 Paragraph C
  A Europe allocates a greater proportion of its advertising budget to magazines than the world average.
  B Belgium and Germany spend more on magazine advertising than other European countries.
  C The figures for magazine advertising in Europe are decreasing.

4 Paragraph D
  A Across Europe, people read very different kinds of magazines.
  B The idea of a 'European' magazine is becoming popular.
  C Magazines that cover popular activities can become best sellers.

5 Paragraph E
  A Cigarette advertising is banned in some countries.
  B Magazines advertise a smaller range of products than television.
  C There are fewer limitations on magazine advertising than TV advertising.

IELTS Reading test practice	Global reading question

Often a set of multiple choice questions ends with a global question. Global questions test how well you understand the main theme of the *whole* passage by asking about the writer's purpose / a suitable title / the main idea. Sometimes the passage does not have a title or subheading, if there is a global multiple choice question.

3

What is the purpose of the writer of the passage on page 54?

  A to compare European and world magazines
  B to attract more magazine readers
  C to review the continuing popularity of magazines
  D to illustrate the advantages of electronic magazines

Some texts have a clear theme in each paragraph. IELTS tests your understanding by asking you to match each paragraph with a heading chosen from a list. The list of headings is given before the passage so that you can read through the headings before you read the passage. Use global reading skills to do the task below.

How to approach the task

- Read through the list of headings to familiarise yourself with them.
- Take ten minutes to read the passage, underlining what you think are the *main ideas* and *key words* in each paragraph.
- Re-read paragraph **A** and the example heading.
- Re-read paragraph **B** and select the heading that best fits this paragraph. If you think there is more than one, mark them both and come back to this paragraph later.
- Repeat this procedure with the rest of the paragraphs.

4 ⏱ Take five minutes to answer questions **1–7**.

Test tip

There are always some extra headings that you do not need to use.

There is sometimes an example answer.

The reading passage has eight paragraphs, **A–H**.

Choose the correct heading for each paragraph from the list of headings below.

List of Headings

i	Benefiting from an earlier model
ii	Important operative conditions
iii	Examining the public confusion
iv	Where to go from here?
v	How it's all linked up
vi	How a suitable location was found
vii	Comparing wind speeds in Australian cities
viii	Matching operational requirements with considerations of appearance
ix	What makes Esperance different?
x	More than just a source of power

Example	*Answer*
Paragraph **A**	**x**

1 Paragraph **B** ....
2 Paragraph **C** ....
3 Paragraph **D** ....
4 Paragraph **E** ....
5 Paragraph **F** ....
6 Paragraph **G** ....
7 Paragraph **H** ....

Australia's first commercial wind farm

It's some years since the rotor blades began spinning in Esperance.

A Harvest time in Esperance is constant. As long as the wind blows – which is pretty much all the time – nine identical synchronised wind turbines reap the benefits of the dependable winds that gust up around the southern coastline of Western Australia. These sleek, white, robot-like wind turbines loom up on the horizon forming part of Australia's first commercial wind farm. They're not only functional machines that help provide electricity for this secluded coastal town, but increasingly, they're also drawcards for curious tourists and scientists alike.

B Because of its isolation, Esperance is not linked to Western Power's grid which supplies electricity from gas-, coal- and oil-fired power stations to the widespread population of Western Australia. Before the wind turbines went in, Esperance's entire electricity needs were met by the diesel power station in town.

C The $5.8 million Ten Mile Lagoon project is not Esperance's first wind farm. The success of a smaller, experimental wind farm, at a spot called Salmon Beach, encouraged the State's power utility to take Esperance wind seriously. Today, the wind turbines at Ten Mile Lagoon work in conjunction with the diesel power station, significantly reducing the amount of the town's electricity generated by expensive diesel power.

D The wind farm is connected to the power station by a 33-kilovolt powerline, and a radio link between the two allows operators to monitor and control each wind turbine. The nine 225-kilowatt Vestas wind turbines produce a total generating capacity of two megawatts and provide around 12 per cent of the energy requirements of Esperance and its surrounding districts.

E The power produced by a wind turbine depends on the size and efficiency of the machine and, of course, on the energy in the wind. The energy in the wind available to the wind turbines is proportional to wind speed cubed. Thus, the greater the wind speed, the greater the output of the turbine. In order to achieve optimum wind speeds, the right location is imperative. 'You have to accept the nature of the beast,' Mr Rosser, Western Power's physicist, said. 'As surface dwellers our perceptions of wind speeds are bad. As you go higher, wind speed increases significantly.'

F The most favourable wind sites are on gently sloping hills, away from obstructions like trees and buildings and where the prevailing winds are not blocked. Computer modelling was used to select the optimum site for Esperance's wind farm. Scientists were concerned not only with efficiency, but also with protecting the coastal health environment which is rich in plant life and home to tiny pygmy and honey-possums, and a host of bird species. In addition, the wind farm is adjacent to Esperance's popular scenic tourist drive.

60 **G** Strict erosion controls have been implemented and access to the wind farm is limited to selected viewing areas. The wind turbine towers are painted white and devoid of corporate logos or signage. According to Mr 75 Rosser there is something of a worldwide backlash
65 against wind farms with regard to their visual impact. 'But because wind turbines perform best in the most exposed positions, they will always be visible. There is a very real need to balance environmental and 80 technical requirements. I think the Ten Mile Lagoon
70 Wind Farm sets the standard for environmentally friendly developments.'

H In fact, the project has become something of a tourist attraction in itself. Esperance shire president Ian Mickel said the wind turbines had been well accepted by locals. 'We have watched the wind farm develop with great interest, and now we find visitors to Esperance are equally enthusiastic about it,' he said. The aim now is to identify other remote locations where wind turbines will be a feasible means of supplementing existing power stations.

- There is always more than one question type for each IELTS Reading passage. Thematic questions such as paragraph headings should help you find the answers to other questions more quickly because they help you see how the passage is structured.

IELTS Reading test practice   Sentence completion

In these questions, ideas from the passage are rewritten in short sentences and there are gaps for you to fill. Like other completion tasks, you need to read the instructions carefully to see how many words you can use. The answers come in passage order.

How to approach the task

- Find the part of the passage that contains the idea and then work out what the missing words are. This makes it easier to find other information.
- Pay attention to the grammar of the sentence and make sure it is correct when your answer is added.

5 ⏱ Take six minutes to answer questions **1–6** about *Australia's first commercial wind farm.*

> **Test tip**
> There may be two gaps in a sentence and this may be worth one or two marks.
> The word 'both' in the sentence or summary signals that two answers may be required.

Complete the sentences below.

*Choose **NO MORE THAN THREE WORDS AND/OR A NUMBER** from the passage for each answer.*

1 Esperance used to rely totally on .... for energy.

2 About .... of Esperance's energy needs are met by the wind farm.

3 Both the .... of a wind turbine affect its energy output.

4 & 5 Wind farms should not be built near barriers to the wind, such as ....
or ....

6 Scientists chose the best location for the wind farm at Esperance with the aid of
....

Getting gapfill answers right

In all the completion tasks, it is easy to lose marks by writing too many or too few words,
copying words incorrectly or selecting the wrong information.

6   Here are some answers that students have given to questions **1–6** above.
For each answer, state which question the student was doing and say why the
answer would be marked wrong.

a	computer moderlling	**b**	tree or building	**c**	around 12 per cent
d	the diesel power	**e**	Western Power's grid	**f**	$5.8 million
g	scientists	**h**	on gently sloping hills		

> **Test tip**
> IELTS questions are written using different words and phrases from those used in the passage. This is known as paraphrasing.

7   Match the words and phrases below from questions **1–6** in exercise **5** with
phrases in the passage.

	Question phrasing	Passage
A	used to rely totally on	
B	energy needs	
C	its energy output	
D	not be (built) near	
E	barriers to the wind, such as	
F	chose the best location	
G	with the aid of	

IELTS Reading test practice   Global reading question

In IELTS Reading, global questions will usually be the last question you have to answer about a
passage.

8

What is the main purpose of the writer of the article?

A to respond to criticism of a project
B to review the success of a project
C to explain his role in a project
D to predict the future of a project

Reading

5 Summarising

- Why is summarising important?

If you can summarise a passage or a section of a passage, this shows that you have understood the content and can paraphrase it (i.e. write it in your own words). Summarising is a key reading skill in academic study.

- What types of summary questions are there in IELTS?

IELTS summaries can test your understanding of a whole text (i.e. global reading skills) or your understanding of the details within a part of the text.

Understanding summaries

Summaries aim to provide a shortened version of the information given in a text. To do this, summaries often paraphrase the information.

1 Read this opening paragraph from a newspaper article on music and then complete the sentence below, which summarises the main idea of the paragraph.

> Gerard Leonhard has seen the future of the music business – and it's incredibly dull. In his book *The Future of Music: Manifesto for the Digital Revolution*, co-authored by Dave Kusek, he predicts that music will be consumed exactly like water or any other household utility.

A new book on music compares it to a _____ .

2 Read the second paragraph of the article to find the words missing from sentences **1** and **2** which follow.

> For a monthly subscription fee of, say, $5, anyone will be able to tap into the 'celestial jukebox', a continuously updated collection that spans the history of recorded music. And given the increasing ubiquity of the Internet, the music will flow easily to listeners, via computers, TV sets, mobile phones and other devices not yet invented. Artists, in turn, will be paid using a subscription pool based on 'pro rata, per second' usage. Free from the constraints of having to manufacture and distribute plastic discs, any musician with a laptop can release whatever, whenever. This will drive musicians to engage listeners – in terms of both price and quality – as never before. In the process, music will become more of a service and less of a product.

    1 According to the writer, fees to musicians will come from _____ .
    2 In future, the two issues of _____ will be very important to consumers.

3 Underline the relevant sections of the paragraph above where you found the missing words. How have the ideas in the paragraph been paraphrased in sentences **1** and **2** in exercise **2**?

4 A summary of the two paragraphs above might look like this:

Flowing like Water

A new book on music compares it to a .... According to the writer, fees to musicians will come from .... and listeners will probably pay for their music on a monthly basis. The loss of discs will mean that in future, the issues of ....will be highly significant to consumers.

- There are two types of summary task in IELTS. In both types you will have a summary with numbered gaps to complete. However, you may have to use words from the passage to do this (rather like sentence completion), or you may have to select the correct words from a box of options labelled **A**, **B**, **C**, etc.

IELTS Reading test practice   **Summary completion**

This type of summary is made up of a number of gapfill sentences that you need to complete using words from the passage. Read the instructions carefully to see how many words you can use.

How to approach the task

- Read the summary heading and mark the part of the passage it relates to.
- Read through the summary first and try to predict the missing words.
- Use key words in the summary to help you find the information you need.
- Make sure you copy words or numbers correctly from the passage and don't include unnecessary words.
- Re-read the summary with your answers to check for content and grammar.

5 Take eight minutes to complete the summary (on page 62) of the rest of the music passage.

There are signs that the brave new world of subscription music is not that far off. A recent survey found interest in subscription services highest among consumers in the all-important 18–24 age group and those aficionados who spend large sums of money on music each year.

Musicians themselves are also adapting to a service model. The key is to build online communities of fans who feel engaged in the creative process, giving 'users' an unprecedented degree of participation in the music they listen to. Some famous artists, such as Metallica, Prince and David Bowie, maintain online collections of live concert downloads, exclusive digital-only tracks, videos, online journals and interactive forums where like-minded fans can meet.

Young listeners, it seems, are increasingly unimpressed with the album format – however cleverly the songs are arranged and attractively designed the cover art is. The album is 'traditional not inevitable' according to William Higham of Next Big Thing, a London-based youth trend consultancy. The next generation of music fans is growing up in a 'compilation culture', he says, pointing out that the single-track purchases make up a much larger percentage of digital music sales than singles do for 'offline' music purchases.

Complete the summary below.

*Choose **NO MORE THAN THREE WORDS AND/OR A NUMBER** from the passage for each answer.*

The Young Market

Selling music by **1** .... is popular among buyers, particularly young ones aged **2** .... Musicians are aware that they need to encourage large groups of their **3** .... to take part in music-making through live concert downloads and other **4** .... activities. The fact is that young people are losing their appreciation of the **5** .... even though it may be well produced and packaged. According to one expert, in the world of digital music sales, **6** .... are much more common.

6 Complete the table to see which parts of the passage have been paraphrased and which parts have used the same words in the summary.

Gap	Words in summary	Words in passage
1	Selling music / buyers	*subscription music / consumers*
2	young ones aged	
3	encourage large groups / take part in music-making	
4	live concert downloads / activities	
5	are losing their appreciation of / well produced / packaged	
6	one expert / world of digital music sales	

7 Work with a partner. Make a list of any wrong answers you had in exercise **5** and then discuss the reasons for this.

Vocabulary builder

8 Before you read the passage on page 63, complete the meanings for each of the words in this table using no more than two words.

Words	Meaning
antibiotic	a type of .... that destroys bacteria in the body.
micro-organism	a very small organism that must be seen using a ....
microbe	a micro-organism that can cause ....
bacteria	very similar to ....
resistance	ability to .... against something, e.g. ....
toxin	something that is poisonous, e.g. ....
epidemic	outbreak of disease among a lot of people or animals, e.g. ....

9　⏱ Take seven minutes to read the passage and answer questions **1–5** on page 64.

Prehistoric insects spawn new drugs

by Steve Connor

A Insects entombed in fossilised amber for tens of millions of years have provided the key to creating a new generation of antibiotic drugs that could wage war on modern diseases. Scientists have isolated the antibiotics from microbes found either inside the intestines of the amber-encased insects or in soil particles trapped with them when they were caught by sticky tree resin up to 130 million years ago. Spores of the microbes have survived an unprecedented period of suspended animation, enabling scientists to revive them in the laboratory.

B Research over the past two years has uncovered at least four antibiotics from the microbes and one has been able to kill modern drug-resistant bacteria that can cause potentially deadly diseases in humans. Present-day antibiotics have nearly all been isolated from micro-organisms that use them as a form of defence against their predators or competitors. But since the introduction of antibiotics into medicine 50 years ago, an alarming number have become ineffective because many bacteria have developed resistance to the drugs. The antibiotics that were in use millions of years ago may prove more deadly against drug-resistant modern strains of disease-causing bacteria.

C Raul Cano, who has pioneered the research at the California Polytechnic State University at San Luis Obispo, said the ancient antibiotics had been successful in fighting drug-resistant strains of staphylococcus bacteria, a 'superbug' that had threatened the health of patients in hospitals across the globe. He now intends to establish whether the antibiotics might have harmful side effects. 'The problem is how toxic they are to other cells and how easy they are to purify,' said Cano.

D A biotechnology company, Ambergene, has been set up to develop the antibiotics into drugs. If any ancient microbes are revived that resemble present-day diseases, they will be destroyed in case they escape and cause new epidemics. Drug companies will be anxious to study the chemical structures of the prehistoric antibiotics to see how they differ from modern drugs. They hope that one ancient molecule could be used as a basis to synthesise a range of drugs.

E There have been several attempts to extract material such as DNA from fossilised life-forms ranging from Egyptian mummies to dinosaurs but many were subsequently shown to be contaminated. Cano's findings have been hailed as a break-through by scientists. Edward Golenburg, an expert on extracting DNA from fossilised life-forms at Wayne State University in Detroit, said: 'They appear to be verifiable, ancient spores. They do seem to be real.' Richard Lenski, professor of microbial ecology at Michigan State University, said the fight against antibiotic-resistant strains of bacteria such as tuberculosis and staphylococcus could be helped by the discovery.

F However, even the use of ancient antibiotics may not halt the rise of drug-resistant bacteria. Stuart Levy, a micro-biologist at Tufts University in Boston, warned that the bacteria would eventually evolve to fight back against the new drugs. 'There might also be an enzyme already out there that can degrade it. So the only way to keep the life of that antibiotic going is to use it sensibly and not excessively,' he said.

The passage contains six paragraphs, **A–F**.

Which paragraph contains the following information?

NB   You may use any letter more than once.

1 two examples of bacteria that are no longer killed by modern antibiotic drugs
2 a reference to the length of time we have been using antibiotic drugs
3 the original source of the new drugs being developed
4 the location of the studies into the new antibiotic drugs
5 examples of other studies similar to Cano's

IELTS Reading test practice	Summary completion with a box

One type of summary is made up of a number of gapped sentences that you have to complete using words from a box of options.

How to approach the task

- Read through the summary first and try to predict the missing words.
- Go back to the passage and decide what the summary covers – a section of the passage or the ideas across the whole passage.
- Use key words to help you decide on the correct option from the box.
- Re-read the summary when you have finished to make sure you have selected the right words, and that the words you have chosen fit the grammar, as well as the meaning, of the sentence.

10 ⏱ Take eight minutes to complete the summary below.

Test tip

There are extra words in the box that you do not need to use.

You cannot use any of the words more than once.

*Complete the summary using the list of words, **A–P**, below.*

NEW DRUGS

Scientists believe that microbes that may supply new antibiotic drugs have been **1** .... in the bodies of fossilised insects. Raul Cano says these microbes may help us destroy some of the bacteria that have become **2** .... to current medicines. What needs to be done first, however, is to make sure the antibiotics are **3** .... When doing this, microbes that seem to have the characteristics of modern diseases will have to be **4** .... Cano has been **5** .... by some scientists; others are already saying that the use of any new antibiotics should be **6** ....

A combined	**E** deadly	**I** rejected	**M** praised
B connected	**F** criticised	**J** placed	**N** real
C alive	**G** killed	**K** preserved	**O** immune
D safe	**H** limited	**L** prescribed	**P** welcomed

11 Look carefully at the summary again then underline the parts of the passage which give you the answers. Note how the words have been paraphrased in the summary.

Reading

6 Understanding argument

- **What is argument?**

  Many texts contain arguments; that is, views or opinions either of the writer or of people that he/she refers to. These arguments are often used to support the writer's claims. They may also be used to present both sides of an issue.

- **Why do I need to understand argument?**

  At least one of the passages in the IELTS test will contain some detailed, logical argument.

Recognising text types

Some texts are factual; for example, texts in an encyclopedia, or factual reports. IELTS **Section 1** passages are often quite factual.

1 Work with a partner. Together, discuss why **A** is a factual text. Can you underline the fact that supports the main idea?

(A) Photographs taken as recently as 30 years ago are already fading in the nation's family albums. Millions of images taken since the invention of modern colour photography are changing because of the way their dyes break down. Just as we now tend to view the 19th century in delicate shades of sepia, there is a fair chance that future generations will look back on the last three decades of the 20th century as the era of purple lawns and red skies.

Other texts may be argumentative, but good arguments are still supported by factual information (for example, research-based texts, which combine data with views and claims). Still other texts may be discursive and the arguments may be less well supported.

2 Read paragraphs **B** and **C** and underline the main ideas.

  a Are the arguments supported? If so, how?
  b Which text presents a fully supported/justified argument and which is more discursive?

(B) Despite 119 years of refinement, the modern car remains astonishingly inefficient. Only 13 per cent of its fuel energy even reaches the wheels – the other 87 per cent is either dissipated as heat and noise in the engine or lost to idling and accessories such as air conditioners. Of the energy delivered to the wheels, more than half heats the tyres, road and air. Just 6 per cent of the fuel energy actually accelerates the car (and all this energy converts to brake heating when you stop). And, because 95 per cent of the accelerated mass is the car itself, less than 1 per cent of the fuel ends up moving the car.

(C) Go into a coffee bar, sit down, relax, have a large drink, try to meet someone or have an argument, or combine the two. It may look to others as though you are wasting your time. It may even feel that way to you. But so long as you are doing this in a foreign country, where you speak the language badly or not at all, you are probably acquiring a new language better than you ever could by formal study with a teacher and a textbook. It is full of native speakers asking you questions, telling you to do things and urging you to take part in conversation.

Recognising arguments in texts

It is important to identify the arguments and follow these, so that you can understand the overall organisation of the passage.

3 Read the passage which follows once to get an overview.
Go back to the two underlined sections and decide whether they present an argument or fact and then answer the questions below.

  a Why do you think this article was written?
  b What do you notice about the views presented in it?
  c What overall message is presented?
  d What would be a suitable subheading for the article?

❚ Penguins show signs of stress ❚

Previous research by scientists from Keil University in Germany monitored Adelie penguins and noted that the birds' heart rates increased dramatically at the sight of a human as far as 30 metres away. But new research using an artificial egg, which is equipped to measure heart rates, disputes this. Scientists from the Scott Polar Research Institute in Cambridge say that a slow-moving human who does not approach the nest too closely is not perceived as a threat by penguins.

The earlier findings have been used to partly explain <u>the 20 per cent drop in populations of certain types of penguin near tourist sites</u>. However, tour operators have continued to insist that their activities do not adversely affect wildlife in Antarctica, saying they encourage non-disruptive behaviour in tourists, and that the decline in penguin numbers is caused by other factors.

Amanda Nimon of the Scott Polar Research Institute spent three southern hemisphere summers at Cuverville Island in Antarctica studying penguin behaviour towards humans. "A nesting penguin will react very differently to a person rapidly and closely approaching the nest," says Nimon. "First they exhibit large and prolonged heart rate changes and then they often flee the nest leaving it open for predators to fly in and remove eggs or chicks."

The artificial egg, specially developed for the project, monitored both the parent who had been 'disturbed' when the egg was placed in the nest and the other parent as they both took it in turns to guard the nest.

<u>However, Boris Culik, who monitored the Adelie penguins, believes that Nimon's findings do not invalidate his own research.</u> He points out that species behave differently – and Nimon's work was with Gentoo penguins. Nimon and her colleagues believe that Culik's research was methodologically flawed because the monitoring of penguins' responses entailed capturing and restraining the birds and fitting them with heart-rate transmitters. Therefore, argues Nimon, it would not be surprising if they became stressed on seeing a human subsequently.

IELTS Reading test practice | **Choosing from a list**

Often this type of question is used to test ideas and arguments across the passage, rather than in one small area. You need to underline the key words in the questions and then skim the passage for similar ideas.

4 ⏱ Take five minutes to answer questions **1–3**.

> *Questions 1–3*
> *Choose **THREE** letters, **A–E**.*
>
> Which **THREE** of the following arguments are stated in the passage?
>
> **A** Penguins are <u>not afraid</u> of <u>people</u> who <u>behave calmly</u>.
> **B** Penguins are becoming an endangered species.
> **C** Tourists are not responsible for the fact that there are fewer penguins nowadays.
> **D** Penguins are harder to research when they have young.
> **E** Penguins will not leave a nest with eggs in it.
> **F** A penguin's behaviour may depend on its species.
> **G** Penguin stress may result from being with other aggressive penguins.

Test tip
Here there are three questions and so the three answers would be worth three marks in the exam. Sometimes one question asks you for two or three answers, and then you would need to get all the answers correct for one mark.

5 Underline the parts of the passage which give you the three answers and explain why the other four options are wrong. Then check your answers with the key.

IELTS Reading test practice | **Classification**

In classification tasks you have to match statements to categories. There may also be *both* and/or *neither* categories. Classification questions can range from testing detail (for example, features of animals) to testing ideas and arguments.

How to approach the task

- Underline the key words in each question.
- Check the passage for the first type of penguin and write **A** next to the question if it is true for that type.
- Do the same for the second type of penguin, and write **B**.
- The final answer will depend on how many letters you have next to the question: none, one or two.

6 ⏱ Take eight minutes to answer questions **1–5**.

> *Classify the following statements as being true of*
>
> **A** *the research on Adelie penguins*
> **B** *the research on Gentoo penguins*
> **C** *both research projects*
> **D** *neither research project*
>
> *Write the correct letter, **A**, **B**, **C** or **D**.*
>
> **1** An individual species of penguin was tested.
> **2** Penguins were caught for the experiment.
> **3** Physical changes occurred when a human was nearby.
> **4** Tourists were permitted to observe the experiments.
> **5** Heart rates were measured by an item manufactured for the experiment.

Test tip
The questions are not in passage order.

Dealing with a range of views

7 Skim the passage on page 69 and answer questions **a–c**.

   a What is the passage about?
   b How many people are referred to in the passage? Do they agree with each other?
   c What words or phrases are used to introduce the arguments?

IELTS Reading test practice	Matching

A matching task is used in IELTS to test how well you can understand different arguments or opinions from different sources such as people or organisations. It is best to do these questions in the order of the people in the box, NOT in question order.

How to approach the task

Test tip

Some options from the box may be used more than once, while others may not be used at all.

- Start by reading the passage and highlighting the people's names **A–G**. The names in the box will be in passage order, so you will find *Jason Alexandra* first.
- Read the list of statements, **1–8**, which are paraphrases of the arguments presented in the passage. These are not in passage order. Underline the key words.
- Skim through the passage until you get to the first name and their view.
- Skim through the list of statements looking for one that matches. In the first instance, *Jason Alexandra*'s view is paraphrased in **4**. So the answer to **4** is **A**.
- Continue reading the passage until you come to *Robert Hadler*, and so on. In this way, you will save yourself some time.

8 Take ten minutes to answer questions **1–8**.

> *Look at the following statements (Questions 1–8) and the list of people below.*
>
> *Match each statement with the correct person, **A–G**.*
> **NB** *You may use any letter more than once.*
>
> **1** Current conservation concerns are focused on a broad range of problems.
> **2** Conserving land is too expensive for farmers.
> **3** Holding farmers responsible for land misuse makes no sense.
> **4** Australia should review its import/export practices.
> **5** More conservation funds should be put into helpful, practical projects.
> **6** Much of the land in Australia is unspoilt.
> **7** Weather research can help solve conservation problems.
> **8** Those involved in conservation are working together more efficiently than before.
>
> | **List of People** |
> |---|
> | **A** Jason Alexandra |
> | **B** Robert Hadler |
> | **C** Dean Graetz |
> | **D** Helen Alexander |
> | **E** Neil Clark |
> | **F** Michael Pitman |
> | **G** Steve Morton |

9 Underline the words in the passage that have a similar meaning to these words and phrases from questions **1–8**.

1 a broad range	**5** helpful, practical projects
2 too expensive for farmers	**6** unspoilt
3 makes no sense	**7** weather research
4 import/export	**8** working together

Australia's Growing Disaster

Farming is threatening to destroy the soil and native flora and fauna over vast areas of Australia. What price should be put on conservation?

Australia's National Greenhouse Gas Inventory Committee estimates that burning wood from cleared forests accounts for about 30 per cent of Australia's emissions of carbon dioxide, or 156 million tonnes a year. And water tables are rising beneath cleared land. In the Western Australian wheat belt, estimates suggest that water is rising by up to 1 metre a year. The land is becoming waterlogged and unproductive or is being poisoned by salt, which is brought to the surface. The Australian Conservation Foundation (ACF) reckons that 33 million hectares have been degraded by salination. The federal government estimates the loss in production from salinity at A$200 million a year. According to Jason Alexandra of the ACF, this list of woes is evidence that Australia is depleting its resources by trading agricultural commodities for manufactured goods. In effect, it

sells topsoil for technologies that will be worn out or redundant in a few years. The country needs to get away from the "colonial mentality" of exploiting resources and adopt agricultural practices suited to Australian conditions, he says.

Robert Hadler of the National Farmers' Federation (NFF) does not deny that there is a problem, but says that it is "illogical" to blame farmers. Until the early 1980s, farmers were given tax incentives to clear land because that was what people wanted. If farmers are given tax breaks to manage land sustainably, they will do so. Hadler argues that the two reports on land clearance do not say anything which was not known before. Australia is still better off than many other developed countries, says Dean Graetz, an ecologist at the CSIRO, the national research organisation. "A lot of the country is still notionally pristine," he says. "It is not transformed like Europe where almost nothing that is left is natural." Graetz, who analysed the satellite photographs for the second land clearance report, argues that there is now better co-operation between Australian scientists, government officials and farmers than in the past.

But the vulnerable state of the land is now widely understood, and across Australia, schemes have started for promoting environment friendly farming. In 1989, Prime Minister Bob Hawke set up Landcare, a network of more than 2000 regional conservation groups. About 30 per cent of landholders are members. "It has become a very significant social movement," says Helen Alexander from the National Landcare Council. "We started out worrying about not much more than erosion and the replanting of trees but it has grown much more diverse and sophisticated."

But the bugbear of all these conservation efforts is money. Landcare's budget is A$110 million a year, of which only A$6 million goes to farmers. Neil Clark, an agricultural consultant from Bendigo in Victoria, says that farmers are not getting enough. "Farmers may want to make more efficient use of water and nutrients and embrace more sustainable practices, but it all costs money and they just don't have the spare funds," he says.

Clark also says scientists are taking too large a share of the money for conservation. Many problems posed by agriculture to the environment have been "researched to death", he says. "We need to divert the money for a while into getting the solutions into place." Australia's chief scientist, Michael Pitman, disagrees. He says that science is increasingly important. Meteorologists, for example, are becoming confident about predicting events which cause droughts in Australia. "If this can be done with accuracy then it will have immense impact on stocking levels and how much feed to provide," says Pitman. "The end result will be much greater efficiency."

Steve Morton of the CSIRO Division of Wildlife and Ecology says the real challenge facing conservationists is to convince the 85 per cent of Australians who live in cities that they must foot a large part of the bill. "The land is being used to feed the majority and to produce wealth that circulates through the financial markets of the cities," he says. One way would be to offer incentives to extend the idea of stewardship to areas outside the rangelands, so that more land could be protected rather than exploited. Alexander agrees. "The nation will have to debate to what extent it is willing to support rural communities," she says. "It will have to decide to what extent it wants food prices to reflect the true cost of production. That includes the cost of looking after the environment."

69

Reading

7 Identifying the writer's views and claims

- What are views and claims?

- Why do I need to identify views and claims?

Many articles are based upon the writer's views, i.e. his or her opinion. Information may be presented as fact, but in some cases it may be a claim, i.e. it is claiming to be a fact.

IELTS questions often test your understanding of the writer's views and claims. This is done through *YES, NO, NOT GIVEN* questions, but also through multiple choice and other question types.

Interacting with the passage

Good readers think about what a passage is saying and compare this with what they know about the subject. This approach helps them understand the passage better.

1 Read the title and subheading of this article. What type of text do you think it will be? Why?

Talk your way into another language

Need to learn another language for a job abroad?
Textbooks and tutors may be the worst approach

2 Consider some of your own views on the best way to learn a new language. Make a note of two or three of your ideas and then read the complete article.

3 Work with a partner. Choose a paragraph and discuss the views expressed.

Go into a coffee bar, sit down, relax and try to talk to someone. It may look to others as though you are wasting your time. It may even feel that way to you. But so long as you are doing this in a foreign country, where you speak the language badly or not at all, you are probably acquiring a new language better than you ever could by formal study with a teacher and a textbook.

The social situation, properly used, beats the classroom hollow. It is full of native speakers asking you questions, telling you to do things, urging you to take an active part in conversation, and using gestures freely to make their intentions clearer – just like your parents did when you were an infant. So plunge in. All you have to do is talk back.

The proposition that infants can acquire languages by prolonged exposure to them is self-evidently true: it is the only way available to them. Older children and teenagers who move to a different country can pick up a new language with a speed that baffles their parents. But in adulthood we find ourselves envying our rare contemporaries who can still acquire languages easily.

There may be biological reasons why the capacity to learn languages falls away with age, even more than the capacity to learn other things. The brain may be designed to do its best language-learning in infancy, and then to redeploy its resources at puberty. But psychological factors play a big part too. As we get older, we get more self-conscious, more inhibited, more dependent on other people's judgements. This process may undermine our capacity to acquire a new language, because language underpins our sense of personality and identity. We fear to make mistakes in it.

Stephen Krashen, an expert on second-language acquisition, makes a strong case for the dominance of psychological factors. According to Mr Krashen, people with outgoing personalities do best at learning a new language because 'they have the ego to make the necessary mistakes involved in learning'.

When we want to learn a new language in mid-life for reasons of career or curiosity, we commonly but wrongly tackle it with the sense of doing something difficult and unnatural. We turn to grammar books and compact discs expecting a fight. We are going to 'struggle' with the language. We will 'master' it, unless it defeats us. And with that sort of attitude, it probably will.

All other things being equal, the best learner will be the person who is the most relaxed in conversation, and the most self-confident.

IELTS Reading test practice	Matching sentence endings

This task tests your understanding of key ideas within a passage. You have to read the beginning of a sentence and then decide how it should be completed by choosing the correct ending from a list in a box. The finished sentence will form a paraphrase of an idea in the passage.

How to approach the task

- Use key words in the questions (part sentences) to locate the idea in the passage.
- Read the idea in the passage very carefully.
- Select the correct sentence ending.

4   ⏱ Take eight minutes to answer questions **1–5**.

---

*Complete each sentence with the correct ending, **A–H**, below.*

1 For adult language learners, an informal setting is better than
2 It is obviously the case that children learn language as a result of
3 Adults who have a natural talent for new languages are generally
4 Confident people learn languages fast because they are not afraid of
5 Middle-aged language learners are often unaware that they are

A taking a negative approach.	**E** losing all sense of identity.
B demonstrating an unusual ability.	**F** producing errors in front of others.
C worrying about the views of others.	**G** moving to another country.
D being in a classroom situation.	**H** living with other speakers of the language.

Test tip

The questions (or part sentences) come in passage order. There are some extra options in the box that you do not need to use.

Analysing the passage

You have already learned how to overview a passage and look at paragraph and text structure (see Reading Units **1–3**). It is also important to try to understand exactly what view is being put forward.

5 Read this passage and then answer the questions.

> **a** What type of reader would be most interested in this passage? Where might you find it?
>
> **b** Does the passage present facts, views or a mix of the two?

Books, Films and Plays

a The novelist's medium is the written word, one might almost say the printed word; the novel as we know it was born with the invention of printing. <u>Typically the novel is consumed by a silent, solitary reader, who may be anywhere at the time.</u> The paperback novel is still the cheapest, most portable and adaptable form of narrative entertainment. It is limited to a single channel of information – writing. But within that restriction it is the most versatile of narrative forms. The narrative can go, effortlessly, anywhere: into space, people's heads, palaces, prisons and pyramids, without any consideration of cost or practical feasibility.

b <u>In determining the shape and content of his narrative, the writer of prose fiction is constrained by nothing except purely artistic criteria.</u>

This does not necessarily make the task any easier than that of the writer of plays and screenplays, who must always be conscious of practical constraints such as budgets, performance time, casting requirements, and so on. The very infinity of choice enjoyed by the novelist is a source of anxiety and difficulty. But the novelist does retain absolute control over his text until it is published and received by the audience. He may be advised by his editor to revise his text, but if the writer refused to meet this condition no one would be surprised. It is not unknown for a well-established novelist to deliver his or her manuscript and expect the publisher to print it exactly as written.

c However, <u>not even the most well-established playwright or screenplay writer would submit a script and expect it to be performed without any rewriting.</u> This is because plays and motion pictures are collaborative forms of narrative, using more than one channel of communication.

The production of a stage play involves, as well as the words of the author, the physical presence of the actors, their voices and gestures as orchestrated by the director, spectacle in the form of lighting and 'the set', and possibly music. In film, the element of spectacle is more prominent in the sequence of visual images, heightened by various devices of perspective and focus. In film too, music tends to be more pervasive and potent than in straight drama. So, although the script is the essential basis of both stage play and film, it is a basis for subsequent revision negotiated between the writer and the other creative people involved;

d <u>in the case of the screenplay, the writer may have little or no control over the final form of his work. Contracts for the production of plays protect the rights of authors in this respect.</u> They are given 'approval' of the choice of director and actors and have the right to attend rehearsals. Often a good deal of rewriting takes place in the rehearsal period and sometimes there is an opportunity for more rewriting during previews before the official opening night.

In film or television work, on the other hand, the screenplay writer has no contractual right to this degree of consultation. Practice in this respect varies very much from one production company to another, and according to the nature of the project and the individuals involved. In short, while the script is going through its various drafts, the writer is in the driver's seat, albeit receiving advice and criticism from the producer and the director. But once the production is under way, artistic control over the project

e tends to pass to the director. <u>This is a fact overlooked by most journalistic critics of television drama, who tend (unlike film critics) to give all the credit or blame for success or failure of a production to the writer and actors, ignoring the contribution, for good or ill, of the director.</u>

6

> Which of these subheadings would be most appropriate?
>
> **A** Why does the future look good for writers of books, plays and films?
> **B** What do audiences want from these three forms of entertainment?
> **C** How do these forms of media compare for those involved in producing them?

7 Work with a partner. Together, read the five underlined sentences, **a–e**, in the passage and then discuss the questions.

   1 Do you agree with the view in sentence **a**?
   2 Is the claim made in sentence **b** well supported by the writer?
   3 What reason does the writer give for making the claim in sentence **c**?
   4 What does *in this respect* refer to in **d**? What is the key issue in this section?
   5 Is the final claim in **e** true in your country?

IELTS Reading test practice	*YES / NO / NOT GIVEN*

As in *TRUE / FALSE / NOT GIVEN*, it is important to understand the difference between a *NO* answer and a *NOT GIVEN* answer. Remember that if you write *NO* as your answer, you are saying that the view or claim contradicts (is the opposite of) the information given in the passage. This is quite different from a *NOT GIVEN* answer, which says that you can find nothing in the passage about this view.

How to approach the task

- Read each statement carefully, noting the key words and phrases and think carefully about what they mean.
- Skim through the article to see whether you can find the key words in the first statement, or a paraphrase of them.
- Read around this part of the passage and decide whether there is a similar idea to the one in the question.
- If there is nothing similar, take some time to decide whether the answer is *NO* or *NOT GIVEN*.
- Look at the first question. The key words are *novelists*, *fewer restrictions* and *other artists*. The statement is a paraphrase of the last sentence in the first paragraph and part of the first sentence in the next paragraph.

8 Take nine minutes to answer questions **1–8**.

Do the following statements agree with the claims of the writer in the Reading Passage?
Write

YES	*if the statement agrees with the claims of the writer*
NO	*if the statement contradicts the claims of the writer*
NOT GIVEN	*if it is impossible to say what the writer thinks about this*

   1 Novelists have fewer restrictions on their work than other artists.
   2 Novelists must agree to the demands of their editors.
   3 Playwrights envy the simplicity of the novelist's work.
   4 Music is a more significant element of theatre than cinema.
   5 Experience in the theatre improves the work of screenplay writers.
   6 Playwrights are frequently involved in revising their work.
   7 Screenplay writers usually have the final say in how a TV drama will turn out.
   8 TV critics often blame the wrong people for the failure of a programme.

Test tip
The questions are in passage order.

- There is a summary of IELTS Reading strategies on page 90.

Reading

- What are the texts like in **Section 1**?

In **Section 1**, you will be tested on your ability to find or identify factual information. Texts in **Section 1** of the General Training (GT) Reading module are short and may take a variety of formats. The GT Reading module presents a series of graded texts and accompanying questions that test a variety of reading skills.

- What sort of questions will I get?

The questions are similar to those used in the Academic module and **Section 3** of the GT module is the same as an Academic Reading passage. However, the texts in GT **Sections 1** and **2** are very different from those in the Academic module.

Using titles and subheadings

Nearly all publicity and advertising material you read will have a title or a heading.

1   Work with a partner. First, take one minute to read the titles and headings for the advertisements **A** and **B**. Then close your book and discuss what type of information each advertisement gives you.

A

THE CHOCOLATE MUSEUM

The story of chocolate through the ages

- **Experience chocolate-making from cocoa bean to chocolate bar**
- **Enjoy the smell, taste and texture of freshly made chocolate**

OPENING HOURS

Tues–Fri	10am to 6pm
Sat & Sun + public holidays	11am to 7pm

Closed on Mondays, Christmas Day and during Carnival week.

ENTRANCE FEES

Adults	€6.00
Concessions	€3.00
Groups (of 15 people or more)	€5.50

MORE THAN A MUSEUM!

The Panorama Restaurant can cater for all your corporate events: business lunches, anniversaries, weddings and parties. Groups of 30–300 people welcome.

B

→ **WELCOME**

TO AUCKLAND MUSEUM

"Nau mai haere mai"

Auckland Museum has a constantly changing feast of fresh events and new exhibitions reflecting the culture of New Zealand. This year is no exception.
Click here to find out **more >>**

Latest news

Be inspired by *The da Vinci Machines* exhibition and design and build your own original flying machine. The best entry will win the budding inventor a helicopter ride over Auckland for a family of four!

Avoid the traffic, enjoy hassle-free parking and view the exhibits in peace and quiet on Wednesday evenings! Open till 7.30pm
From 28 November until 4 March there will be no public access to the Reading Room.
Click here to find out **more >>**

Museum opening hours
10am–5pm daily (except Christmas Day)

IELTS Reading test practice   Short-answer questions

Short-answer questions often begin with *wh-* words because they are designed to test whether you can find concrete facts, such as names, times or places. You should read the questions carefully before you start so that you know what you are looking for. Also check how many words you can use in your answers.

Test tip
You must copy words correctly as accurate spelling is essential.

2 Take three minutes to read through questions **1–6** below.
First, underline the key word(s) in each question that tell you what you need to find. Note the type of words you need, e.g. *a number, a noun*, etc. Then answer questions **1–6** for advertisements **A** and **B**.

Answer the questions below.
*Choose **NO MORE THAN THREE WORDS AND/OR A NUMBER** from the passage for each answer.*

1 <u>When</u> is the Chocolate Museum closed for more than a day?
2 What process is on show at the Chocolate Museum ?
3 How many people do you need to get the group concession?
4 What is the prize for designing the best machine?
5 When is the best time to visit Auckland Museum?

Type of words
1 *a time/date*
2
3
4
5
6

IELTS Reading test practice   Multiple choice

Multiple choice questions can test a range of reading skills. They require detailed reading.

3 Read the text below and answer the multiple choice question. Before you check your answer in the key, answer the questions **a–d** below.

a What does the question ask you to do?
b In what way are the options **A**, **B**, **C** and **D** similar?
c Which words in the text help you to find the answer?
d Why are the three other options close but not correct?

*Choose the correct letter, **A**, **B**, **C**, or **D**.*

This is a client ID card issued by

A a travel agency.
B a telephone company.
C an insurance company.
D a medical centre.

SAFE AND SOUND TRAVEL COVER   YOUR ACE Assistance Card

◆ Worldwide Service
◆ We accept all reverse
  charge calls
◆ Emergency Assistance
  overseas (e.g. lost luggage,
  medical expenses)
◆ 24 hours, 7 days a week
◆ Phone 61 2 8907 5958

ACE Assistance
John R. Smith
Card no. 291 201 202

| IELTS Reading test practice | *TRUE / FALSE / NOT GIVEN* |

This type of task tests your ability to scan for specific information as well as identify main ideas. The question will look like this, followed by a number of statements.

Do the following statements agree with the information given in the Reading Passage?
Write

TRUE   *if the statement agrees with the information*
FALSE   *if the statement contradicts the information*
NOT GIVEN   *if there is no information on this*

Always read the statements carefully so that you understand the difference between a **FALSE** answer and a **NOT GIVEN** answer. If you choose **FALSE** as your answer, you are saying that the information expressed in the statement is the opposite of that presented in the text. If you choose **NOT GIVEN** as your answer, you are saying that this information is not covered in the text.

4 Read the text below, then take seven minutes to decide whether the information in sentences **1–6** is *TRUE*, *FALSE* or *NOT GIVEN*.

Visit the island state of *TASMANIA*

Getting there
Tasmania is well serviced by air, but the cost of flights varies enormously, so make sure you shop around for the best price. The over-sea route to Tasmania is covered by two fast ships from Melbourne. These vessels offer an overnight service in both directions, seven days a week, all year round, with additional daytime services in the high season (December–January). Ships also sail from Sydney and ticket prices vary seasonally. The ferry takes cars and motorbikes.

Getting around
Coach services link all the main towns, as well as bus tours geared for independent travellers, though services can be limited in the low season, so check with the bus company. Cycling is a good option for people with strong legs, and several excellent tours cater for cyclists throughout the island. Car rental is sometimes the best choice to go further and at your own pace. For general info on getting around Tasmania, contact Tourism Tasmania (03) 6230 8235.

1 It is a good idea to <u>investigate the airfares</u> carefully.
2 There is a <u>reduced ferry service from Melbourne in December</u>.
3 <u>The price</u> of travelling <u>by boat from Sydney</u> is <u>the same throughout the year</u>.
4 There is <u>a charge</u> for <u>transporting vehicles</u>.
5 The <u>buses may run less frequently when</u> there are <u>fewer visitors</u>.
6 <u>Renting a car</u> is <u>recommended</u> for <u>longer trips</u>.

5 Now check your answers by looking for words in the text that have a similar meaning or the opposite meaning to the underlined words in each question. Remember that if there are no words in the text with either a similar or an opposite meaning, the answer will be *NOT GIVEN*.

| **IELTS Reading test practice** | **Sentence completion** |

This task focuses on specific information. However, you also need to pay attention to the grammar of the sentence and make sure it is correct when your answer is added. In this type of task, you must complete the sentences with words taken directly from the texts.

6   Quickly skim the texts to get an idea of the topics.

5 *very* different things to do this weekend

Opera in the park

Last but not least in the season of outdoor concerts is this stunning production of *Madame Butterfly*, with Russian soprano Elena Prokina. Performance starts 8pm.

Admission: Free

Chinese New Year

Ring in the Year of the Dog this weekend as the local Chinese community kicks off Chinese New Year. Belmore Park is the venue for a kids' fair (music, acrobats, a show of Chinese dog breeds) and a market with Asian cuisine. Runs over the two days, 11am to 6pm, with more activities scheduled for later in the week in China Town.

Skateboard lessons

Use the last weekend of the school holidays to improve your board skills: four sessions, today and tomorrow, from 10am to 6pm. $30 a lesson. Helmets & knee pads recommended. Moore Park Skate School. Booking essential 1800 509 956.

Nigel Kennedy

The UK violinist who meshes a rock star persona with violin virtuosity brings his magnificent repertoire of Vivaldi's music to town tonight (8pm) and Monday night (7pm). For bookings ring 02 8215 4699 or reserve your seats online and save the telephone booking fee. Tickets also available at the door. Opera House Concert Hall.

Feathered images

These paintings and sculptures emerged from Trevor Walker's time spent at the Natural History Museum of France, whose collection includes some 80,000 specimens of birds. Daily 8.30am to 5pm. Free. Eden Gardens, Lane Cove Road, North Ryde.

Adapted from *Sydney Morning Herald 'Good Weekend'*

7   Read questions **1–6** below and decide what type of information is missing, e.g. a place, a type of performance.

8   Take eight minutes to complete the sentences below with words taken from these advertisements.

Write **NO MORE THAN TWO WORDS AND/OR A NUMBER** for each answer.

1 The opening celebrations for Chinese New Year are being held at ....
2 The children's fair lasts for ....
3 Tickets for Nigel Kennedy cost less if you buy them ....
4 Today's performance of *Madame Butterfly* is the last in the series of ....
5 You cannot turn up for the skateboarding lessons without a ....
6 Trevor Walker was influenced by the different types of .... in the French Natural History Museum.

---

9   Check your answers in class. Did you copy words correctly and are the completed sentences grammatically correct?

Reading

9 General Training Reading Section 2

- What are the texts like in General Training Reading **Section 2**?

- How many words are there in **Section 2**?

Section 2 of the General Training Reading module also tests your ability to find factual information.

The texts will total approximately 750 words.

---

1 Skim through the advertisements on page 79 (more practice on skimming and scanning is in Reading Unit **2**, page 43). What are all the advertisements for? How many of the places are expensive?

2 Read the question below and features **1–5** which follow. Underline the key words in the features to help you find the information in the texts, **A–H**.

Which residence has the following features?
1 <u>views</u> of the <u>countryside</u>
2 immediate bookings
3 help in finding a room-mate
4 a set of standards for behaviour
5 young management

Words in text with same meaning
bedrooms <u>look out</u> on the surrounding <u>farmland</u> (E)

IELTS Reading test practice	Matching

How to approach the task

- Read questions **1–5** below and underline any key words.
- Read the first advertisement and skim the questions to see if any of them matches. The questions are not in the same order as the advertisements.

3 ⏱ Take ten minutes to answer questions **1–7**.

---

*Answer questions **1–7** by writing the correct letter, **A–H**.*
NB *You may use any letter more than once.*

For which accommodation are the following statements true?

1 It offers a double room and full board at a reasonable price.
2 Long-term accommodation is available, with on-the-spot sports facilities.
3 It provides inexpensive accommodation for people with a family.
4 It offers low-budget, furnished accommodation to share with a friend.
5 You can get a room close to the university with clean linen provided weekly.
6 You must be prepared to help keep the place clean.
7 The management expects residents to obey the house rules.

Student Accommodation Guide

For students new to the city, here is a range of places you could stay.

A Banbury House ★★

Enjoy mixing with other students in luxury accommodation 30 minutes from the station and close to all main bus routes. Single and double rooms. Students provide own food but all cleaning services offered. Please bring your own linen.

B Home from Home ★★

Single or double rooms for students. Fully air-conditioned with all amenities including sheets and laundry service. Only a few minutes on foot to the city centre and close to colleges. All services and meals included. The management do not provide room-mates for individuals seeking double occupancy.

C Three Seasons ★

We can provide all types of accommodation for all types of single student. Rooms are fully furnished with linen and have reasonable rates. Full board possible. 55 minutes from main universities and city by bus. Please observe code of conduct.

D Downtown Digs ★

Do you worry that you won't have enough money to see the term out? Don't waste it on expensive housing. This is a hostel for students run by students. No references and no rules. Shared bathroom, dormitory accommodation. Must provide own linen. All cleaning operates on a rota system. Singles only.

E Sturtin Hostel ★★★

Set in beautiful rural surroundings, all bedrooms look out on the surrounding farmland. Relax after a long day by swimming in the pool or using the exercise gym located on the premises. Quiet study area available. No children. Rent reductions for stays of over 6 months.

F Star Lodgings ★

This is a hotel but it offers apartment style housing so that you can retain some independence. Single or double rooms available with separate bathroom. All unfurnished. Children welcome.

G First Stop ★

Ideal for new students, we provide fully equipped double rooms. If you wish, we can offer assistance in finding a suitable person to share a room with. All washing and cleaning services offered at extra charge. Large canteen and three bathrooms on each floor. Sports centre next door. Short stay only.

H Highdown House ★★

Bed and breakfast hotel offers student accommodation for limited period only. Vacancies for on-the-spot reservations usually available. Own bathroom and laundry facilities but no cooking on premises. Sports room and small pool.

Key		
★ cheap	★★ reasonable	★★★ expensive

Test tip

When you skim through a text or a number of short texts like this for the first time, it is a good idea to make use of any pictures or keys, and of all headings, titles, etc. to help you get an overview of the content and topic.

IELTS Reading test practice	Choosing headings for paragraphs

A heading captures the *main idea* of a paragraph. Use your global reading skills to do these tasks first. Refer back to Reading Unit **4** page 56 for advice on this skill.

4   Read *Course IT 062 2200* and then answer the questions below.

Course IT 062 2200

Overcome your fear of computers and step into the world of IT. At the end of two days you will be able to differentiate between the various types of computers, identify the hardware components of a computer, move and resize windows, create a document using commercial software and work with a mouse. You will also learn how to use basic email.

---

a Which of these three headings covers the main idea of the paragraph?

i   Identifying types of computers
ii Computing skills for beginners
iii Learning about software

b Why are the other two options wrong (i.e. not suitable as headings)?

5   Now read this paragraph and then answer the questions below.

Courses are suitable for everyone aged 16 or over. You don't need any special qualifications to enrol, unless mentioned in the course outline. Please choose your course carefully as we cannot refund your course fee unless we cancel the course. If you wish to transfer or withdraw, you must advise us in writing at least two weeks before the course start date. You will receive a credit note to the full value of the course.

---

a Which of these three headings covers the main idea of the paragraph?

i   How to withdraw from a course
ii Qualifications required
iii Enrolment conditions

b Why are the other two options wrong (i.e. not suitable as headings)?

6   Answer questions **1–5** on page 81 for the *Everybody loves fish* passage. Follow the guidelines below to help you.

How to approach the task

- Skim through the passage once to get a general idea of the topic.
- Read it a second time and underline any key words or ideas in Paragraph A.
- Discuss why vi is the correct heading for this paragraph and all the others are wrong.
- Go on to Paragraph B. Discuss the key ideas and then select the best heading for this paragraph.
- Take ten minutes to do the rest of the exercise (questions 2–5) on your own.

List of Headings

i Trying it yourself	vi Rationale for a seafood school
ii Buying the right ingredients	vii Picking the fish for your dish
iii Mixing your seafood	viii How to enrol
iv Watching the experts at work	ix A range of levels
v A changing student base	

The reading passage has six paragraphs, **A–F**.

Choose the correct heading for each paragraph from the list of headings above.

Example Paragraph **A** *Answer* **vi**

1 Paragraph **B** ....
2 Paragraph **C** ....
3 Paragraph **D** ....
4 Paragraph **E** ....
5 Paragraph **F** ....

Everybody loves fish but do they love cooking it or know how to, for that matter?

A The Seafood School, located at the fish market, first opened its doors in 1989 to provide advice to consumers on how to prepare a wide variety of seafood dishes at home. The School is now widely regarded as one of the country's leading cooking schools with over 10,000 students a year attending classes.

B The classes were initially aimed at the local residents who regularly shopped at the fish market, but more recently the school has found a market in teaching visitors from other states, as well as from overseas.

C While fish dishes are still the main focus of most classes, recipes involving mussels, octopus, crabs and lobster are also very popular. Asian flavours are in high demand and one very popular class begins with a shopping expedition to Chinatown to find out where to purchase the best herbs and spices for each individual recipe.

D All classes commence with a demonstration of how the dishes are prepared. As anyone who has ever observed a good chef knows, it may look easy in their skilled hands but prove much more difficult at home.

E This is where the Seafood School is unique. After the demonstration, students roll up their sleeves, put on an apron and, in groups of five, recreate the dishes they have just seen being prepared. Under the watchful eye of the demonstrator and assistants, each student helps to create a meal to be proud of, and then they all sit down to sample their seafood feast.

F The Seafood School conducts a wide range of classes for all degrees of competency, from a four-session course in seafood basics to the more complex weekend workshops with some of the nation's leading chefs taking the classes. A vast array of cuisines and cooking styles is covered, including the School's most popular class, 'Seafood BBQ', which is scheduled up to four times a month to keep up with demand!

For a program of classes Click here >>

7 Underline the words in each paragraph that helped you to find the right answer to questions **1–5**.

IELTS Reading test practice   **Choosing from a list**

In this type of task you choose the correct answers from a list of options. Note how many questions there are as this will tell you how many marks each one is worth.

8 Look at the text below and answer these questions.

    a What is the text about?
    b Who was it written for?

9 🕐 Take five minutes to answer questions **1** and **2**.

> **Test tip**
> These two questions are worth one mark each.

Questions 1 and 2
Choose **TWO** letters **A–F**.

*Which **TWO** things will students learn how to do on the course?*

A to give presentations   **D** to handle themselves in social situations
B to create new ideas   **E** to work as a team
C to sell a wide range of products   **F** to run a small business

---

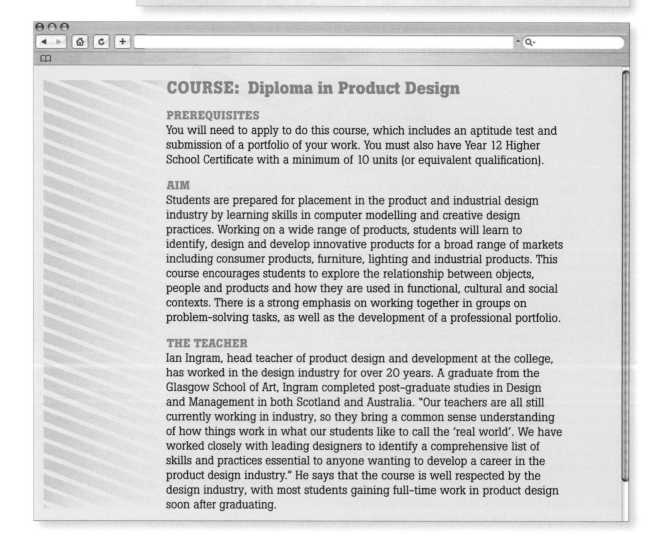

COURSE: Diploma in Product Design

PREREQUISITES
You will need to apply to do this course, which includes an aptitude test and submission of a portfolio of your work. You must also have Year 12 Higher School Certificate with a minimum of 10 units (or equivalent qualification).

AIM
Students are prepared for placement in the product and industrial design industry by learning skills in computer modelling and creative design practices. Working on a wide range of products, students will learn to identify, design and develop innovative products for a broad range of markets including consumer products, furniture, lighting and industrial products. This course encourages students to explore the relationship between objects, people and products and how they are used in functional, cultural and social contexts. There is a strong emphasis on working together in groups on problem-solving tasks, as well as the development of a professional portfolio.

THE TEACHER
Ian Ingram, head teacher of product design and development at the college, has worked in the design industry for over 20 years. A graduate from the Glasgow School of Art, Ingram completed post-graduate studies in Design and Management in both Scotland and Australia. "Our teachers are all still currently working in industry, so they bring a common sense understanding of how things work in what our students like to call the 'real world'. We have worked closely with leading designers to identify a comprehensive list of skills and practices essential to anyone wanting to develop a career in the product design industry." He says that the course is well respected by the design industry, with most students gaining full-time work in product design soon after graduating.

IELTS Reading test practice	**Summary completion**

In the summary completion task, you must choose words from the text to fill the gaps in a summary of what you have read. Reading Unit **5**, page 61, has more information on this task type.

10 Take five minutes to answer questions **3–6**.

> *Questions 3–6*
>
> *Complete the summary below.*
> *Choose **NO MORE THAN TWO WORDS AND/OR A NUMBER** from the text for each answer.*
>
> The head of product design and development has more than **3** .... of experience in the field. The **4** .... are all employed in industry, which keeps them in touch with the **5** .... The course is well regarded and prospects are good for positions in the area of **6** .... for the majority of graduates.

Dealing with unfamiliar words

IELTS texts may contain unfamiliar words, but these should not stop you from being able to understand the text as a whole. Use your knowledge of the subject and the position of the words in the sentence to work out their meaning.

11 Look at the text below and answer the questions.

    a What do you notice about the heading?
    b What is the text about?
    c Where would you expect to read it?

> Sign in / create account
>
> **Your continued donations keep Wikipedia running!**
>
> # What is Podcasting?
>
> **Podcasting** is the distribution of audio or video files, such as radio programs or music videos, over the Internet, for listening on a mobile device and personal computers. The term **podcast**, like 'radio', can mean both the content and the method of delivery. Podcasters' websites may also offer direct download of their files, but the way the new content is delivered is what distinguishes a podcast from a simple download. Usually, the podcast features one type of 'show' with new episodes at planned intervals, such as daily or weekly.
>
> Subscribing to podcasts allows a user to collect programs from a variety of sources for listening or viewing either online or off-line through a portable device, whenever and wherever it is convenient. By contrast, traditional broadcasting provides only one source at a time, which is specified by the broadcasters. While podcasts are gaining ground on personal sites and 'blogs', they are not yet quite so widespread.
>
> *Adapted from Wikipedia, the free encyclopedia*

12 Work with a partner. Together, make a list of any unfamiliar words in the text and then try to work out their meaning.

Reading

- What are the texts like in **Section 3**?

  You will have to read one long text in General Training (GT) Reading **Section 3**, so you need to leave at least 20 minutes for this. The text will be divided into a number of paragraphs, each with a main idea. There will also be a title to introduce the topic of the text.

- What is the general theme of the **Section 3** texts?

  There is no general theme but the text will be descriptive or discursive and on a topic of general interest across a wide range of subjects.

- How many words are there in GT Reading **Section 3**?

  The text will be a maximum of 1,000 words long.

IELTS Reading test practice **Mixed task types**

1 Skim through the text below and then answer the questions.

  a What is the passage about?
  b The text can be divided into three parts. Where does the text divide?
  c What does each part deal with and how does this relate to questions **1–7** on the following page?

COWS THAT MILK THEMSELVES

Australian agricultural authorities have announced they are to trial a new milking system they believe could revolutionise life for the average dairy farmer. Relying on computer technology, the system allows cows to milk themselves without any human input.

The first automatic systems for milking cows emerged in Europe in the 1990s. The system has taken off in countries such as the Netherlands and Britain and two automated milking machines will be put through their paces in Australia next year.

Most systems rely on cattle walking into specially designed milking booths on their way between feedlots. A microchip implant in each beast identifies it to a computer system. Farmers can later find out which cow is producing the most milk and which animal has been milked.

Once in the milking booth, a robotic arm is used to wash and sterilise the cow's udder before milking begins. While milking is under way, classical music plays to soothe the cows. If they want a rub-down they can nudge a switch above their food with their noses to activate a series of brushes and rollers. A fan can be used to blow away flies and if a cow develops a problem during milking, its owner can be notified by a text message.

There are about 9000 dairy farms in Australia that produce about 10 billion litres of milk per year. European cattle are kept in feedlots and food is used to encourage them into the machines. In Australia, however, cattle are more likely to graze in open pastures, providing fewer opportunities to funnel them into the milking machines. A spokesman for the scheme, Sean Kenny, said that the trials would try to find ways to make the machines suitable for Australian dairy farms, which tend to be larger than their European counterparts.

2 Take seven minutes to answer questions **1–7**.

Complete the notes below.

*Choose **NO MORE THAN TWO WORDS** from the text for each answer.*

New milking system:

dependent on	**1**	....
no need for	**2**	....
widely used in	**3**	.... and ....

Label the diagram below.

*Choose **NO MORE THAN THREE** words from the passage for each answer.*

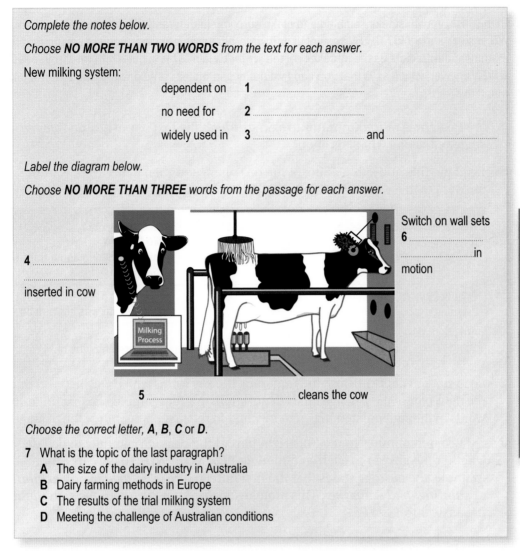

Switch on wall sets
6 ....
....in
motion

4 ....
....
inserted in cow

Milking Process

5 .... cleans the cow

*Choose the correct letter, **A**, **B**, **C** or **D**.*

7 What is the topic of the last paragraph?
  A The size of the dairy industry in Australia
  B Dairy farming methods in Europe
  C The results of the trial milking system
  D Meeting the challenge of Australian conditions

Test tip

You label the diagram with words taken from the text. They may not be in the same order as they appear in the text and you must write the exact words, so make sure you copy the spelling carefully.

- Writers often use synonyms within a text to add variety and avoid repetition. Being able to recognise this technique can help you follow the meaning of the text.

Vocabulary builder

3 Read through the text *Cows that milk themselves* again.

 a What three words does the writer use to avoid repeating *cow*?
 b Find a verb in the text which has a similar meaning to these definitions.
    The verb may be in a different form.

1	make a huge difference to	**6**	have a calming effect
2	first appeared	**7**	tell someone about something
3	become popular	**8**	give confidence to someone or something
4	recognise	**9**	eat grass in an open field
5	disinfect / make very clean	**10**	test something out

IELTS Reading test practice   *YES / NO / NOT GIVEN*

In this task, you must take some time to make sure you understand the difference between a *NO* answer and a *NOT GIVEN* answer. If you write *NO* as your answer, you are saying that the statement contradicts (is the opposite of) the writer's claim. This is quite different from a *NOT GIVEN* answer, which says that you can find nothing in the passage on what the writer thinks about this.

4 🕐 Take three or four minutes to skim through the text opposite and then write a sentence saying what it is about.

5 Read the title and subheading of the text again and then look carefully at the answers to these three *YES*, *NO*, *NOT GIVEN* questions.

Question	Answer
Did people stay in the Russian ice palaces?	*NOT GIVEN* there is nothing about this in the passage
Are ice palaces still popular?	*NO* 'the fashion was short-lived'
Are ice hotels becoming popular now?	*YES* 'they are catching on'

6 Read statements **1–7** below and underline the key words which will help you find the right part of the passage for each question. In **1** for example, the first underlined words in the statement match *first ice hotel* in the first paragraph of the passage.

7 🕐 Take ten minutes to read the right part of the passage carefully to decide whether the answer to each statement is *YES*, *NO* or *NOT GIVEN*. In **1** for example, the passage states that the first hotels were used *to house an exhibition of paintings and sculptures*. This matches *to display artworks* in the statement, so the answer to **1** is *YES*.

Test tip
Make sure you identify where the ideas or concepts in the statements are located.

Do the following statements agree with claims of the writer of the passage?
Write

YES   *if the statement agrees with the claims of the writer*
NO   *if the statement contradicts the claims of the writer*
NOT GIVEN *if it is impossible to say what the writer thinks about this*

1 The original ice hotel was built to display artworks.
2 Most people who visit the hotel spend the night there.
3 From the inside, the walls have a fragile appearance.
4 The ice sculptures are difficult to carve.
5 The walls are built around moveable frames.
6 The river adjacent to the hotel is unpolluted.
7 The fibre-optic cables have to be specially produced.

ICE HOTELS

For more than two centuries, ice palaces were popular in Russia and then later in North America but the fashion was short-lived. Now ice hotels are catching on. Gabrielle Walker reports from Sweden on this unusual but fast-growing tourist destination.

Every winter, for the past two decades, the Swedish village of Jukkasjärvi, 200 kilometres north of the Arctic Circle, has been the site of a hotel made entirely of snow and ice. The first ice hotel was built in 1989 to house an exhibition of paintings and sculptures. A few hardy souls decided to spend the night inside the ice construction, and from there the idea took off. Now there are more than 6,000 overnight guests in a season, and many more day visitors. Some come to get married in the ice chapel. Others come for the dare, or out of pure curiosity to witness the closest living relative of the old ice palaces.

So how do you build a 37-room hotel to last 5 months from such an unpromising raw material? The first rule of snow building is that there are no vertical walls. Instead, the hotel is made up of interconnecting arched hallways, the arches not quite semicircular. The white, sloping walls of the entrance hall are reassuringly solid, and the ceiling is propped up by cylindrical columns of ice, some flecked with bubbles, some perfectly clear. The first impression is one of dazzling whiteness. Round the corner stretches a long hallway, with ice sculptures set into alcoves along the walls.

The arches are made from a combination of snow and ice which the designers call *snice*. They start in November at the beginning of winter, using snow-making machines. First they line up a row of metal frames and coat them with a mix of snow and water. In temperatures that can drop to −30°C or less, the *snice* takes only a couple of days to become rock solid. The frames can then be slid out and moved on to make the next part of the hotel. The ice for the columns – and for the windows and sculptures for which the hotel is famous – comes from the Torne river, which runs alongside the hotel. Because there are no hydroelectric plants or factories nearby to pollute the water, the ice it produces is as clear as glass.

One major challenge is to produce light without heat, which melts the ice, so the chandelier in the bar is lit from a projector on the roof, which feeds into a bundle of fibre-optic cables. Below the sculptures are low wattage lamps and the bar has a gentle neon strip light. The owner, Arne Bergh, explains that they avoid too many colours as it makes the ice look like candy: "We want it to look like ice." To power the lighting, the hotel walls contain many kilometres of cables, frozen into the ice. Bergh adds, "It's quite a job installing electricity into a living building of ice and water."

8 ⏱ Take 12 minutes to read the text below and answer questions **1–8** which follow.

Art in Everyday Life

A Art is everywhere in our lives. Every man-made object is linked with art – a house, a motor car, a bridge, a chair, a teapot, a screw or a piece of cloth. Throughout history, humans have made articles for a wide variety of purposes; generally for everyday utilitarian requirements. The style of utilitarian objects reflects the outlook and the spirit of the times in which they are made and in consequence style is constantly changing.

B It seems that humans possess a natural urge to enhance constructed objects with elaborate decoration: sometimes for beautification, sometimes with religious motives, sometimes to show off their wealth and power, and sometimes to tell a story. Decoration is not art in itself. Unnecessary decoration can ruin the form and perhaps the function of an object, but when decoration is used with care and discretion, it can beautify, produce variety, and add interest.

C The first essential in every creation is that it should properly fulfil its purpose; for instance, a teapot should pour perfectly, an easy chair should provide comfortable relaxation, a block of flats should be a pleasant place in which to live, and a factory or commercial building should be a suitable building in which to work.

D The second essential is that an object should please the eye with its form, line, proportion, colour and texture, and it should be capable of stirring the emotions. Louis Sullivan (1856–1924, American architect) coined the apt phrase 'form follows function'. In other words, it is more important for things to be functional than decorative. For example, contemporary furniture designers must think of form, function and structure, and for the last half century have taken their lead from the outstanding Scandinavian designs of Denmark, Finland and Sweden, whose preference was for simple functional furniture to suit the architectural environment of the day. Heavy ponderous furniture is no longer desirable, and by contrast, modern furniture is often characterised by its good proportion, pleasing lines, simple fittings and attractive fabrics.

E Pottery is an example of form and function coming together. Pottery is the art of fashioning an object in clay, firing it in a kiln to harden the material and then glazing the object to produce a waterproof coating. As well as fulfilling its function, the object should exhibit a pleasing form. A teacup needs to be easy to drink from, the handle should provide a comfortable safe grip and the shape should prevent the loss of heat from the liquid. When hand-made pottery does not perform a strict utilitarian function, but is produced purely as a work of art, it should stir the emotions with its inherent beauty. The merging of the Eastern and Western traditions shows in the work of the English potter Bernard Leach, who worked as a potter in Japan for several years and always considered 'the mood, or nature of a pot to be of first importance'.

Ancient pieces of pottery excavated from archaeological sites indicate that the desire to produce pots which were both functional and beautiful at the same time is by no means a new concept.

F Motor vehicles are a perfect example of how design has changed to suit function. Early car design was greatly influenced by the horse-drawn carriage, but today we find functional design fulfilling every requirement of utility and good appearance. Designs in the 1980s and 1990s incorporated streamlining to reduce wind resistance in fast-moving vehicles, and, at the same time, satisfy an important art principle – rhythm. But the cars of today, often half the size of their predecessors, have taken the concept of industrial design way beyond simple strength, comfort and beauty. They now incorporate a raft of safety and ecological features, reflecting the need to be environmentally friendly through, for example, reduced fuel consumption, while at the same time satisfying the need to be stylish, modish and appealing to the eye. For many people, the 21st-century car represents the ultimate work of art.

Questions 1–5
Which paragraph contains the following information?
NB You may use any letter more than once.

1 an expert's expression that is considered appropriate for all art objects
2 the process required to make a certain type of object
3 the main reason why people have always produced objects
4 reference to an artist who combines different artistic styles
5 mention of the fact that a particular object is smaller than it used to be

Questions 6–8
*Choose the correct letter, **A**, **B**, **C** or **D**.*

6 What point does the writer make about decorating objects?
   A It is something people have always done.
   B It always improves the appearance of an object.
   C It is usually done to make the object more noticeable.
   D It can indicate that the object has a range of functions.

7 Which of the following is a characteristic of contemporary furniture?
   A It is strong and lasts well.
   B It combines several important features.
   C More of it is made in Scandinavia than elsewhere.
   D Much of it is designed these days for individual homes.

8 The writer refers to the motor car because
   A it is an art form which raises concern about the environment.
   B it shows how far humans have progressed.
   C it has a longer history than many other art objects.
   D it has been appropriately altered according to need.

Summary of IELTS Reading strategies

	Approach	Reason
	Spend 20 minutes on each passage and its questions. This should include the time you need to write the answers on the answer sheet.	Treat each passage as a separate test. In 20 minutes you should be able to cover all the questions that you find straightforward.

	Approach	Reason
The passages	Start with the first passage.	The first passage may not be the easiest for you but you need to do them all, so get going!
	Read the title and subheading and consider what you expect the passage to be about.	You need to 'get into' each passage, so predicting the text type, content and structure will help you do this. If there is no title or subheading, use the opening paragraph to find the topic.
	Think about what you know on the topic.	Your own knowledge of the topic will help you follow the passage and understand the questions better. However, always check carefully that your answers to the questions come from the passage and not your own ideas.
	Read the passage quickly before you start the questions.	As you do this, you can underline the key ideas in each paragraph. This will give you an overview of the content.

	Approach	Reason
The questions	Start with the first set of questions.	The questions have been arranged in a logical order, i.e. the first set of questions usually focuses on the first part of the passage or on the main ideas in the passage.
	Read the instructions very carefully.	It is silly to lose marks because you didn't check the instructions; for example, gapfill questions can have a limit of one, two or three words.
	Use the strategies that you have learned, to help you do each set of questions.	Some IELTS questions are very different from others. You can work faster if you know and understand these differences. For example, which questions follow the order of information in the passage and which don't?
	Try to check all your answers.	You may not have time to check all the answers but in written answers make sure that you have spelled words correctly, especially those that you copy from the passage. You will lose marks for misspelling.

The Writing module

As a student at college or university, you will have to produce a lot of written material. As someone who may soon be living or working in a country where English is widely used, an ability to communicate effectively in writing will also be essential. Some writing may be in the form of letters, emails, short essays or reports. Other pieces of writing will be longer and will require considerable planning and attention to detail.

It will therefore be important for you to be able to express yourself clearly, write in a variety of styles and organise your ideas carefully. You will also need to be fairly accurate in your writing, so that your message is not obscured by grammatical errors.

The IELTS Writing modules test your ability to produce two quite different pieces of writing in a fairly short period of time. Before applying to sit the test, you need to decide whether to take the Academic or the General Training module. Each module is divided into two parts and you have only one hour to complete both pieces of writing.

In both Academic and General Training modules, Task 2 is longer than Task 1, and worth more marks. You are therefore advised to spend approximately 40 minutes on Task 2 and 20 minutes on Task 1.

The Writing examiners mark your work on a scale of **1–9** in four areas: content, organisation, vocabulary and grammar (see pages 92 and 93). This book explains what these terms mean and how they are applied in the Writing test.

Academic Writing Task 1

In the first part, you are given a task based on some graphic or pictorial information. You are expected to write a summary of the information provided, in at least 150 words.

Academic Writing Task 2

The second task is more demanding. You are expected to produce a written argument on a given topic and to organise your answer clearly, giving some examples to support your points. You have to write at least 250 words.

General Training Writing Task 1

In the first part, you always have to write a letter based on a situation described to you in the task. You are expected to write a letter of at least 150 words in an appropriate style.

General Training Writing Task 2

Task 2 is an essay based on a given topic. You should organise your answer clearly, giving some examples to support your points. You have to write at least 250 words.

If you are studying for the General Training module, you should begin with Writing Units **5** and **6**. Then go on to Units **7–10** for Task 2.

Writing

There are four areas (called the *assessment criteria*) which the examiner will focus on when marking **Task 1** of the Academic Writing test. These same four areas are also used to assess the General Training Writing module, even though **Task 1** in General Training and Academic are different. In both modules, each of the four areas is worth a quarter of the total marks for **Task 1**.

In Academic Writing **Task 1**, the diagrams, charts, graphs or tables are always introduced on the question paper. You are then instructed to:

> *Summarise the information by selecting and reporting the main features, and make comparisons where relevant.*

1 Look at the table and the box below. The table shows the four assessment criteria for Writing **Task 1** and the box shows a list of skills and strategies Academic Writing candidates must use in order to get a good mark. Match each of the skills and strategies, **A–R**, to one of the four assessment criteria. The first two have been done for you.

Assessment criteria	Skills and strategies
Content	N
Organisation	A
Vocabulary	B
Grammar	

Skills and strategies

A   Use linkers appropriately
B   Choose the right words
C   Use the correct punctuation
D   Choose words that go well together
E   Include data to support points
F   Use the right tense and voice
G   Use paragraphs appropriately
H   Provide an overview of the information
I   Use words in the correct form
J   Use complex sentences
K   Use reference words to avoid repetition
L   Use the right prepositions
M   Spell words correctly
N   Select the most important information
O   Use comparative structures correctly
P   Use precise words and expressions
Q   Write at least 150 words
R   Present information in a logical order

2 Work with a partner. Together, discuss these questions.

    a What do you think are the most important skills for a good writer to have?
    b Which of the four criteria do you find most difficult when writing in English?

■ General Training Writing Task 1 is dealt with in Writing Units **5** and **6**.
■ Exercises to help you improve your writing in these areas can also be found in the Workbook.

The instructions for Academic and General Training **Task 2** are the same. You have to write a discursive essay of at least 250 words. There may be more than one part to the task.
As in **Task 1**, there are four equally weighted criteria and each one has up to nine bands. However, the skills and strategies for *content* are different in **Task 2**.

Assessment criteria	Skills and strategies	What you must not do
Content	Show a clear position or clear, balanced views	Write less than 250 words
	Present sufficient main ideas	Use bullet points or note form
	Add support to main ideas	Only address half the task
	Introduce and conclude the topic	Give irrelevant answers

■ Under *Organisation*, more emphasis is placed on paragraphing in **Task 2** than in **Task 1**.

> *You cannot score above Band 5* if you do not use any paragraphs.
> *You cannot score above Band 6* if your paragraphs do not have a clear central topic.

Otherwise, the criteria for *Organisation*, *Grammar* and *Vocabulary* are the same as **Task 1**.

3   Work with a partner. Together, see which of the skills and strategies (**A–R** on page 92) you can add to the table below from your work on **Task 1**.

Assessment criteria	Skills and strategies
Organisation	Link main and supporting points well
Vocabulary	Use less common vocabulary
Grammar	Use a range of sentence types

4   Why do you think the marking criteria for content are different in **Task 2**?

Writing

1 Interpreting charts, tables, graphs and diagrams

- Why do I have to interpret graphic information in **Task 1**?

  Being able to understand and describe graphic information is an important academic skill. You need to show that you can interpret this type of factual information clearly and accurately.

- What do I need to know?

  You need to develop a good understanding of different types of visual data. Collect some examples of graphs, charts and diagrams to help you do this.

Interpreting visual information

Here are some examples of the main types of charts, tables, graphs and diagrams that you may get in IELTS Writing **Task 1**. Make sure you know how to interpret them.

Bar charts

In a bar chart, the values are given along one axis and each bar represents what is being measured along the other axis. The bars can then be compared.

> **Test tip**
> You need to be able to describe the information accurately, using a range of different structures.

- Charts, tables and graphs present facts, which are objective and often involve measurement. For example, the bar chart on the right shows what a group of students think about a film they have just seen. We can interpret the information by saying that *half the students did not like the film* or by saying that *fifty per cent of the students did not like the film*. We can be even more specific and state that *fifteen out of thirty students did not like the film*.

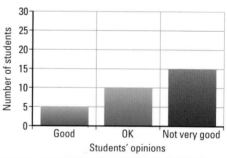

1 Find out some factual information about your class members or your friends and family. How many of them enjoy taking part in the activities shown in the table on the right? Put a tick (✓) against each activity the people like doing and then write the total in the *Total* column.

Activity	Total
Skiing	
Cooking	
Playing badminton	
Shopping	
Painting	
Listening to music	

2 Use the information in the table to make a bar chart.

3 Make some factual statements about the data. Try to use the following structures.

NUMBER *Five out of ten*
PER CENT *Fifty per cent of* *people enjoy …*
FRACTIONS *A third of the*

4 Now make some general observations using the same data. For example:

The most
The second most *popular activity is …*
The third most
The least

The majority of
A large number of
Most *people enjoy …*
Very few
Hardly any

Pie charts

A pie chart is another way of presenting information but the segments are always percentages of a whole. Together they represent 100%.

5 Draw the bar chart on the previous page as a pie chart.

6 Read the *Test tip* and the *Improve your writing* box. Use the information in the pie chart of sales opposite to complete sentences **1–4** below.

Bob's Music Store: sales

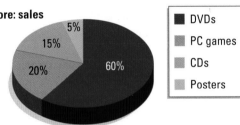

Test tip
You must get the facts right or you will lose marks.

Improve your writing
Make sure you know how to use *per cent* and *percentage*.
- *per cent* comes after a number.
- *percentage* comes after words like *the, a, this, that,* etc. and is often preceded by an adjective, e.g. *A high percentage of customers …*
- Both go with the preposition *of.*

Common error!
Nearly 30 percentage of the books were new. ✗

When writing numbers or percentages, use words up to the number ten, e.g. *eight per cent,* and then figures, e.g. *12 per cent.* However, always write a number at the beginning of a sentence in words, e.g. *Twelve per cent …*

1 According to the chart, _____ of the shop's sales are DVDs.
2 CDs account for a much smaller _____ of sales.
3 While PC games account for _____ of the store's sales,
the _____ of CDs sold is only 15.
4 Posters represent the _____ of goods sold.

7 Draw a pie chart to show roughly what percentage of time you spend on the following activities in an average week: *watching TV, working, studying, sleeping, using the Internet, doing sport, doing 'other' activities.*

8 Swap charts with a partner and look at what he or she does in an average week. Write some sentences that describe your partner's chart.

Tables

Tables present information about different categories. Sometimes tables can be turned into charts but sometimes the categories are too different to do this.

9 A number of secondary schools in three countries conducted a survey about how their students travel to school. Here are the results.

Method of travel by %		Britain	Australia	Singapore
	Walking	19	15	25
	Car	65	65	10
	Public transport	16	20	65

Work with a partner. Together, discuss the similarities and differences in the table and then say whether you could turn this table into a chart.

10 The sentences below describe the facts in the table in exercise **9**. Complete the sentences using the information in the table and the words in the box.

per cent   on foot   percentage   figures   most/least common   popular

1 The car is the .... means of transport for British and Australian schoolchildren, with .... of students in both countries getting to school in this way.

2 In contrast, only .... of Singaporean students use cars, and this is the .... method of transport there.

3 There are considerable differences in the .... for public transport.

4 A large .... of students in Singapore use public transport.

5 In Britain and Australia figures for public transport are lower, being .... and .... respectively.

6 Less than .... of students walk to school in Britain and Australia.

7 For Singaporeans, walking is the second .... option, with a quarter of the students travelling to school ....

11 Guess what the figures might be for your own country and add them to the table in exercise **9**. Write some sentences comparing the figures with another country.

Line graphs

Line graphs show how information or data change over time. They highlight trends.

- The line graph on the right shows the changing trend in the level of car ownership in Britain. It looks very simple but it may not be.

12 Work with a partner. Together, discuss the questions.

   a Is the graph about people or vehicles?

   b What do the numbers along the horizontal axis represent?

   c What do the numbers on the vertical axis represent?

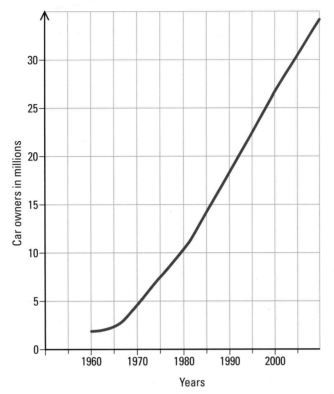

Test tip

You must make sure you understand what the two axes represent before you start writing. However, you do not need to describe the axes in your answer.

Test tip

Statements like: The number of cars has increased or Car ownership has increased from 2 to 20 are incomplete because they do not provide accurate descriptions of the data. Your description should tell the reader the exact figures, so that he or she can visualise the graph line.

Improve your writing

Use the present perfect tense when you are describing a trend that began in the past and is still continuing. Sentences like this may include *since*. For example:

Temperatures have risen worldwide since 2000.

Remember how to form the present perfect:

SUBJECT + *has/have* + PAST PARTICIPLE

13 Write a short, overall statement about car ownership in Britain.

14 Re-write your statement in two new sentences which include these words and phrases:

   a *since*

   b *over a … period between 1960 and 2005*

15 Now re-write your two sentences, **a** and **b**, to include the number of car owners. You will have to re-organise your sentences to do this.

97

Diagrams

In **Task 1**, you will not always be asked to interpret factual information from a chart, table or graph. You may be asked to describe a diagram which illustrates a process or which shows how something works. You should examine the diagram and any information you can see carefully. You must make sure you understand the diagram before you write your answer.

16 Work with a partner. Together, discuss the questions.

    a What does the process diagram below show?
    b What do the arrows represent?
    c What does the scale at the side of the diagram describe?

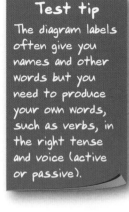

Test tip
The diagram labels often give you names and other words but you need to produce your own words, such as verbs, in the right tense and voice (active or passive).

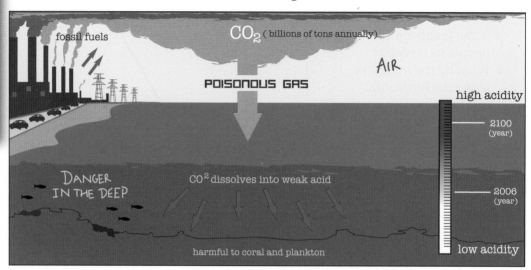

17 Complete this short description of the diagram by first choosing the most suitable verb from the box for each gap and then putting it in the correct form.

reduce	pass	happen	rise	develop	burn	destroy
pollute	become	release	give	allow	attack	

This diagram shows how carbon dioxide **1** .... the world's oceans. Billions of tons of carbon dioxide and other toxic substances **2** .... into the air every year from the fossil fuels that **3** .... in our factories, homes and cars. These gases eventually **4** .... into the oceans and form a weak acid, which **5** .... plankton and the shells of marine creatures, causing serious damage.

Experts predict that the acid levels of the oceans **6** .... considerably between now and 2100. If this happens and the Earth's seas **7** .... too acidic, much of the coral and plankton that live there could **8** .... within a few decades.

Writing

2 Describing trends

- **What should I think about before I start writing?**

  You need to ask yourself *What is the main purpose of this chart/table/graph? What is the overall trend?*

- **What should I do first?**

  State what the chart, table or graph shows in your own words. Then consider how to organise the rest of your answer, which should include the most important features and the overall trend(s).

- **What is a trend?**

  Trends are noticeable changes in a situation or in the way something usually behaves, e.g. downloading music from the Internet is now much more common than buying CDs.

Writing an overview

An overview is an overall summary of the information and is different from an introduction, which simply states what the diagram or chart shows. The examiner will expect to find an overview as part of your answer to **Task 1**.

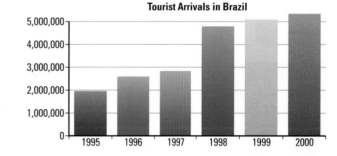

Tourist Arrivals in Brazil

1 Look at the bar chart and say what information is being shown.

Here are two descriptions of the overall trend shown in the bar chart.

The number of tourists visiting Brazil rose.

The chart shows an increase in the number of tourists visiting Brazil.

2 Add *considerably* to the first sentence and *considerable* to the second sentence. What effect do these words have?

3 Re-write the two sentences about tourism in Brazil to include a reference to time and to the number of tourists in figures.

4 Look at the table below and say what information is being shown. Write two sentences which describe the information and provide an overview.

Test tip

When you write your introduction, avoid copying whole phrases from the question. The examiner may not include these words in the final word count. This means you may lose marks if your answer is less than 150 words.

Total Number of Japanese Tourists Travelling Overseas					
2005	**Jul**	**Aug**	**Sep**	**Oct**	**Nov**	**Dec**
Number of tourists	1,422,200	1,634,000	1,634,400	1,502,700	1,500,700	1,401,800
2006	**Jan**	**Feb**	**Mar**	**Apr**	**May**	
Number of tourists	1,343,600	1,398,700	1,577,400	1,280,000	1,385,000	

Using appropriate vocabulary

The examiner will want to see that you know a range of words to describe and interpret visual information and that you can make precise statements in your answer using adjectives, adverbs and phrases.

5   Look at these words and phrases which will help you describe trends.

	↗	↘	↗↘	〰️➔	➔	⤴
Nouns	a rise an increase a surge a growth	a fall a drop a decline a dip	a peak	a fluctuation a variation	a period of stability	a plateau plateaux
Verbs	to rise to increase to surge to grow	to fall to drop to decline to dip	to peak	to fluctuate to vary	to stabilise	to plateau

Phrases	to show an
	   upward trend
		to show a
		   downward trend
		to hit the lowest
		   point
		to hit a trough
			to reach a
			   peak
				to show some
				   fluctuation/
				   variation
					to remain
					   stable/
					   constant
						to reach a
						   plateau
						to level off
						to flatten out

Adjectives and adverbs	sharp(ly) dramatic(ally) significant(ly)	steady(ily)	relative(ly)	considerable(ably)	the second highest the third lowest	slight(ly) gentle(ly) a little	gradual(ly)

Test tip

Practise using different verb and noun phrases to describe trends. Your ability to write a good Task 1 summary will improve as a result.

6   Use the nouns and adjectives from the table to help you describe the trends in line graphs **2–6**.

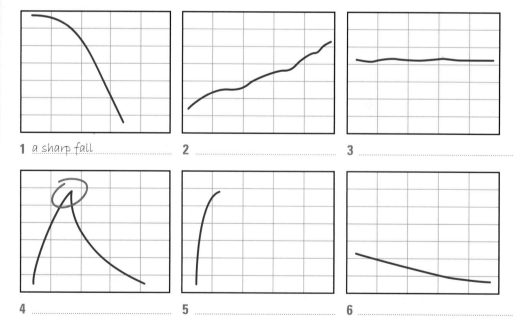

1 _a sharp fall_

2 ....

3 ....

4 ....

5 ....

6 ....

7   Describe each trend again, this time using the verbs and adverbs from exercise **5**, e.g. **1** *It falls sharply.*

8 Look at **A–C**, which present different kinds of information about a large multinational company. Write three short paragraphs about the information. For each graph or chart, first write a sentence which describes what it shows. Then write another sentence which describes the overall trend you can see. Finally, write a sentence which includes some specific data.

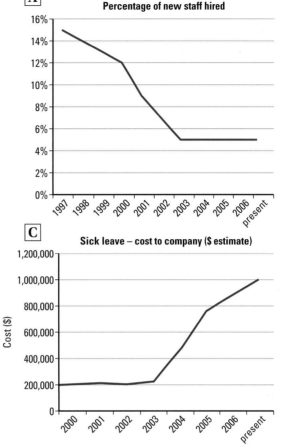

9 Look at the graph below and answer the questions.
   a What does the graph show?
   b How is the overall trend in this graph different from the others you have looked at in this unit?
   c What tense will you use to describe it?

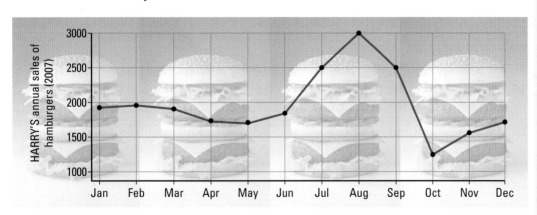

10 Write four or five sentences about the trends you can see in the graph of *HARRY'S annual sales of hamburgers*. Try to include the words *stable*, *fewer*, *rise*, *sales*, *peak* and *drop*.

11 Write a general observation about the popularity of hamburgers over the year.

Test tip

The examiner will be checking to see whether you can describe the important features of the graph. You should not try to describe every detail of a graph.

For example, if you write twelve sentences about annual sales of *HARRY'S* hamburgers – one for each month – your answer will be repetitive and more importantly it will NOT be describing the main trends.

IELTS Writing test practice   **Picking out significant trends**

12 State what is being shown in the graph below in your own words. Circle the most important trends.

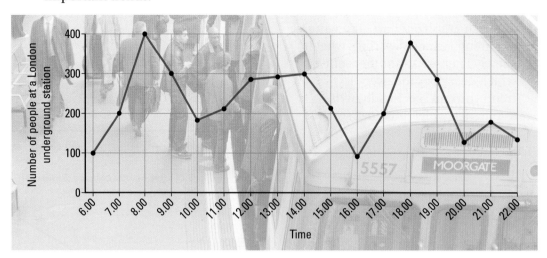

13 Read a student's description of the graph and the advice on how to approach **Task 1**.

> At 6am the station had 100 people. At 8am there was a big increase to 400 people. Not many people went there at 10am. The same thing happened after 8pm. It declined a lot to 120 and 180 people at 9pm and 10pm respectively.
> Between 12 noon and 2pm the number of people was stabilised at 300.

How to approach the task

- State the purpose of the graph or chart.
- Provide an overview.
- Select the key trends or features.
- Illustrate these with figures.
- Make a simple, relevant rounding-off point – if appropriate.

14 Work with a partner. Together, discuss the description of the graph above. How successfully has the writer used the advice on how to approach **Task 1**?

15 ⏱ Take 20 minutes to write a better description of the graph in exercise **12**, using the advice to help you. Then compare your answer with the model answer in the key.

16 Work with a partner and discuss which of the numbered and underlined parts of the model answer provide:

  a an introduction to the chart
  b the key trends
  c an overview of the trends

17 Look at the model answer in the key again and circle the words and phrases the writer uses to link the different points.

Writing

3 Summarising information

- What does *summarising* involve?
- How do I do this?

You need to show the examiner that you can select the main points and illustrate these with relevant details or data.

This means giving more attention to some parts of the graph, table, chart or diagram than to others.

Selecting main points

In **Task 1**, there may be a lot of information to describe in a limited number of words, so you cannot include every feature and all the data.

1 Work with a partner. Together, take two minutes to examine the chart below. What does the vertical axis represent?

2 Discuss what the chart shows and identify some important points.

3 Consider which tense you will use most for your answer.

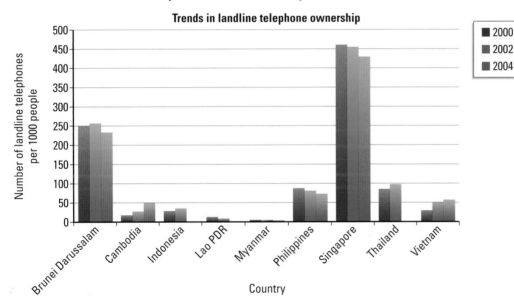

Trends in landline telephone ownership

> **Test tip**
> This chart does not provide information about population size. If you choose to include information in your answer that is not given in the task, you will not get extra marks. In fact, it may be considered irrelevant and you may be penalised if you make detailed comments about information that is not provided in the chart.

4 Follow the instructions **1–6** to write a description of the chart.

  1 Write one sentence which states what the chart shows.
  2 Write two sentences which give an overview of the chart.
  3 Write two sentences about Singapore.
  4 Write one sentence about Brunei Darussalam.
  5 Write one sentence about Cambodia and Vietnam.
  6 Conclude with a final sentence about the remaining countries.

5 Swap answers with a partner. Read your partner's description of the chart and compare it with the model answer in the key.

6 Now look at your partner's description and the model answer again and answer questions **1–6** for both. Did your partner

    1 give the overall time period in the first sentence?
    2 use a suitable verb and adverb to describe the trend in the second and third sentences?
    3 provide some figures for Singapore?
    4 use *fluctuate* with an appropriate figure for Brunei Darussalam?
    5 note a contrast in the trends?
    6 get the figures correct overall?

IELTS Writing test practice	Illustrating main points

You need to add some data to support the main points in your summary, otherwise you will lose marks.

7 Underline the data in the first paragraph of this summary, which introduces the graph and provides an overview.

Obesity prevalence among adults: by sex, England

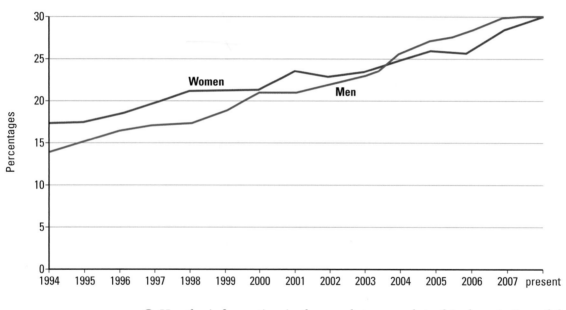

The graph shows how obesity levels have increased in England since 1994. Clearly, figures have doubled over this period, reaching a current high of around 30 per cent for both male and female adults.
(34 words)

8 Use the information in the graph to complete this description of the trend for women.

Looking more closely at the trend for women, it can be seen that a steady increase took place between 1994 and 1998, with obesity levels rising by **1** .... to 21 per cent. This was followed by a **2** .... period of stability. Then, after the year 2000, levels rose again, reaching a peak of **3** .... in 2001. Since then, apart from a slight fluctuation, the percentage of obese women in England has increased significantly.
(77 words)

9 Draw two vertical lines on the graph to show how the writer divided up the overall trend for women.

10 Divide the male trend into three parts by drawing two more vertical lines on the graph. Then write a paragraph about the male pattern and provide an overview summarising the trends. Count the number of words in your paragraph.

11 Look at the graph below and then write a summary of the main trends, using some of the structures from the answers to exercise **10**. Remember to say what it shows and include an overview. Count your words at the end.

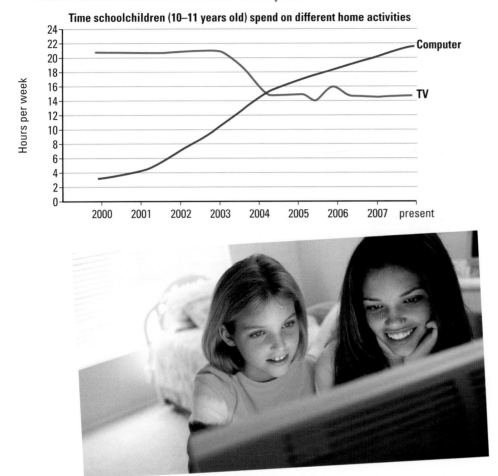

Time schoolchildren (10–11 years old) spend on different home activities

---

IELTS Writing test practice   **Highlighting the main stages of a process**

Just as you select the main points of a chart, you need to summarise the main stages of a process, as they are shown in the diagram.

How to approach the task

- Look at the start and end of the process and consider what it shows overall.
- Divide the process into a number of logical stages.
- Think about how you could rephrase some of the labels.
- Decide on some verbs and tenses to use.
- Consider how you could round off your answer.

12 Work with a partner. Together, look at the task on the next page and then discuss these questions.

    a Can you rephrase the task introduction in your own words?
    b Which key words in the labels do you not need to rephrase?
    c Which words could you try to rephrase?
    d What other vocabulary do you know that would be useful to describe the equipment or process?
    e What linking words might you use?

The diagram below shows how raw materials are used to make plastic products.

Summarise the information by selecting and reporting the main features, and make comparisons where relevant.

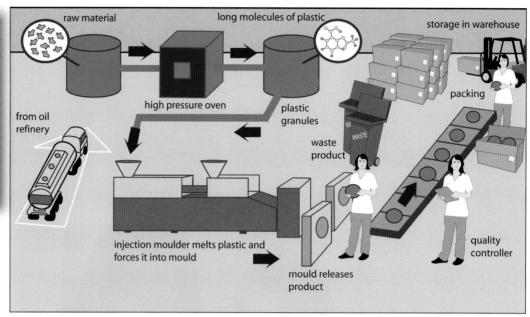

13 Complete this plan and then write a summary of the process shown in the diagram.

		Notes
Para 1	Introduction and overview of diagram	complex process / number of steps / equipment / people
Para 2	How process begins up to production of long molecules	
Para 3	From molecules to mould	
Para 4	What happens to finished product	

14 Swap your plan and your summary of the process with a partner. Read your partner's answers and then compare them with the model answer in the key. Does the model answer include any of your vocabulary or linking words from your answers to exercise **12**?

Writing

4 Comparing and grouping information

■ Why is it important to group and compare information?

Summarising charts always involves making comparisons. Some diagrams also require comparisons, particularly if you have to describe stages or have more than one piece of visual material. Part of the task of organising your answer involves deciding how to categorise or group the information you need to compare.

Comparing information

You need to make sure that you can form comparative and superlative adjectives and use expressions such as *more/less ... than*; *the same as ...* ; *as ... as*; *the second/third most*; *twice, three times*, etc. You may need to use these expressions in some long noun phrases, for example:

the most
the second/third most   *popular tourist destination*
the least

1   Fill in the gaps **1–9** in the summary of the chart below and on the next page. For some of the gaps, there is a word in brackets to help you.

World languages with the highest numbers of first-language speakers
(millions of speakers)

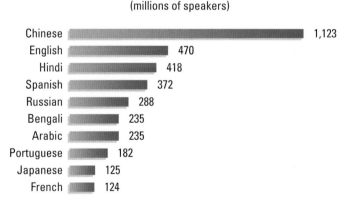

Chinese — 1,123
English — 470
Hindi — 418
Spanish — 372
Russian — 288
Bengali — 235
Arabic — 235
Portuguese — 182
Japanese — 125
French — 124

According to the chart, Chinese is by far the **1** ＿＿＿＿＿ widely spoken first language, with 1,123 million speakers. This is more than **2** ＿＿＿＿＿ the number of speakers of any other language. English has the **3** ＿＿＿＿＿ (*high*) number of speakers, with a total of **4** ＿＿＿＿＿ , closely followed by Hindi, which is spoken by the **5** ＿＿＿＿＿ (*large*) number of people.

Further down the list, it is interesting that Bengali has **6** ....
number of speakers **7** .... Arabic: 235 million.

Of the top ten languages in the chart, the **8** .... widely spoken is
French, with 124 million speakers, which is only slightly **9** .... than
Japanese, which has 125 million.

2 Change the noun phrases into comparative phrases, as in the example.

Example	fertility of land areas	the most **fertile** area	the second most **fertile** area	the least **fertile** area
1	frequency of grammatical errors			
2	height of smog levels			
3	density of populated areas			
4	significance of reasons for disease			
5	length of study periods			

■ There are linkers that signal a comparison or contrast. The most useful ones are *while,
whereas, although, however, similar(ly), unlike, equally, both/neither, compared to,
in contrast with, different (from), the same (as).*

3 Complete sentences **1–6**, which are based on the table below, by using a
comparative or superlative adjective, a comparative expression, or a linker in
each gap.

	Rooms	Star rating	Distance from city centre	Value for money
Kendal Hotel	225	☆☆	1 km	✓
Premda Hotel	225	☆☆☆☆	2 km	✓✓
Cord Hotel	156	☆☆☆☆☆	5 km	✓✓

> **Test tip**
>
> Using appropriate linkers is important, but don't start every sentence with one – exercise 3 is just for practice.
> Remember that words like *this, the, which* and *it* and comparative/superlative structures also link ideas.

1 Compared to the Kendal Hotel, the Premda is .... value for
money.
2 Both the Premda and the Cord Hotel are .... good value for
money.
3 While the Cord Hotel has .... star rating, it is ....
from the city centre.
4 .... the Cord Hotel, the Kendal is close to the city centre.
However, it has a .... star rating.
5 Although the Kendal Hotel and the Premda Hotel have ....
number of rooms, their star ratings are ....
6 The Cord looks like .... hotel, even though it has
.... rooms than the others.

When organising your answer, it may be necessary to group some of the information, particularly when there is a lot of data.

4   Work with a partner. Together, discuss what difficulties you may have in answering this **Task 1**.

The graphs below compare the average weekly earnings of male and female graduates and non-graduates.

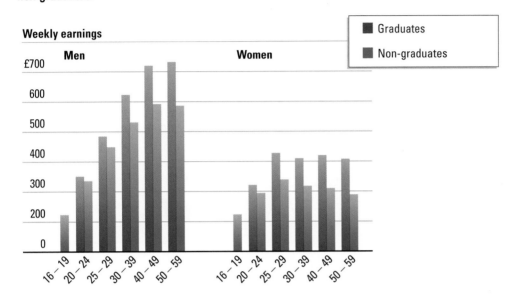

- There are too many age groups for you to include all of the information from both charts in your answer. You will therefore have to group some of the information to make your answer easier to read and understand.

5   With your partner, work through the advice on how to approach the **Task 1** in exercise **4** and make some notes.

How to approach the task

- Consider what the graphs show and think about the vocabulary and tenses you will use to summarise them.
- Decide on an overview.
- Select three significant features of the graphs to write about.
- Note some points about the earning power of male graduates by grouping the ages; for example, grouping 40–49 with 50–59.
- Note some points about the female graduates by grouping the ages.
- Think about a general observation summarising the main comparison(s).

6   Take about 15 minutes to write about the information above. When you have finished, count the number of words you have used (there must be at least 150) and allow three minutes to correct any mistakes. Check that you have used all the data correctly.

7   Look at the model answer in the key and underline:

- the comparisons
- any linkers that signal a comparison or contrast.

IELTS Writing test practice	Describing how something works

Take the same approach as you would with a process diagram and decide where to begin your description. Provide an opening sentence that summarises the overall function of the diagram.

8 Work with a partner. Take turns to describe how the dredger works and discuss the table and how the information could be combined. What is the best way to begin writing this task? What information should your overview include?

The diagram below shows how a dredger can remove mud from the bottom of canals. The table compares features of the canal dredger with those of a coastal dredger.

Summarise the information by selecting and reporting the main features and make comparisons where relevant.

Test tip

Never write your Task I answer in bullet points. You will lose marks if you do this. Always use continuous text and always use paragraphs to organise your points.

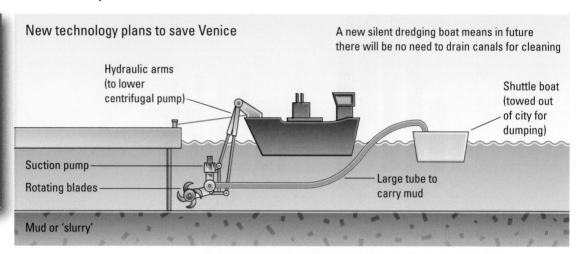

New technology plans to save Venice

A new silent dredging boat means in future there will be no need to drain canals for cleaning

Hydraulic arms (to lower centrifugal pump)

Shuttle boat (towed out of city for dumping)

Suction pump

Rotating blades

Large tube to carry mud

Mud or 'slurry'

	Canal dredger	Coastal dredger
Hull length	22 m	85 m
Hull breadth	6.69 m	14 m
Depth	1.87 m	35 m
Area of operation	Canal/lagoon	North Sea

How to approach the task

- List some of the verbs that you can use in your answer.
- Suggest some suitable linkers.
- Decide what tenses you will use.
- Consider how to group some of the information in the table.
- List some of the comparatives you could use.
- Consider how you could round off your answer.

9 ⏱ Take about 15 minutes to write an answer to this task. When you have finished, count the number of words you have used and allow three minutes to correct any mistakes.

10 Work with a partner. Together, compare your descriptions. Look particularly at the comparatives and linkers used in each answer. Then look at the model answer in the key and discuss how it has been organised and what each paragraph contains.

Writing

Planning a letter

- What kind of writing will I have to do for **GT Task 1**?
- How will I know what to write about and how to organise my answer?

General Training (or GT) **Task 1** is always a letter. This could be in a formal or informal style, depending on the purpose of the letter.

The instructions in the task will describe a situation and tell you exactly who to write to. This is followed by three clearly bulleted key points which help you organise the content of your letter. You need to write a total of 150 words.

Studying the task

When you read the situation described in the task, you need to think about why you are writing the letter and what it should include.

1 Read this typical **GT Task 1** and answer the questions. Who is the letter to? What is the purpose of the letter? Parts of the task have been underlined to help you.

An old car was left on the street near your apartment block several weeks ago. You telephoned the local Council to get them to take it away, but nothing has been done about it. The car is now causing a problem for residents.

Write a letter to the Council. In your letter

- *describe the car*
- *outline the problems it is causing*
- *tell the Council what you want them to do*

Opening and closing a letter

How you begin and end your letter depends on the person it is written to and how well you know them. Letters can be formal or informal and we begin and end each type of letter in a different way. Formal letters are for official or commercial situations, written to people you do not know well, or have never met. Informal letters are generally to friends or relatives.

2 Which beginning and ending should you use in the letter to the Council?

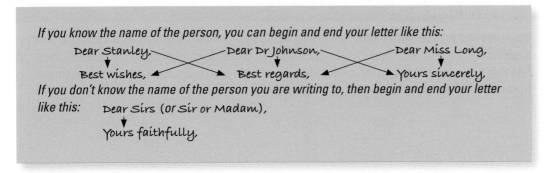

If you know the name of the person, you can begin and end your letter like this:

Dear Stanley,   Dear Dr Johnson,   Dear Miss Long,

Best wishes,   Best regards,   Yours sincerely,

If you don't know the name of the person you are writing to, then begin and end your letter like this: Dear Sirs (or Sir or Madam),

Yours faithfully,

The purpose of the letter

When you are deciding what to include in your letter, you should keep the purpose of the letter in mind. You will lose marks if you do not make the purpose clear. In formal letters the purpose is usually stated in the opening sentence.

3   Underline the key words and phrases in this task and then say what the main purpose of the letter is.

> *You are applying for a job and need a letter of reference from someone who knew you when you were at school.*
>
> *Write a letter to one of your old teachers asking for a reference. In your letter*
>
> - *say what job you have applied for*
> - *explain why you want this job*
> - *suggest what information the teacher should include*

Test tip

You should use your imagination to build on the situation outlined in the task. Try to make the best use of all the information provided.

4   Complete these notes to help you write the letter.

> Decide on a **1** .... for the teacher.
>
> Mention **2** .... since leaving school.
>
> Describe the **3** .... and what it involves.
>
> Give reasons for **4** ....
>
> Suggest some **5** .... to mention.

5   Work with a partner to complete the table below. Together, brainstorm ideas for three different sets of information you could use to answer this **GT Task 1**.

Test tip

If you fail to cover any of the three key points in the task, you will not score more than Band 4 for content.

Since leaving school	Job applied for	Why I applied	What to mention

6   Compare your ideas in groups.

7   Make a similar table of ideas for the letter to the local Council in exercise **1** on page 111.

Beginning your letter

You need to start your letter with something that is appropriate for the situation and that will capture the reader's attention. If it is a formal letter, you should mention the purpose in the opening paragraph. If it is an informal letter, you should start with a more general opening paragraph; for example I hope you're well and … **or** Sorry for not writing sooner but …

8 Look at these different ways of beginning a letter and say which of them are suitable for a formal letter and which for an informal one.

1 I am writing with regard to / in connection with …

2 I am writing in the hope that …

3 It was lovely to see you and your family last month …

4 I would like to express my concern about …

5 Apologies for not writing for so long, but I've been really busy …

6 I am a resident of … and I would like to draw your attention to …

7 It was great to get your postcard … and I'm thrilled to hear you are …

8 It's been a long time since we saw each other.

9 Write an opening paragraph for the letter in exercise **3** to one of your old teachers. Use your own words and remember to state the purpose of your letter clearly. Compare your finished paragraph with the model answer in the key.

Organising your points logically and clearly

You can use the three key points to create the main part of your letter and each one can form the basis of a paragraph. Then you need to work out how to organise each paragraph.

10 Read this example of a **GT Task 1** and the notes which follow. Put the remaining points (**1–9**) in the order you think they should be mentioned in the letter (**a–i**).

> *Last year you went on a camping tour with your family. A friend has contacted you about the tour and asked you whether you would recommend it.*
>
> *Write a letter to your friend about the trip. In your letter*
>
> - *say where you went and how you travelled*
> - *describe the place and the accommodation*
> - *suggest why he/she should go on this holiday*

Test tip

Although you must cover all three key points, you do not have to put them in the same order as they appear in the task instructions. The important thing is to cover all the points in a logical order.

1	~~flight to Darwin~~
2	amazing bird life
3	prices going up next season
4	~~Kakadu National Park~~
5	wilderness may change
6	~~by four-wheel drive vehicle~~
7	crocodiles in river
8	cabins with bunk beds
9	great fun

a	Kakadu National Park, Australia
b	flight to Darwin
c	by four-wheel drive vehicle
d	
e	
f	
g	
h	
i	

11 Work with a partner to create a table similar to the one in exercise **5**. Together, brainstorm ideas for the camping tour task above, using your own experience or imagination.

12 Take seven minutes to write the opening paragraph and then the second paragraph of your letter.

Explaining the situation

The introduction to the **GT Task 1** and the first one or two key points which follow always present you with a situation. Creating a bubble diagram can help you develop ideas so that you can set the scene clearly for your reader at the start of your letter.

13 Read this task and look at the bubble diagram of the situation it describes.

> *You recently bought a camera while travelling overseas. When you got to your destination you discovered that some important items were missing from the box.*
>
> *Write a letter to the local representative of the company. In your letter*
>
> - *give details of the camera and where you bought it*
> - *explain what has happened*
> - *say what you want him/her to do about it*

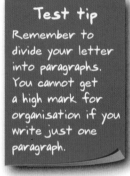

Test tip

Remember to divide your letter into paragraphs. You cannot get a high mark for organisation if you write just one paragraph.

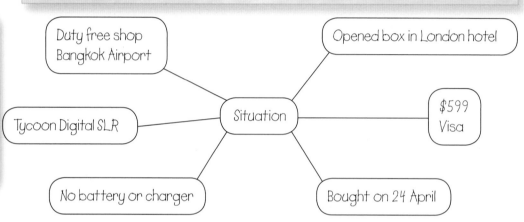

14 Take ten minutes to write the first two or three paragraphs of this letter, explaining the situation (i.e., cover your purpose and the first two bullets). When you have finished, compare your letter with the model answer in the key.

Concluding your letter

You need to conclude your letter with something brief and appropriate to the overall tone.

15 Look at these different ways of concluding a letter and say which of them are suitable for a formal letter and which for an informal one.
  1 Thank you very much for your attention.
  2 I'm really looking forward to …
  3 I hope the situation will be resolved soon.
  4 Bye for now.
  5 See you at the weekend.
  6 Hope to hear from you very soon.
  7 Take care!
  8 I look forward to hearing from you.

16 Take ten minutes to write the last paragraph of the missing camera parts task. Base this paragraph on the third key point and decide which of the endings from exercise **15** is most appropriate to the overall tone of the letter.

■ You will find more help on how and where to use formal and informal language in the next unit.

Writing

6 Communicating your message

- What is *tone*?

The tone and level of formality that you use in your **GT Task 1** letter will affect how successful you are at communicating your message.

The tone of your letter depends on who you are writing to. If you are writing a formal letter, your language should be clear and polite, while a letter to a friend may contain less formal expressions and be more direct.

- How can I make sure that my meaning is clear?

You need to use the right expressions to convey your message, and your vocabulary should be appropriate and varied.

Using the right tone

You need to use appropriate language in your letter to give it the right tone – formal, neutral or informal.

1   Read the list of sentences below in the *Requests and suggestions* box. What do you notice about them?

2   Work with a partner. Together, discuss how a reader would react if they received these statements in a letter.

Requests and suggestions

Send me a brochure.
I want a ticket for tonight's show.
I think you should employ more staff.
You should give up smoking.
I want to get a place at your school.
You always park too close to me!
I need to use you as a referee.

Polite expressions

I would like to
I am interested in … -ing
Could I suggest that …
I would be grateful if …
Perhaps it would be better if you …
I would recommend that you …
I would appreciate it if …
You could consider … -ing
I was wondering if …

---

3   Improve the tone of each request and suggestion by rewriting it using a structure from the *Polite expressions* box.

Choosing the right language and expressions

Informal letters are often quite personal, while formal letters need to be more distant, but there are many feelings that you may wish to convey in both types of letter and often it is best to be neutral (neither too formal or informal).

4 Read expressions **1–15** and match them to the uses described in **A–G**.

Test tip

When you are considering the purpose of your letter, you also need to think about what you have to do in the letter, e.g. complain, advise, etc. This will affect the language and expressions that you choose.

Expressions	These are used to …
1 I was (so) sorry to hear about … **2** I would (very much) like to know … **3** I'm sorry that I … **4** I would be grateful if you could … **5** I was delighted/glad to hear … **6** I am writing to express my concern about … **7** I'm (extremely) grateful to you for … **8** I very much appreciate your … -ing **9** Unfortunately/Regrettably I … **10** Even though *I phoned you about* … **11** Please accept my apologies (for …) **12** … was very *enjoyable*. **13** … is very *disappointing*. **14** I regret that … **15** Would it be a good idea to …	**A** apologise for something **B** ask for information **C** express satisfaction **D** complain about something **E** thank somebody for something **F** express sympathy **G** make suggestions

5 Now say when it is appropriate to use each expression. Write **f** for formal, **i** for informal and **n** for neutral next to each expression. If you are not sure, write **n/f** for expressions which are more formal and **n/i** for expressions which are more informal.

6 Work in groups. Together, make a list of other feelings you might want to express in a letter.

7 Read the *Test tip* and then look at the extracts **A–D**. Decide what is wrong with the underlined words.

Test tip

You need to use the right tone throughout your letter. You will lose marks if you use an inappropriate tone or if you use the wrong tone in parts of your letter.

A

Dear Jenny,

It was absolutely fantastic to see you at the school reunion last week. You haven't changed a bit since we last met! I only have your old email address, so <u>kindly send me your contact details so that I can forward you the photographs I mentioned</u>.

B

Dear Mr Parsons,

<u>How's it going? Still at the old school, I hope, because I need you to do something for me!</u>

I've been working in hospitality for the last 5 years, as an apprentice chef, but now I've decided that I'd like to take up full-time study again, <u>so I'd like you to be a</u> referee for me.

C

> Dear Sirs,
>
> I've received a reminder notice from your company, saying I have not paid my phone bill and threatening to cut off the phone.
> <u>You guys have got it wrong because I know I paid this bill.</u>
> I enclose a copy of my credit card statement showing that the payment was made on 26 February.

D ⊙⊙⊙ ⊖

> ... I'm really looking forward to our holiday together. I know we're going to have a great time.
> <u>Thank you for your kindness in doing the organising.</u>
> <u>Yours faithfully,</u>

8 Rewrite the underlined sentences using the right tone.

Using appropriate vocabulary – brainstorming

The examiner will be looking for a range of words and phrases related to the topic and purpose of the letter.

9 Look at this task and the notes a student has started to make. Complete the notes with other expressions and relevant vocabulary you could use. Make sure you use appropriate words to match the situation. As you do this, note the verb tenses and forms you should use.

> *You have a friend who lives in a city overseas. You have decided you would like to apply to do a course at one of the colleges in this city.*
>
> *Write a letter to your friend. In your letter*
>
> - *ask what the city is like*
> - *say what work or study you are doing now*
> - *explain why you would like to do this course in the future*

Test tip

Examiners will ignore any sections of text copied directly from the question. Remember that this will reduce your total word count and may also reduce your marks.

● ask what the city is like		
Can you tell me I'd be interested to know	weather transport	present tense ....
● say what work or study you are doing now		
I am currently ... -ing I've just completed For the past 3 years, I've been ... -ing	nursing hospital	....
● explain why you would like to do this course in the future		
I believe it would I'm keen to	improve my English get a good job	....

10 Read the four GT Writing tasks **A–D** below and decide what type of letter you will need to write (formal or informal) and what feelings you need to convey.

A

You play sport (e.g. football) for a local team. You recently heard that a player in your team is in hospital.

Write a letter to your team mate. In your letter

- *say how you feel about the news*
- *ask about the treatment in the hospital*
- *suggest some ways of cheering him/her up*

B

You recently stayed in a hotel in another city. When you got home you discovered that you had left something of value in the room.

Write a letter to the hotel. In your letter

- *describe the item that you left behind and say where you left it*
- *ask the hotel to arrange to send it to you*
- *suggest a way to pay for the postage*

C

Two days ago you had a meal at a well-known restaurant. Unfortunately, you were very ill after the meal.

Write a letter to the restaurant. In your letter

- *describe what you ate*
- *say how you feel about the situation*
- *ask them what they can do about it*

D

A friend recently invited you to a special party. You intended to go but at the last minute you were unable to attend.

Write a letter to your friend. In your letter

- *apologise for not going to the party*
- *explain what prevented you from going*
- *suggest a way of making up for this*

IELTS Writing test practice	**General Training Task 1**

How to approach the task

- You should spend 20 minutes on planning and writing Task 1.
- Decide on the important points, the level of formality and the purpose.
- Consider the information you need in order to cover the three key points.
- Decide how you will organise the paragraphs.
- Begin with an appropriate opening in the correct tone.
- Keep the tone consistent and use appropriate language for feelings, etc.
- Use an appropriate ending.
- Check for mistakes in vocabulary, grammar and punctuation.
- Count the words to make sure you have written at least 150 words.

11 Choose one of the tasks **A–D** and make detailed notes like those in exercise **9**. Then take 20 minutes to write your letter. You do **NOT** need to write any addresses.

Writing

7 Approaching the task

- What am I expected to do in Writing **Task 2**?

- How can I develop good ideas?

IELTS Writing topics vary but you are always expected to produce an essay on the topic, and to cover all parts of the task.

To prepare for this Writing task, you need to analyse and brainstorm different essay topics so that you have a range of ideas on IELTS-type questions.

Analysing the task

The examiner will check the relevance of the ideas that you include in your answer. It is therefore important to read the task very carefully and make sure you understand it.

1 Read this example of a **Task 2** and answer the questions which follow.

> *These days everyone seems to have more and more possessions (e.g. computers, cars, mobile phones, etc.). Our strong desire to own these things is making us less aware of important personal qualities such as kindness and concern for others.*
>
> *Do you agree or disagree?*
>
> Give reasons for your answer and include any relevant examples from your own knowledge or experience.

- **a** What is the topic?
- **b** Can you turn the statements in the task into one question?
- **c** How useful is the information in brackets?
- **d** What do the words *such as* tell you?
- **e** Is there one correct answer?

2 Read this second example of a **Task 2** and answer the questions which follow.

> *Mobile phones have changed the way many people communicate. Nowadays people cannot live without them if they want to be a part of society.*
>
> *To what extent do you think this is true?*
>
> *Why do you think some people have not adapted to this type of communication?*
>
> Give reasons for your answer and include any relevant examples from your own knowledge or experience.

Test tip

If the task instructions have two parts and you fail to write about one of them, you cannot get more than Band 5 for content.

a What is the topic?

b How many parts does the task have? What are they?

c When you are asked *to what extent* you agree, which of the following can you do in your essay?

    A completely agree with the statement (by giving reasons/ideas)

    B completely disagree with the statement (by giving reasons/ideas)

    C present both sides of the argument (by giving reasons/ideas)

d If a task has two questions or parts, what proportion of your essay should you give to each part?

    A 50–50   **B** 60–40   **C** 80–20   **D** it doesn't matter

3 Now read another example of a **Task 2** and answer the questions which follow.

> *These days Internet-based courses have become a popular alternative to university-based courses. Some students prefer this type of learning because they do not need to attend lectures. Others argue that it is important to study at university.*
>
> *Discuss both these views and give your opinion.*
>
> Give reasons for your answer and include any relevant examples from your own knowledge or experience.

Test tip

You cannot score more than Band 5 if some of your main ideas are not relevant to the task (even if they are about the topic).

a How many parts do you need to cover?

b How much of your essay should you give to each part?

c Can you only agree with one of the views in your answer?

Generating ideas

Your examiner will award marks for the clear presentation of a number of relevant main ideas. You can collect ideas on a topic by brainstorming.

4 Analyse this task and decide how many parts it has.

> *Children over 15 should be allowed to make decisions about their lives without the interference of their parents or teachers. Society should accept that children mature at a younger age these days and should adjust the law accordingly.*
>
> *Do you agree or disagree?*
>
> Give reasons for your answer and include any relevant examples from your own knowledge or experience.

5 Brainstorm this task by making a bubble diagram of ideas like the one on page 114.

6 Work with a partner. Compare your diagrams and answer the questions.

a How similar or different are your ideas ?

b Do you have more arguments for *agree* or *disagree*?

c Has your personal view changed after seeing your partner's arguments?

7 Analyse this task and then decide how many parts it has.

> *There are more cars on the roads these days and more accidents. As a result, some politicians have suggested that people should take regular driving tests throughout their lives, rather than one single test.*
>
> *What do you think are the advantages of repeat driving tests? Do these outweigh the disadvantages?*
>
> Give reasons for your answer and include any relevant examples from your own knowledge or experience.

8 Work with a partner. Together, read the list of advantages for making regular driving tests compulsory and then make a list of disadvantages.

Advantages	Disadvantages
• Useful in the case of older drivers • Good for people who don't drive regularly • Keeps drivers up-to-date with road rules • Raises driving standards • May prevent young men driving too fast • Reduces accidents	

> **Test tip**
>
> Make sure you know the difference between your main ideas and your supporting ideas when you write. The examiner will check that you have included both.

■ Listing the advantages and disadvantages of a task is another way of brainstorming ideas before you write.

Main and supporting ideas

You need to group your ideas into main and supporting ideas. Main ideas act like a theme that links your supporting ideas; supporting ideas provide evidence that either justifies or proves your main idea. In other words, they are reasons for or examples of your main idea.
For example:

Supporting ideas	**Main idea**
Useful in the case of older drivers May prevent young men driving too fast Good for people who don't drive regularly	Certain groups of people would benefit.

9 Together, decide on a main idea that links the three remaining ideas from the *Advantages* list.

Raises driving standards
Keeps drivers up-to-date with road rules
Reduces accidents

10 Compare your main and supporting ideas with your partner's.

11 With your partner, decide on two main ideas and some supporting points from the list of disadvantages you made in exercise **8**. You may need to add some more ideas.

Writing a coherent paragraph

Paragraphs are often built around one main idea and its supporting points.

12 Read this paragraph from an answer to the task in exercise **4** on page 120. Can you identify which is the main idea and which are the supporting ideas?

> One of the reasons why the law should not be changed is that children need to be protected. Although some children go out to work at fifteen or look after the family at this age, they are really too young to be shouldering such heavy responsibilities. Some adults may think it is alright to let children work if we change the law but then this might prevent children from getting the important education and care that they need.

13 Write a paragraph using one of your main ideas for the task in exercise **7** on page 121.

14 Compare your paragraph with the model answer in the key. Underline the words that are used to introduce each of the supporting points.

15 Work with a partner. Together, brainstorm some ideas on one or both of the questions which follow the **Task 2** IELTS topics **A–D**, below. Divide your ideas into main and supporting ones.

A
Cities
- Why do people prefer to live in cities?
- How should cities be designed?

B
Air pollution
- What are the main causes of air pollution?
- What steps can we take to reduce it?

D
Tourism
- What are the benefits of tourism for the individual and society?
- How does tourism affect the environment?

C
Education
- How important is a university education?
- How has education changed over the years?

16 Use your notes to write some paragraphs. Make sure your paragraphs include one main idea and at least two supporting ideas.

Writing

8 Planning your essay

- How should I begin my essay?

  You should start by introducing the topic and the points for discussion in your own words. You may also wish to state your position.

- How should I organise my ideas?

  Your ideas need to be presented in a logical sequence. This is done through the use of paragraphing. The examiner will be looking for a clear, convincing argument that supports your position and leads to a logical conclusion.

Writing your opening paragraph

Your examiner will want to know what your view (or position) is on the topic. You can decide on your position at the end of your essay, after you have given all your arguments, but it is often a good idea to state your basic position as part of your introduction.

1 Read this opening paragraph to a task on obesity in children. The writer's position has been underlined. Can you guess what the wording of the task was?

> It is certainly true that some children these days eat too much fat and that this may have a negative effect on their health when they become adults. However, I don't agree that it is always the fault of the parents. Many adults have busy lifestyles and do not have time to prepare a proper meal when they get home, so they are forced to turn to convenience food.

Test tip

Your position is important to the content of your answer. If the examiner cannot find a clear position in your answer, you will lose marks.

2 Work with a partner. Read the task and opening paragraphs **A–C**. Underline each writer's position and then explain it in your own words.

> *Although many countries are becoming richer, these societies still have members who are poor and struggle each day to survive.*
>
> *Why do you think this happens and what can wealthy societies do to help their poorer citizens?*

Test tip

Remember there is no correct answer, so there will be different ways that you can answer the question(s).

A

> It's easy to see that poor people are everywhere. Even developed countries like the USA have citizens who cannot afford to buy clothes or food, so I agree with the statement in the task. I think that many societies already have systems to help poor people but perhaps they do not run these well enough.

B

> It is true that some people are comparatively poor, even though they live in a rich country, but I think it may be their own fault. Developed countries already do a lot to help poor people, so I think the problem cannot be solved by giving them more state benefits.

C

> Why are there so many poor people in the world? This is a very good question and I think the problem has many different root causes. People have to take some responsibility for their own welfare but, at the same time, some people cannot work for good reasons, so they need some support.

3 With your partner, discuss what you would expect the main argument to be about in each of the three essays, **A–C**.

- When writing your essay, it is important not to copy from the question paper. Your examiner will ignore any sections of copied material and will not include these words in the total word count.

4 How many of the words in paragraph **D**, below, will the examiner not count as part of the student's answer to the task in exercise **2**?

D

> There are a lot of rich countries in the world whose members are poor and struggle to survive each day. It is hard for them to survive. They have to look for food and sometimes they can't find anywhere to sleep. I think it is hard for them and sometimes nothing is done to help them.

Test tip

Your examiner will expect to be able to identify your main ideas easily. Paragraphs help do this.

5 Read paragraph **D** again and see if you can identify the student's position.

Organising ideas

Do not start the second paragraph until you know which main ideas you are going to use in each paragraph to develop your position.

How to approach the task

- Select two to four main ideas to form the paragraphs that come between your introduction and your conclusion.
- Think of some supporting points for each main idea.
- Decide which order the ideas should go in.
- Consider whether you can add any examples from your own experience of the topic.

6 Work with a partner. Together, discuss the task below. Think of some different positions you could take when answering this task.

> *Many childhood diseases can now be prevented through the use of vaccines.*
>
> *Should parents be made by law to immunise their children against common diseases or should individuals have the right to choose not to immunise their children?*

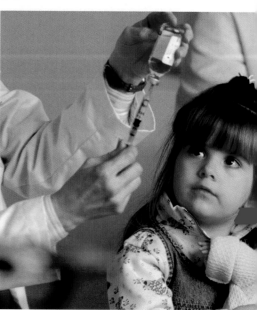

7 Read the introduction and paragraphs on the next page which form part of an answer to the task in exercise **6**. As you read, complete the table by making notes on:
- the writer's position on the immunisation of children
- the writer's main ideas
- the writer's supporting points and examples.

Position	1st main idea	Supporting points
....	Preventative medicine most effective	....
	2nd main idea	**Supporting points**
	....	....

Some people argue that the state should not make parents immunise their children. However, I feel that without vaccinations all these diseases could return and, therefore, laws should be made forcing parents to use them.

Preventative medicine has proved to be the most effective way of reducing the number of fatal childhood diseases. As a result of the widespread practice of immunising young children, many lives have been saved and some diseases, such as polio, have been almost wiped out.

Medical practices like immunisation are part of human progress. In previous centuries some diseases were the result of poor hygiene but nowadays water is cleaner and sanitation is better. Nobody would suggest that we should reverse this good practice, so why would we stop immunising children?

8 Think of another main idea for the fourth paragraph of this essay. Take ten minutes to write the paragraph.

9 Read the alternative answer to the task in exercise **6** in the key. This answer presents the opposite point of view to the essay above. Underline the main ideas and supporting points and make notes, as you did for exercise **7**.

Balancing views

Many tasks invite you to produce a balanced argument showing that you are aware of both sides of an issue.

10 Work with a partner. Together, discuss the task below. What does *this view* refer back to?

> *Many people decide on a career path early in their lives and keep to it. This, they argue, leads to a more satisfying working life.*
>
> *To what extent do you agree with this view?*
>
> *What other things can people do to try and have a satisfying working life?*

11 Read the notes below, which show the position and a main idea of a student.

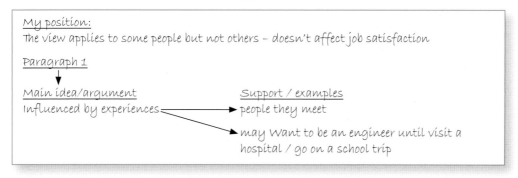

My position:
The view applies to some people but not others – doesn't affect job satisfaction

Paragraph 1
↓
Main idea/argument   Support / examples
Influenced by experiences ——→ people they meet
                            ↘ may want to be an engineer until visit a
                              hospital / go on a school trip

■ You can use a counter-argument to present an opposing view. In this way, you can show that you see both sides of the argument. If you choose to write a counter-argument, it is a good idea to use concessional language (see page 128).

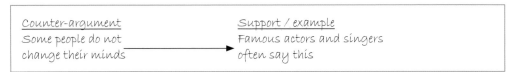

> <u>Counter-argument</u>
> Some people do not
> change their minds ⟶
>
> <u>Support / example</u>
> Famous actors and singers
> often say this

12 Use the student's notes in exercise **11**, to fill in the gaps in the essay below.

> Young children are often asked what they want to be when they grow up and most of them have an answer. However, while some people do not change their minds about this over the course of their lives, many others do. Yet this does not mean that their jobs are not **1** ....
>
> The main reason why people's ambitions change is that, as they grow up, they are affected by their **2** .... For example, a child may want to be an engineer until he goes on a school trip to a hospital and then decides he would rather be a doctor. Similarly the people we meet as children can have a big impact on our goals and ambitions.
>
> Having said that, there are some people who …

■ *Having said that,* … is a useful linking phrase to introduce a counter-argument.

13 Use the student's notes above to complete the counter-argument in the third paragraph of the essay.

14 ⏱ Take ten minutes to think of a main idea that relates to the second question in the task in exercise **10** and then write the fourth paragraph. Compare your finished paragraph with the model answer in the key.

Writing a conclusion

Your conclusion should summarise your position for the reader and, if appropriate to the task instructions, present your final decision on a question. You can also be impartial, i.e. take no side, or state that you have no conclusion to draw.

■ Phrases like those in the box below can be useful in a conclusion.

To sum up, *people are all different.*	In conclusion / To conclude
Overall / All in all	Ultimately
In the final analysis	In the end
Clearly	Taking everything into consideration

15 Write a conclusion to the student's essay that began in exercise **12**. Compare your finished conclusion with the model answer in the key.

Writing

9 Turning your ideas into written arguments

- How can I turn my ideas into arguments?

Once you have got your ideas and decided how to organise them, you need to think about how to turn them into arguments.

There is a range of expressions that you can use to express arguments. It is a good idea to use some of these expressions because they act as signposts and help the examiner follow the development of your essay. They also help you write fuller, more varied sentences in an appropriate essay style.

Presenting ideas

Your ideas will form the basis of your argument and they need to be expressed clearly and appropriately.

- You may need to give your personal opinion.

> In my view, school uniforms ...

- You may want to give other people's opinions, e.g. when you are asked to consider an argument from both sides.

> Some people argue that school uniforms ...

- Sometimes a more general statement is needed.

> It is generally believed that school uniforms ...

- To support your argument, you will often need to state facts.

> In my country most people have to wear school uniform ...

Here are some expressions to help you present ideas.

I would argue/say that ...	Some/Most people argue/think/say that ...
In my view ...	It is understood that ...
It seems (to me) that ...	It is generally accepted that ...
I tend to think that / I feel that ...	There is a tendency to believe that ...
As far as I am concerned ...	One of the main arguments in favour of / against ...

Test tip
Words like *tend, seem* and *feel* are often used to soften the tone of the writer's argument.

1 Work with a partner. Together, use the expressions in the box to present some ideas on the topics **A–D**, below.

    A Having large or small families   **B** The growing popularity of football
    C Travelling to new countries   **D** Using a mobile phone in a public place

2 Write some of your sentences down and discuss them in class. Did the writers use appropriate expressions? If not, why not?

Making concessions

Good writers often consider other arguments that are different, before presenting their own views. For example:

Although some people would like to have a lot of children (concession), *the cost of raising them has to be considered first* (writer's view).

The following expressions are useful when making concessions.

While/Although …	It could be argued that …
Despite the fact that …	Admittedly / Certainly … but / However …
Even though …	It may be true that …

3 For each statement **A–C**, write a short paragraph arguing against the ideas.

Statement	For	Against
A Television is beneficial for children.	Educational programmes	Adverts – brands / expensive consumer goods
B There is too much packaging in supermarkets.	Shoppers want it	Creates waste
C We need to build more roads around cities to reduce traffic problems.	Less traffic in cities	More cars and lorries will use them

4 Now rewrite your paragraphs to include a concession. Begin with a sentence containing your main idea and then express your argument with a concession. For example:

A *It seems to me that television has few benefits for children.* **While** *I agree that there are some good educational programmes, far too much advertising is targeted at children. This encourages them to want expensive goods that their parents may not be able to afford to buy.*

■ A concession is often useful when you are writing a conclusion, because it can sum up pros and cons. For example: *All in all, despite the fact that there are some interesting programmes, much of the time children spend watching TV would be better spent on other activities.*

Refuting an argument

This is a forceful way of expressing a view. It means that you present an argument or view by first rejecting an argument that you do not agree with.

The following expressions are useful in refuting an argument.

I am unconvinced that …	There is little evidence to support the view that …
I don't believe that …	It is unjustifiable to say that …
Some people find it hard to accept that …	I disagree with the view/argument that …
It is doubtful whether …	I am uncertain whether …

5 Write four sentences refuting the arguments **B–D** in the table below. In the first part of the sentence, use one of the expressions on the previous page to refute the argument in the first column. Then complete the sentence using *when* and the counter-argument in the second column. For example:

A

I **don't believe that** footballers should be paid such high salaries **when** they are just doing a job like everyone else.

Test tip
These expressions will help you show the examiner that you can write complex sentences.

Argument	Counter-argument
A footballers – deserve high salaries	**A** just doing a job like everyone else
B Internet – a useful resource for children	**B** so much uncensored material
C running – good for you	**C** so many physical injuries
D gambling – legal	**D** so much misery and poverty

6 Choose one of the following topics and write two or three sentences like those in exercise **5**.

Building more homes in urban centres	Buying iPods for children
Encouraging young people to go to university	Encouraging people to have credit cards
Putting money into space research	Putting a space research station on the moon

Defining and explaining

If you are using general terms that could be understood in many different ways, it is a good idea to define or explain what you understand by that term. This will form part of your supporting argument.

7 Underline the explanation in this example from a student's essay.

> I would argue that many young people today see using a computer as a leisure activity. By this I mean that they seem to spend all their free time downloading Internet material or looking up websites when they could be doing something more active such as taking exercise.

The following expressions are useful in helping you be more precise.

By this I (don't) mean …	In other words, …	To be more precise, …
In fact, …	That is to say, …	Here I'm (not) referring to …
That is not to say that …		

8 Use one of the expressions above to add another sentence to the following arguments.

   1 In my opinion, extended families are more successful than nuclear families.
   2 It is often said that young people are more tolerant than older people.
   3 I am convinced that choice is important in the school curriculum.
   4 Job commitment is not always the key to success.

9 Discuss with your class the structure and content of some of your sentences.

10 Read this opening paragraph to a **Task 2** essay on whether examinations are useful or not. Underline and explain the different ways that the writer expresses his views.

> I would argue that examinations have a positive influence on learning and by this I mean that they lead to a better understanding of the subject. This is essential in areas such as medicine. While I admit that they can create a lot of pressure for students and can cause stress, I am convinced that these problems can be largely avoided, if the approach to examinations is handled well by teachers and students. Overall, students are motivated by examinations and this motivation can only benefit them.

IELTS Writing test practice   Task 2

11 ⏱ Take 40 minutes to write an essay of at least 250 words on the following task. Use some of the phrases and structures that you have practised in this unit to express your views.

> *Disruptive school students have a negative influence on others. Students who are noisy and disobedient should be grouped together and taught separately.*
>
> *Do you agree or disagree?*
>
> Give reasons for your answer and include any relevant examples from your own knowledge or experience.

12 Work with a partner. Together, read the model answer in the key and then, using the text in *italics* to help you, discuss some of the expressions the writer uses to present arguments.

Writing

10 Linking your ideas

- **Why do I need to link ideas?**

  You need to ensure that you can get your meaning across to the reader. Good writing relies on the ability to be coherent – to use the right linking and reference words in complex sentence forms.

- **What are linking words?**

  Linking words and phrases are used to add supporting points and examples to your main ideas. You need to signpost these clearly so that it is easy to follow your argument(s).

Making the main argument clear

1 Read this extract from a student's essay on *Why cars should be banned from city centres* and then answer the questions which follow.

> I don't think cars should be banned from city centres because we need to travel by car. Otherwise how can we get around? Public transport is not good in my city so I need my car. In some cities, e.g. London, you must pay to enter the city centre by car. People with money can pay this anyway. There are not enough car parks so people must park their cars on the streets and this causes traffic jams.

   a Can you clearly identify the main and supporting ideas?
   b What is the problem with this paragraph?

2 Now read this extract from another student's essay on the same topic and then answer the questions below.

> Most world cities were designed long before the motor car and so, naturally, they were not meant to handle the large volumes of traffic so common today. For instance, the streets in the centre of Tokyo, where I come from, are narrow and the traffic moves very slowly, particularly at rush hour. Cities such as Jakarta and Bangkok are famous for their traffic jams and, in fact, a 10 km journey can take up to two hours.
>
> Understandably, governments look for ways to reduce traffic jams, and one way is to ban cars from entering city centres altogether or, alternatively, to charge them a steep fee. A good example of this is the Congestion Charge in London, which has successfully reduced the number of vehicles entering the city between 7am and 6.30pm on weekdays. Indeed, it has been so successful that the Mayor of London is planning to extend the zone to encourage people to use public transport. In my experience, this is a sensible way to tackle the problem of traffic congestion and one which other world cities could easily copy.

   a What is the writer's main point in each paragraph?
   b Underline the words which link the main points to the supporting ideas.

Using linking words and expressions

There are many ways in which you can link your main and supporting arguments. It is important to try to vary the words and structures you use.
Here are some useful expressions.

For example / For instance …	In fact / Indeed …
Of course …	If this is/were the case …
Firstly / For one thing …	Naturally / Understandably …
A good example of this is …	In my experience …

3 Link the following arguments using an appropriate expression from the box above. Use a different expression in each gap.

1 It is impossible to predict what type of holidays people will be taking in 100 years' time. It is possible, **a** _____ , that space travel will be a realistic option in the future. **b** _____ , it would completely transform our traditional view of a holiday.

2 I would argue that supermarkets are a good thing. **a** _____ in some countries they can offer so many products that it's hardly necessary to shop anywhere else. **b** _____ there are sometimes instances of local opposition, but this is usually short-lived.

3 Statistics show that the worst drivers in the world are young men. _____ , if you look closely at any car that is going too fast, overtaking in the wrong place or driving too close to the car in front, there will be a young man in the driver's seat.

4 I strongly approve of the preservation of historic buildings. **a** _____ , they are a part of our heritage and secondly, they are often very beautiful. Too many have already been destroyed. **b** _____ my home town, where whole streets of lovely houses were knocked down in order to build high-rise flats.

■ You can also use simple reference words to link ideas together.

4 Fill in the gaps in paragraphs **1–5**, below, *either* with a reference word from the box only *or* with one of the reference words and one of the nouns in brackets. There are more reference words than you need.

e.g. this these those others such one another who which where	

1 Generally speaking, air travel has come down in price over the past five years. **a** _____ has been the result of airlines offering a 'no-frills' service, **b** _____ passengers pay for refreshments. (*reduction*)

2 Just under 40% of people in the UK and 50% of Americans say that work is the most important part of their lives. **a** _____ increase further when you include retired people looking back on their working lives. **b** _____ may be changing, however. (*figures, attitudes*)

3 When a group of schoolchildren was interviewed, the majority said they preferred their teachers to be humorous but also kind. However,
a .... are not as highly rated by the teachers themselves.
b .... suggested that commitment to their subject was more important. (*qualities*)

4 The cost of petrol has risen steeply in the last few years. **a** .... is due to a combination of things, such as shortages of oil and higher government taxes. Unfortunately, it looks unlikely that **b** .... will be reversed. (*rise, trend*)

5 People's views vary on the subject of recycling waste. **a** .... who live near recycling centres usually support it, while **b** .... who have to travel long distances to recycle their rubbish often just don't bother.

5 Read paragraphs **1–5** in exercise **4** again and underline any other words or expressions that help to link the ideas.

6 Read the following extract from an essay. Underline any *reference words* which help link ideas together. Use a different colour to underline any other linkers in the text.

There is always controversy over whether it is important to spend large sums of money on medical research or whether more of this money should be directed towards treating patients.
Obviously some medical research is essential. Without it, we would have no vaccinations against diseases such as polio, no drugs such as antibiotics and no treatments like x-rays and radiotherapy. Nevertheless, the field of medical research is very competitive and this has financial disadvantages. Take, for example, the current research being conducted on the HIV virus. In this field it is arguable that money is being wasted in that scientists throughout the world are working independently towards the same ultimate goal, to find a cure for AIDS, and with the same hope of becoming famous in the process. Surely it would be more productive and less costly if these scientists joined forces and an international research team was set up with joint international funding.

Building complex sentences

You cannot produce complex sentences without linking your ideas.

7 Work with a partner. Together, read the sets of sentences **1–4** and see if you can link each set together into one complex sentence, as in the example. The result will probably be shorter than the set of sentences together. There are several possible ways to do this in each case.

Example
The World Cup is the largest sporting event in the world.
The World Cup is played every four years.
The event is hosted by a different country each time.
The event generates huge amounts of money.

The World Cup, which is held in a different country every four years, is the largest sporting event in the world and generates huge amounts of money.

1 Mobile phones used to be very expensive.
Only wealthy people had mobile phones.
Today mobile phones are extremely common.

> **Test tip**
> It is important to show that you can write complex sentences and link your ideas.

133

2 Many young people are overweight.
Many young people spend their evenings in front of the TV.
Advertisements for unhealthy food are shown between 5.00pm and 8.00pm.

3 Few people communicate by 'hard copy' mail these days.
'Hard copy' letters are used mainly in formal situations.
Emails have become the most common form of written communication.

4 Some people believe human beings are responsible for global warming.
Other people think global warming is caused by climatic factors.
The influence of climatic factors cannot be altered by lowering pollution levels.

IELTS Writing test practice   Task 2

8 ⏱ Write an answer to this task in 40 minutes. When you have finished, count the number of words you have used and allow three minutes to correct any mistakes.

> Write about the following topic:
>
> *Young people today are better qualified than they were in the past. Some people argue that this is because competition for jobs is greater than it used to be. Others say that people only continue their education because the opportunities exist for them to do so.*
>
> *Discuss both these views and give your own opinion.*
>
> Give reasons for your answer and include any relevant examples from your own knowledge or experience.
>
> Write at least 250 words.

9 Work with a partner. Swap answers and then use the checklist below to make some notes as you read your partner's essay. Then together, discuss your notes.

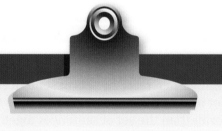

Can you follow the argument?	How well are the views expressed?
What is the position?	How are the main ideas presented?
What is the main idea in each paragraph?	How are they linked to the supporting ideas?
How are the main ideas supported?	Are there any examples?
What is the conclusion?	Can you find some vocabulary related to the topic?
Can you summarise your partner's view on the topic?	Has your partner copied too much from the task?

	Approach	Reason
	Spend 20 minutes on Task 1 (150 words) and 40 minutes on Task 2 (250 words).	Task 2 is longer than Task 1 and is worth twice as many marks.
Before you write	Read the task and make a mental summary of the key points and overall trends/stages.	If you misinterpret the data or diagram, you will lose a lot of marks for content.
As you write	Introduce the information, in a sentence or two, using your own words.	If you copy the question, the examiner will not count these words.
	Summarise the key points and use data to illustrate these.	You will lose marks if you miss key points or fail to illustrate them.
	Include an overview of the information – either in your introduction or conclusion.	You will lose marks if your answer does not contain an overview.
How you write	Try to show that you can use your own words (wherever possible) and a range of grammatical structures.	You will get more marks for vocabulary and grammar if you can do this.
	Divide your answer into paragraphs and use linkers to connect your ideas.	You will get more marks if you can organise your answer well and use a range of linking and reference words.
When you have finished	Count your words to make sure you have written enough.	Short answers lose marks. (There are no extra marks for long answers.)
	Check your grammar, spelling and punctuation.	Mistakes in these areas can reduce your marks.

Approach	Reason
Spend 20 minutes on Task 1 (150 words) and 40 minutes on Task 2 (250 words).	Task 2 is longer than Task 1 and is worth twice as many marks.

	Approach	Reason
Before you write	Read the task carefully to decide how many parts it has and what your position is.	You will lose marks if you do not address all the parts of the question relevantly.
	Make a quick plan either mentally or on rough paper. Decide on your main ideas.	The examiner will be looking for a number of clear main ideas.

	Approach	Reason
As you write	Introduce your answer in your own words and make your position clear. You may state your position here as well.	The examiner will not count copied material as part of your total word count.
	Present your main ideas clearly and use examples to support them.	You will get more marks if your ideas are clear and well supported.
	Write a conclusion and re-state your position.	Your examiner will expect to find a logical conclusion and a consistent position.

	Approach	Reason
How you write	Try to show that you can use your own words (wherever possible) and a range of grammatical structures.	You will get more marks for vocabulary and grammar if you can do this.
	Divide your answer into paragraphs and use linkers to connect your ideas.	You will get more marks if you can organise your answer well and use a range of linking and reference words.

	Approach	Reason
When you have finished	Count your words to make sure you have written enough.	Short answers lose marks. (There are no extra marks for long answers.)
	Check your grammar, spelling and punctuation.	Mistakes in these areas can reduce your marks.

The Speaking module

The IELTS Speaking test takes the form of a one-to-one interview. There are three parts to the Speaking test. These allow you to demonstrate your spoken English skills through a number of tasks. The tasks are designed so that you can use a range of language on a variety of topics. The whole interview takes between 11 and 14 minutes. Here is an overview of the Speaking test format showing the three parts and the approximate timing of each.

	Interaction
Part 1 **Introduction and interview** 4–5 minutes	You will have the chance to speak on familiar topics. The examiner will ask you a number of straightforward questions about yourself and about familiar topics, and you should find these easy to answer. This is an opportunity to overcome any nerves and demonstrate your basic fluency.
Part 2 **Short talk** 3–4 minutes	You will be asked to talk for 1 or 2 minutes on a topic chosen by the examiner. You will have a minute to prepare and then you will have to speak on the topic without stopping. The topic will be based on your personal experiences and feelings, so your talk should be lively and interesting.
Part 3 **Two-way discussion** 4–5 minutes	You will be asked more abstract questions, broadly linked to the topic introduced in Part 2, and you will be encouraged to discuss these more fully. This is where you can demonstrate control of language, your ability to express abstract ideas, and to support your opinions appropriately. You should aim to give longer replies than you did to the Part 1 questions.
11–14 minutes	

The examiner's role

IELTS examiners have been specially trained to rate spoken English on the IELTS scale. They will be clear and encouraging so that you can do your best on the day of the test. They know that you may be nervous but they can only assess what they hear, so they will expect you to speak up and to produce plenty of language.

The examiners rate your language on a scale of **1–9** in four broad areas: fluency, vocabulary, grammar and accuracy, and pronunciation. This book provides guidance in these four areas and explains how they are assessed in the Speaking test.

The candidate's role

It is important that you listen carefully to what you are asked and provide full and extended answers to the questions. However, you must stick to the topic and avoid rehearsed language or answers which do not relate to the questions.

There are four areas (called the *assessment criteria*) which the examiner will focus on during the Speaking test. You will be rated on the IELTS scale in each of these four areas.

1 Look at the table and the box below. The table on the left shows the four Speaking assessment criteria and the box on the right shows a list of skills or strategies that you need to use when you are speaking.

Match each of these skills and strategies, **A–R**, to one of the four assessment criteria. The first four have been done for you.

Assessment criteria	Skills and strategies
Fluency	A C
Vocabulary	B
Grammar and accuracy	D
Pronunciation	

Skills and strategies

A ✓ Use linking words
B ✓ Choose appropriate words
C ✓ Correct yourself
D ✓ Use articles correctly
E Use the right tense
F Emphasise words to convey meaning
G Get the stress right on long words
H Be able to keep going and talk on the topic
I Find a way to say something when you don't have the right word
J Be able to join your ideas
K Use complex spoken sentences
L Use a variety of words and expressions
M Get the word order right
N Speak clearly
O Produce sounds so that they can be understood
P Choose words that go well together
Q Use idiomatic language
R Use conditionals correctly

2 Work with a partner. Together, discuss these questions.

a Which of the four areas of assessment do you find most difficult when speaking English?

b What do you think are the most important skills for a good speaker to have?

■ Exercises to practice these skills can be found throughout the Workbook.

Speaking

1 Responding to personal questions

- What is **Part 1** of the Speaking test like?

- What sort of topics will I be asked to talk about in **Part 1**?

Part 1 of the test lasts four to five minutes. The examiner will introduce him or herself to you and ask you your name. You must show some photo identification.

The examiner will then ask you several questions on a number of different topics, such as your interests, studies or working life, family, accommodation, etc. You need to give a clear reply and to show that you can develop your answers. However, you are not expected to talk for a long time.

Answering questions on familiar topics

The questions in **Part 1** are always based on familiar topics which relate to your own everyday experience. You should not find it difficult to think of an answer.

1 ⏲ Take one minute to complete the table below. Write appropriate information about yourself in the spaces in each column. You only need to write two or three words in each column.

Home town and family	Hobbies	Favourite food	Languages spoken
	tennis		

2 Use the four topics in the table to ask questions to other students in your class. When you form the questions, you should use the **simple present tense**, e.g. *Where **do** you live? How many languages **can** you speak?* Make notes of two or three words on their answers.

What **are** your hobbies?

3 Report back to the class, telling them what you learned about the people you interviewed.

> Kumiko lives in Kyoto and has one brother. Her favourite food is sashimi but she quite likes Australian meat pies. She speaks Japanese fluently, of course, and English quite well.

4 Take one minute to complete the table below with appropriate information about your past. Again, you only need to write two or three words in each column. Then use the four topics to ask questions to other students and make short notes of their answers.

First house or apartment	A friend from primary school	Entertainment	Past holidays/ travel
	Young Jun		Thailand

> What **was** your favourite TV programme when you **were** young?

> **Did** you **live** in a house or an apartment when you **were growing up**?

Expanding your answers

It is important to give a full answer that flows naturally. So you need to learn strategies to help you to keep going.

5 Think about what you did last weekend and then make a list of at least five activities like the one in the example below.

- checked email
- played football
- got take-away noodles
- ate at a friend's house
- hired a DVD

6 There is a lot more that you can say about activities like these. Use the question words in the box to $E X P A N D\ O N$ (i.e. give additional details for) each of your activities. Here is an example of how you could expand on a topic.

What?
Who?
When?
Why?
How?
Where?

What did you do last weekend?

I went to an Internet café on Saturday to check my emails. It's near where I live and only costs $1.80 an hour. I had lots of messages from …

- You don't need to repeat the words in the question, but it's a good idea to make a link, e.g. *last weekend – on Saturday.*

7 Work with a partner. Take turns to tell each other about what you did last weekend. Try to keep talking for about one minute. If necessary, ask other questions to find out more information and help your partner expand on his or her answer.

8 Work with a new partner. Together, repeat exercise **7**. Practise your expansion strategy until providing more information to your listener becomes automatic!

IELTS Speaking test practice   Part 1

9 Read the question below and take a minute to think about your answer.

What important things did you do last year?

Talk to your partner about this question. Use one of these opening expressions from the box below to help you start talking.

Opening expressions to get going
- One of the most important things I did was to …
- I did a number of important things such as …
- Last year was an important year because I …
- Of all the things I did …

Test tip
If you give very short answers, you will lose marks. Aim to give two to four spoken sentences for each answer.

141

Speaking

2 Becoming more fluent

■ What is meant by *fluency*?

■ How can I become more fluent?

Fluency in speech is the ability to maintain a flow of language without unnatural hesitation, by linking your ideas.

If you can present a number of well-connected ideas and avoid using a lot of hesitation and repetition, the examiner will find your answers interesting and will be able to follow them more easily.

Linking your ideas

One way to keep going is to answer questions by providing some extra information and linking this information to your first response.

1 Read this student's ideas and then notice how she links them together to form a cohesive (i.e. clear and logical) answer to the examiner's question. Try saying her answer out loud so that it flows naturally.

> Do you have any brothers or sisters?

> My brother is studying economics.

> My brother is older than me.

> My brother is at university.

> I have one brother.

> I have an older brother who is studying economics at university.

Linking words or phrases
because, and, if
which, although, as
because, but, also
at the moment, but, one
even though, and, so
because, with
and, but, or, either

2 Now join the sets of ideas **1–7** below in the same way. Use the linking words provided.

1 I need to learn English. English is very important for me. English will help me to get an interesting job. I want to work in the tourist industry.
2 I work in a bank. Working in a bank can be quite interesting. The nature of the job is changing. Many people do their banking on the Internet.
3 My favourite sport is tennis. Tennis is a lot of fun to play. I enjoy watching tennis.
4 I live in an apartment. The apartment is very small. I hope to live in a larger apartment next year.
5 Fast food is very popular in many countries these days. Fast food is bad for our health. Fast food is expensive. I think cooking at home is more sensible.
6 My school was very large. There were hundreds of children at my school. It was impossible to know everyone at the school.
7 I love movies. I like watching TV. I don't like live theatre. I don't like opera.

3 What questions do the sets of ideas **1–7** in exercise **2** answer? For example: *1 Why are you studying English?*

4 Work with a partner. Take turns to give your own answers to the questions for **1–7**.

IELTS Speaking test practice	Part 1

In the Speaking test you may be asked to answer questions on some of the topics below.

5 Choose one of the topics to talk about. Think about how you can expand on your chosen topic.

e.g. *football → supporting my local team → playing with friends*

> your interests
> clothes and fashion
> entertainment
> the climate in your country
> travel plans
> your education

6 Write your chosen topic and your additional ideas on a piece of paper and then give it to your partner.

7 With your partner, take turns to ask each other general questions about the main topic, using the notes as a prompt. For example:

Can you tell me about the climate in your country?

Test tip
When the examiner asks you a question in Part 1, make sure you answer that question. Don't start talking about something else.

Then ask specific questions to draw out the information in the notes.

Does the weather affect what people wear in your country?

How often do you watch or listen to the weather forecast?

Do you prefer a hot or cold climate?

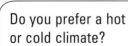

Try to use some of the linking words and phrases on the previous page.

Using vocabulary to link and expand your ideas

In **Part 1** of the IELTS test you will have to respond by giving full and rounded answers. This means you need to know how to use a range of vocabulary.

8 Match the Speaking Part 1 questions 1–8 to the answers a–h which follow.

1 What is the best way to stay healthy?	2 Are you a student or do you work?	3 What kind of music are you interested in?	4 What is your favourite time of the year?

5 How do you feel about living in a big city?	6 Do you prefer watching DVDs at home or going to the cinema?	7 How do people get to work in your home town?	8 What is the most important festival in your country?

a	b
I prefer staying at home. I'm not very keen on crowds and also, it's much cheaper than going to the movies.	Both, in fact. I have a part-time job. But it's not the job I want to do when I finish my course. It's just a way of earning some extra money while I'm studying.
c I think <u>walking</u> is <u>good for you</u>, as well as <u>watching what you eat</u>. So I try to <u>take</u> some <u>exercise</u> every day and on top of that I <u>eat</u> lots of <u>fruit and vegetables</u>.	**d** At first I didn't like being in London, because of the crowds, but now I'm used to it and I think it will be quite hard to go back to my quiet little village.
e By public transport normally. We still have trams in my city and as they're really efficient, a lot of people use them.	**f** Well … I really enjoy listening to songs, particularly songs from my country. And I like to have music playing when I'm studying. In fact, I can't study without music.
g New Year is a very important celebration. For instance, in our family we all get together to enjoy each other's company. It's a very special occasion.	**h** Um … that's hard to answer. I suppose I like summer best of all because I love the warm weather, and I have lots of good memories of summer holidays with my family.

- Your answer will be better if you don't simply repeat the words that the examiner uses. Try to vary your vocabulary by using words with a similar meaning to key words in the question.

9 Read the responses **a–h** again and underline the content words which link back to the question. The first one has been done for you.

10 Use a different colour to underline the linking words which join the two ideas grammatically.

Main idea	*I think <u>walking</u> is <u>good for you</u> as well as <u>watching what you eat</u>.*

Additional information	*So I try to <u>take</u> some <u>exercise</u> every day and on top of that I <u>eat</u> lots of <u>fruit and vegetables</u>.*

IELTS Speaking test practice	**Part 1**

How to approach the task

- Listen carefully to each question so that your answer is relevant to the topic.
- Ask the examiner to repeat the question if you do not understand it.
- Give a short but full reply using the correct tense.
- Try to use different vocabulary from the examiner.

11 Work with a partner. Take three or four minutes to ask each other questions **1–8** in exercise **8** and give your answers. Make sure you give some additional information and try to link it back to the main idea of your answer. If possible, record your answers.

12 If you were able to record your answers, draw a table like the one below and then listen to your recording. Try to complete the table as you listen to your answers.

Speaking

3 Preparing your talk

- What do I have to do in Speaking **Part 2**?

In **Part 2** of the test, you will be asked to give a short talk for one to two minutes on a topic chosen by the examiner. The examiner will remain silent while you are speaking, but *will* stop you when the time is up.

- How can I make the best use of my preparation time?

You will have a minute to think about what you are going to say, and it is important to use this time to note down some helpful points and relevant vocabulary. This will help you structure your talk.

Understanding the topic

Below is an example of a topic for Speaking **Part 2**. The **Part 2** topic will usually focus on a familiar or personal area.

1 Read the topic and the points which follow, and then do the exercises.

> **A**
>
> **Describe a place you have lived in that you particularly liked.**
>
> **You should say:**
> **when you lived there**
> **who you lived with**
> **what was most memorable about this place**
> **and explain why you liked it so much.**

How to approach the task

- Read all the instructions carefully and make a note of the key words, e.g. *Describe, place, particularly liked*.
- Decide which place you are going to describe. If you have lived in a number of different places, then you will need to make a quick decision.
- Try to think of something to say that your listener might find interesting or want to know.
- Make sure you mention something about each of the three points on the card.
- Jot down some key ideas, drawing on your own experience. Don't be afraid to say how you feel about something.
- Jot down any useful vocabulary or expressions that you can use in your talk.

> **Test tip**
>
> Make sure you write something during your minute. Use the time to make notes on key ideas to prompt you while you are speaking. Only make notes, not full sentences.

Here is an example of how to start making notes.

IELTS Speaking test practice	Part 2

While you are speaking, your partner should time you and write down the key points in your talk, and then compare these with your notes.

2 Give your talk on topic **A** to your partner. Make sure you speak for more than a minute. When it is your turn to listen, time your partner's talk and write the key points he or she makes. Below is a list of possible ways to begin your talk on this topic.

> I'd like to talk about …
> I've chosen to talk about …
> I'm going to talk about …
> I've lived in quite a few places, but one place I particularly liked was …
> I've really only ever lived in … so I'll talk about that.

3 Look at the key points your partner wrote during your talk and then compare them with your own notes. Did you use all your notes in your talk?

Brainstorming ideas for Part 2

4 Look at the Speaking **Part 2** tasks **B–E** below and follow this strategy for each of them in turn.

How to approach the task

- Read the task carefully to make sure you fully understand the topic and the three points.
- Make a note of the key words.
- Decide whether you will need to talk about the past, the present or the future.
- Make a note of at least *two* key ideas for each of the three points in each task.
- Make a note of any key vocabulary that you could use.

B

Describe the member of your family who is the most successful.

You should say:
 who this person is
 how often you see each other
 what this person does
and explain why he/she is successful.

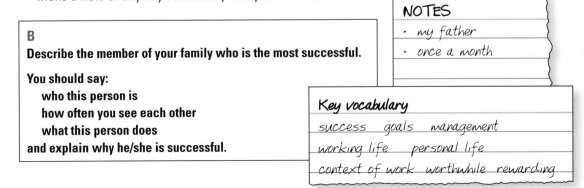

147

C

Describe a job that you would like to do in the future.

You should say:
   why you are attracted to this job
   how much training would be necessary
   what kind of personal qualities it would require
and explain why you would like to do this job.

D

Describe a tourist trip that you have been on which you particularly enjoyed.

You should say:
   where you went
   why you took the trip
   what you remember most about the trip
and explain why you particularly enjoyed this trip.

E

Describe a city that you would like to visit in the futuref.

You should say:
   where the city is
   how you would travel there
   what you would do there
and explain why you would like to visit this city.

Checking your notes

Test tip

Practise giving your talk with a clock or watch in front of you. As you must talk for between one and two minutes in the exam, you need practice at judging this time. If you don't keep talking for at least a minute, you will be wasting a valuable opportunity to show off your skills. You may, of course, look at your watch during the test.

5 Work with a partner. Swap your notes on the topics **B–E**. Use this checklist to decide how well your partner's notes prepare him or her for this part of the test.

Checklist for notes	✓	✗
Has he or she noted the key words from the question?		
Has he or she written something for each point?		
Are there any words which express feelings?		
Is there any useful vocabulary related to the topic?		
Can you improve the notes in any way?		

IELTS Speaking test practice   Part 2

6 Work with a partner. Take turns to give a talk on one of the four topics, **B–E**, in exercise **4**. Choose a topic to give to your partner. While you are listening, use the checklist from exercise **5** to say how well your partner covers the points during his or her talk. Try to talk for two minutes.

Speaking

4 Giving your talk

- How can I do well in **Part 2**?

Use the card to guide you through your talk so that you stick to the topic and say something about each of the three points on the card, using relevant vocabulary. Make sure you have a good idea of how long two minutes lasts so that you can begin and end your talk appropriately.

- What strategy should I adopt if I don't know much about the topic?

You should always be prepared to use your imagination if you haven't had much experience of the topic.

Using your notes

1 Look at this student's notes for one of the **Part 2** topics, **A–E**, from Unit **3**. Which topic has she chosen?

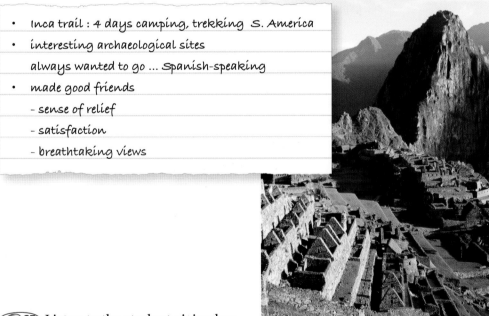

- Inca trail : 4 days camping, trekking S. America
- interesting archaeological sites
  always wanted to go ... Spanish-speaking
- made good friends
  - sense of relief
  - satisfaction
  - breathtaking views

2 (35) Listen to the student giving her talk based on the notes she made. As you listen, answer the questions **1–7**.

1 What information does she start her talk with?
2 What tenses does she use mostly?
3 What words are specifically related to the topic?
4 What words does she use to express her feelings?
5 Does she speak for long enough?
6 Does she cover all three points?
7 How does she deal with the last part of the task?

149

3 Listen again and complete a table like the one below with examples in the student's talk of strategies (**A–R**) from the *Skills and strategies* box on page 138. The first two have been done for you.

A	Use linking words	*... even though you have all the luxuries*
B	Choose appropriate words	*altitudes of ...*
C		

4 🕐 Try giving a two-minute talk of your own on this subject. Follow the procedure for making your own notes and then time your talk.

IELTS Speaking test practice   **Part 2**

5 🕐 Take one minute to prepare a short talk on the **Part 2** topic below. Follow the procedure for making your own notes and time your talk.

> **Describe a family holiday you have been on which you particularly enjoyed.**
>
> **You should say:**
> **where you went**
> **how you travelled there**
> **what you remember most about the holiday**
> **and explain why you particularly enjoyed this holiday.**

6 Work with a partner. Take turns to give a two-minute talk on this topic, using the notes you have made. Time each other's talks.

Using rhythm and timing to help your talk flow

7 Look at another student's notes for one of the other **Part 2** topics, **A–E**, from Speaking Unit **3** on pages 146–148. Which topic are these notes for?

- father / daughter
- what does 'success' mean?
- regular meetings – breakfast once a week
- manages retirement homes
  - personally rewarding
  - professionally satisfying
  - worthwhile

8 (36) Listen to the student giving her talk based on the notes she made. As you listen, answer the questions 1–6.

1 Does her talk follow the order of her notes?

2 Why does she question the idea of success?

3 Why does she mention the weekly meetings?

4 What tense does she mostly use and why?

5 Which words are specifically related to the topic?

6 How does she deal with the last part of the task?

Test tip
Make sure you round off your talk by mentioning the last part of the task.

9 (37) Listen to these extracts from the second student's talk. Note how she groups certain words together to convey her meaning.

10 Now listen carefully to the extracts again and try to mark lines (/) to show which words she groups together, and then mark with a dot (•) which word(s) she stresses in each group. The first one has been done as an example.

Test tip
If you stress the important words in your talk, it will help your examiner follow your answer more easily.

1 so … / My answer/ … is in the context of / working life,/ rather than personal life.

2 He feels like he's accomplishing something

that is obviously personally and professionally satisfying …

3 It's a bit hard to explain exactly what he does.

4 It's a management job really, but working in a context

which is really worthwhile.

5 I see my dad very regularly, about once a week.

6 He enjoys what he does, as well as making a decent living out of it.

11 Check your answers in the key and then read each extract out loud using the same intonation as this student.

IELTS Speaking test practice	**Part 2**

12 Find your own notes for topic **B** from Unit **3**. Try to expand on your notes by including any relevant ideas and vocabulary from the second student's talk.

13 Work with a partner. Take turns to give a two-minute talk on topic **B**, using the notes you have made. Time each other's talks.

Speaking

5 Understanding abstract and analytical questions

- What sort of questions will I get in Speaking **Part 3**?

- What sort of answer is the examiner expecting me to give?

In Speaking **Part 3** you will be asked some abstract or analytical questions. These will be broadly linked to the topic introduced in **Part 2**.

The examiner will be expecting you to provide more discursive answers. You cannot get a high mark if you only provide short answers, so you need to have plenty of ideas on the topics and you need to make these clear to the examiner.

Understanding Part 3 questions

After you have given your talk, the examiner will tell you that he or she is going to ask some questions related to the **Part 2** topic. In Unit **3**, you practised ways of preparing a **Part 2** talk on a number of different topics. The questions **1–6** below are all linked broadly to the **Part 2** topics, **A–E**, in Speaking Unit **3**.

1 How important is it to enjoy your work? Why?

2 Having somewhere to live is a basic right. So should the state provide cheap housing for people who don't earn a lot of money? Why?

3 In what ways do we measure personal achievement in our society?

4 What are some of the advantages of living in a large city?

5 Does tourism bring mainly positive or negative things to a country?

6 Workers in this country are usually entitled to four weeks' paid holiday. What are the benefits of ensuring that people have paid holidays?

1 Read questions **1–6** and match them to the **Part 2** topics A–E in Unit **3** on pages 146–148.

2 Underline the key words in these questions which provide a link to the topics **A–E**.

3 Rephrase the questions in your own words to make sure you understand them.

4 ⟨38⟩ Listen to six students give an answer to the six questions on the previous page. As you listen, complete the *Answer given* column of the table below with the opinions or points that the students make and any reasons or examples they give.

Student	Answer given	Linkers used
1	*very important / we do it for many years / more motivated*	*For one thing / another reason is*
2		
3		
4		
5		
6		

Test tip
Giving reasons for your opinions will help you give a fuller answer.

5 Listen again. Complete the *Linkers used* column of the table with the words that are used to link the speaker's reasons and examples to the opinions and points they make.

6 Work with a partner. Take turns to ask and answer questions **1–6** in exercise **1**.

Making your ideas clear

You need to introduce your ideas and link them together. This will signal each of your ideas clearly for your listener and make your answer flow well.

7 Imagine your examiner has asked you this question after a **Part 2** talk about the weather. Take one minute to think of an appropriate answer.

> Let's move on to the broader subject of climate. To what extent do you think the climate of a country affects the kind of houses or homes that are built?

Test tip
Don't be afraid to say what you think. It's important to express opinions in the discussion. However, make sure you can explain why you think your opinion is correct by giving reasons.

8 Look at the example of a possible answer to this question. Underline the words which:
  ■ introduce an opinion
  ■ link the opinion to the evidence for that opinion.

> Well … in my view, climate probably has a lot to do with the way we design our houses. So … for instance, in countries where it snows a lot, you find houses with something like a steep roof … so that the snow can't settle there, and … you know … damage the roof. But in warm climates, I think the houses are often built to keep the sun out …

IELTS Speaking test practice	**Part 3**

9 Work with a partner. Take turns to answer the question in exercise **7**. Try to use some of the words and phrases in the boxes below to help you. If possible, record your answer.

Ways to begin your answer

When you are sure or agree with the suggestion	**When you would like to put an alternative viewpoint**
I think / I don't (really) think … I believe / I don't (really) believe … Personally, I think … In my opinion / In my view … It seems to me that …	I'm not sure (that) … I'm afraid I think … Well, I don't know for sure but … Possibly, but … I tend to think / believe …

Exploring the theme

Your examiner will ask you a number of questions based on one theme. In the example question about the weather, the theme is global climate.

Test tip
It is important to say something, so make up an answer if you have no experience of the topic.

10 Look at the next question on this theme. How would you begin an answer to this question if you have never lived in a cold climate?

> What do you think are some of the advantages of living in a cold climate?

11 Take a few minutes to think of some possible answers to the question above. Then see how many ideas your class has produced. Link some of these ideas together to form an answer.

12 Repeat exercises **10** and **11** but this time for a **warm climate**.

13 Try answering another question on this theme. If possible, record your answer.

> Many people believe the Earth's climate is changing because we are burning too many fossil fuels. What can governments do about this?

14 What other areas could the examiner ask you about on the topic of climate?

Answering the question

You need to be sure that you answer the examiner's question and not a different question on the same theme.

15 Match each of the questions **1–4**, below, to one of the answers, **A–D**, which follow.

Questions

1 Should young people be allowed to leave school when they like?

2 What age do you think people should be allowed to leave school?

3 Should students who are disruptive in class be barred from going to school?

4 Should senior school students in their last year at school have to attend school all day or only when they have classes?

Answers

A I think they should be able to leave school when they don't have any lessons, because by that age … they should be responsible enough to organise their time.

B Um … probably not, because then they run the risk of becoming even more difficult. I think the school should try to find out why it's happening, rather than trying to get rid of them.

C I don't think so, because young people get bored at school and so many of them would choose to leave at 13 or 14 if they didn't have to be there.

D I think it should be 16. I don't think they should be forced to stay on after that if they don't like it. They might be better off learning a trade or something of that sort.

---

16 Class activity

Look at these two **Part 3** questions on the theme of employment and then follow the instructions, **1–5**, which follow.

> What is the difference between a job and a career?

> Is it right that a footballer should earn more than a nurse?

1 Think of some more questions that you could ask on this theme.

2 Write each of your questions on a separate piece of paper and put them all in a hat with the two questions above.

3 Take turns to go to the front of the class and take a question from the hat. Each student should try to answer the question as soon as they read it.

4 As you listen to each other's answers, make notes and be prepared to ask at least one question after each student has answered.

5 When every student in the class has answered, discuss these questions.

   a Who did you agree with and why?

   b Which answers explored areas of the question you hadn't thought about?

   c Did any answers challenge or change your opinion?

   d Were the answers relevant to the topic?

Speaking

6 Giving a reasoned response

- How can I make my language accurate and appropriate for a formal discussion?

- How important is it to have a personal view on the topic?

This is your opportunity to demonstrate your language skills as well as your ability to express an opinion and justify your ideas. Think about what the examiner is asking you and use appropriate phrases and structures for your answer.

It is very important; having a view helps you develop a relevant, coherent answer. In **Part 3** you will be expected to give your personal views but you may also have to give a counter- or opposite view.

Using the right language

Each question that the examiner asks is designed to encourage you to use language for different purposes. It helps to consider what type of question you have been asked. For example, the examiner may ask you to give an explanation or make a suggestion.

1 Work with a partner. Together, read questions **1–5** and decide what each one asks you to do from the options (**a–e**) below.
  a give an explanation
  b make a suggestion
  c compare two things
  d make a prediction about the future
  e agree or disagree with something

1 City life and rural life
'People who live in cities often like to spend time in the countryside at weekends. How is the countryside different from the city?'

2 Books and young people
'Many children seem to prefer playing computer games to reading. What can we do to encourage young people to read more?'

3 Books and young people
'You mentioned you liked the cinema. But when a book is made into a film, sometimes the audiences are quite disappointed. Why do you think this is?'

4 Health education
'We hear a lot about advances in medicine but do you think governments should spend money on expensive medical treatment and surgery?'

5 Studying at university
'We've been talking about technology in education and the growing popularity of online university courses. Do you think that university lecturers and professors will become redundant one day or will there always be a teaching role for them?'

2 Make a note of some ideas that you could use to answer questions **1–5**.

3 With your partner, discuss which of the words and phrases in the table below you would use for the questions on the previous page. Add some more expressions of your own if you can.

Giving an explanation	Making a suggestion	Comparing two things	Making a prediction about the future	Agreeing or disagreeing with something
Firstly,	I think we should	I think … is preferable to	It's quite likely that	Yes, absolutely (because)
One reason is	It would be a good idea to	better than	It's possible that	Certainly, yes, (because)
That's why I think	What about … ?	more comfortable than	It's not very likely that	Yes, I think we should actually, (because)
So	One idea would be to	less useful than	It's unlikely that	Yes, I personally like … (because)
Consequently,	One thing we could do would be to	I prefer	I doubt whether … will happen.	Not really (because)
That's why		My favourite … is	In the long run	To be honest, no, (because)
As a result of		If you compare … with	In the future, I think	I'm not sure that I agree with
Because of			In years to come	I don't really think
It's possibly due to			By the year	I'm afraid I can't agree with that idea (because)
It may be because of			By the time we are	
It may come from the fact that				

IELTS Speaking test practice   Part 3

4 Follow these instructions for a detailed discussion of the themes in the five questions in exercise **1**.
- Take turns to be the examiner and ask your partner the questions.
- When it is your turn to answer, try to give reasons for all your ideas.
- When it is your turn to be the examiner, ask at least one more question about the ideas and reasons your partner gives.
- Try to establish a genuine discussion on each topic.
- If possible, record your discussions and then listen to them, using the check list on page 79 in Speaking Unit **4** of the Workbook.

Giving two sides of an argument

Sometimes the examiner may invite you to give both sides of an argument.

5 Read this question and the two views on it.

> To what extent is it important for everyone to have a university education?

> Some people don't want to study beyond school.

> Very – we should all have equal opportunities.

6 Now answer the examiner's question using the two views to help you. Begin with: *While I agree that everyone … .* Try using some of the expressions in the box.

> While … may be true, I also think …
> Although …
> It's true that … but on the other hand …
> Some people think … . However, I think …
> Certainly / Obviously … but …

■ You can also make your own argument clearer by presenting a counter-view. For example:

> Is it important to teach children to save money?

> I think so. Obviously, you don't want them to become obsessed with money, but it's important that they appreciate the value of money.

the counter-view

your opinion

your argument

7 Go back to questions **1–5** in exercise **1** and see whether you can answer some of them with a counter-view.

Speculating

The examiner may ask you to think about the future and consider possibilities.

8 Work with a partner. Together, look at the list of jobs and professions on the left below and then discuss briefly what kind of person would be suited to each of these jobs.

9 Draw a table with three columns like the one on the right below. With your partner, make a list of *skills and abilities, personal qualities* and *educational requirements* that are necessary or useful to do the jobs and professions.

accountant	surgeon
advertising executive	journalist
airline pilot	lawyer
computer programmer	nurse
economist	politician
engineer	interpreter
fire fighter	

Skills and abilities	Personal qualities	Educational requirements

10 Take turns to ask each other questions. For example: *What kind of person would make a good airline pilot?* Try using expressions from the box below in your answers.

> I would imagine that *a pilot* needs to *be able to think quickly*.
> I suppose people who take up *nurs*ing need to *be dedicated*. They also need to *be patient and understanding*.
> I'd say …
> As far as I can see …
> It's probably useful for a … to be …
> I think it's important/essential for a … to be …

IELTS Speaking test practice   Part 3

How to approach the task

- Rephrase the question in your own words to help you to explore the issues raised, e.g. *Are homes built to suit the climate?*
- Think about what you are being asked to do: give an explanation, compare, speculate, etc.
- Decide whether any of the key words raise new questions, e.g. *Design of all buildings, or just houses?*
- Quickly develop a few ideas.
- Begin your answer with an appropriate expression.
- Make sure you can support or justify your opinion.

Extending a conversation

11 Look at the bubble diagram on what is important in a job. Take a moment to think about each of the issues shown here. Be prepared to make a useful comment about each of the issues. Make sure you have an opinion on all the ideas.

12 Class activity
  1 Make up sets of eight cards based on the eight ideas in the bubble diagram.
  2 Place a set of the cards face down on the table for each group.
  3 Each student picks a card and must talk on the topic for 45 seconds. Replace the card on the bottom of the pile.

13 Make similar bubble diagrams with other broad themes. For example:
  - Lifestyle - Education - Entertainment - Health

Summary of IELTS Speaking strategies

	Approach	Reason
	Make sure you know what you have to do in the Speaking test and what you are being assessed on.	Even good candidates can lose marks because they are not prepared for the requirements of the different parts of the test.

	Approach	Reason
Part 1	Use this part to develop your confidence and fluency.	The questions are about you and should be straightforward to answer.
	Give full answers but do not talk for too long.	Fuller answers are expected in Part 3.
	Do not memorise answers.	Your examiner will recognise prepared answers and you will not get credit for them.

	Approach	Reason
Part 2	Use the preparation time wisely.	Useful notes will help you speak for longer.
	Refer to the task card as you talk.	The points on the task card are designed to help you structure your talk.
	Be aware of how long 2 minutes is.	You need to produce a rounded talk that is long enough, but not too long.

	Approach	Reason
Part 3	Make sure you know what the discussion topic is.	Your answers need to be relevant to the topic.
	Re-phrase the questions in your mind, so that you know what the examiner expects.	The questions aim to get you to talk about things using a range of language functions.
	Support and extend your answers.	You must show that you can discuss the Part 3 topics fully.

	Approach	Reason
All parts	Listen carefully to each question the examiner asks and think about the tenses and vocabulary you should use in your answer.	You will get better marks if your answer is grammatically correct and shows a range of vocabulary.
	Have some views on typical Part 1 and 3 topics.	You cannot discuss topics if you do not have any views. This is especially important for Part 3.
	Ask the examiner to repeat a question if you do not understand it.	This is much better than talking about something which is irrelevant to the topic.
	Try to develop your answers using linkers and structural markers.	You will get better marks for fluency if you can sequence ideas, rather than repeating them or hesitating over them.
	Speak clearly and use stress and intonation to help you get your points across.	This will help improve your marks for pronunciation. Even good speakers can lose marks if they speak much too quickly.

Recording scripts

Listening 1

Track 02

1 Good morning, everybody. How nice to see so many of you here this morning. My name is Richard Brambles and I'd like to <u>welcome you</u> all to the <u>Brambles International</u> *College of English*. Now let me begin by <u>introducing the teaching staff</u>.

2

MAN Good morning! I'd like to <u>check in</u>, please.
WOMAN Do you <u>have a reservation</u>, sir?
MAN Yes, I do. In the name of Matthews.
WOMAN Let me just check … How do you spell that?
MAN M–A– double T–H–E–W–S.
WOMAN Oh, here we are. <u>Room two-two-six</u>.

3

DRIVER 'Scuse me. Are you giving me a <u>parking ticket</u>?
INSPECTOR Yes, I am. <u>The meter has run out</u>.
DRIVER But I was only in the bank for two minutes. Surely you can allow that.
INSPECTOR Sorry – but the meter ran out of money ten minutes ago.
DRIVER So how much is that going to cost, then?
INSPECTOR There's a fine of $75.

4

MALE Oh, hi Susan. Thank goodness I've run into you! I'm trying to <u>find my way</u> to the Economics building but I seem to be totally <u>lost</u>!
FEMALE Yes, you're on completely the <u>wrong side</u> of the campus, actually. You need to be on the other side of City Road. <u>Go back</u> to the main entrance and then take the pedestrian bridge across the main road. The Economics building is <u>over there</u>.

5

Oh, hello. Is that <u>customer service</u>? … I'd like to organise a service call, please … Yes …Well, the <u>door doesn't close properly</u> and so <u>water pours out</u> the front when you turn it on … Yes, well it should still be under guarantee, we've only had it six months … Right. I see. Oh, well … I'll have to wait till Thursday then, if that's the earliest day your <u>technician</u> can get here.

6

DAUGHTER You would not believe what happened to me today, Dad!
FATHER No. What?
DAUGHTER I got a $75 <u>parking ticket</u> outside the bank. It's so annoying!
FATHER How long had you been <u>parked</u> there?
DAUGHTER Oh. About twenty minutes, but even so!
FATHER Oh well. You won't do that again, will you?

Track 03

Melbourne is situated on the northern shore of Port Phillip Bay in Victoria. The Mornington Peninsula is the eastern arm of the bay and it's a <u>one hundred and twenty kilometre journey</u> by car from Melbourne to Phillip Island along the Bass Highway. It's a very popular holiday destination for people living in Melbourne. You can do the trip by car in roughly <u>two hours</u> and take in the magnificent scenery along the way. You need to get the ferry across to the island. Phillip Island is famous for its little penguins, and many tourists go there just to see them. People like to watch <u>the penguins</u> making their way along the beach at the end of the day. Other visitors enjoy the chance to do some seal-watching from <u>boats</u> or through the telescopes set up on the hill.

Track 04

MAN Good morning! I'd like to check in, please.
WOMAN Do you have a reservation, sir?
MAN Yes, I do. In the name of Matthews.
WOMAN Let me just check … How do you spell that?
MAN M–A– double T–H–E–W–S.
WOMAN Oh, here we are. Room <u>two-two-six</u>.
MAN Thanks.
WOMAN Would you like a wake-up call?
MAN Yes, please.
WOMAN What time?
MAN Um, about <u>7.00 … Actually … half past</u> should be all right.
WOMAN Fine. And a newspaper?
MAN No thanks, I'll get one on the way to the meeting.
WOMAN Breakfast is included in the price, but you do need to book. So will you be having the full breakfast, that's the cooked breakfast, or the buffet … or breakfast in your room?
MAN I'll have the <u>full</u> breakfast thanks.
WOMAN How do you intend to pay, sir? Visa, American Express …?
MAN I think my <u>company</u>'s paying.
WOMAN Oh, sorry, that's fine then.

Recording scripts

Track 05

MOTHER Hello. Justine Cox speaking.

BEN Oh. Hi Mum! It's Ben. Just calling to say that the six o'clock train has been cancelled and we're now getting the 7.15 which gets in at <u>8.30</u>. Can you pick us up from the station?

MOTHER Yes, of course. But can you do me a favour? Can you wait outside <u>under the clock</u>? 'Cos I'll never get parked in the station car park.

BEN Sure. And Mum! Can you bring my leather jacket because it's absolutely freezing and I haven't got a coat.

MOTHER Right …

BEN Oh and yes, I need to pay Charlie back for the train ticket. I had to borrow <u>£13</u> from him, so could you bring that too?

MOTHER OK! See you both soon.

Listening 2

Track 06

A Oh hi, everybody. It's Julia here. It's Thursday afternoon. I'm just ringing to remind you that I'm coming for dinner on <u>Friday night</u>. I'll be there <u>about 7.30</u>. See you soon.

B Johnson's Repairs here. Your <u>DVD player</u>'s now working and ready for collection. You'll need to pay <u>$45</u> for the work that's been done. Bye.

C This is the <u>university bookshop</u> here. I'm afraid we haven't been able to obtain the book you ordered on Asian Economies as unfortunately it's <u>out of print</u>. Sorry about that.

D Dr Boyd's surgery here. I'm afraid we'll have to cancel your appointment tomorrow as unfortunately Dr Boyd has <u>the flu</u>. Could you come on <u>Monday at 3.30pm</u> instead?

E Hello, this is Sam. Message for Ian. We're having a <u>farewell party</u> for Prof. Hall on Saturday. You know he's going to China for two years. Give us a call on <u>98184078</u>.

Track 07

RECEPTIONIST Good morning. City Aquarium, Georgina speaking.

TEACHER Oh hello. I'd like some information about the cost of visiting the aquarium.

RECEPTIONIST Certainly.

TEACHER I'm thinking of bringing a group of people to the aquarium. What would be the cheapest way of doing that?

RECEPTIONIST Well … you have a couple of options. The standard price for a ticket for a child is $14.

TEACHER OK.

RECEPTIONIST But they must be under 15 years of age. Otherwise they rank as an adult, in which case it would be <u>$27</u> for a single admission.

TEACHER Right. I see. Well … they're all over 15, I'm afraid.

RECEPTIONIST So it would be the adult entry fee then. But the good thing about this ticket is that there's <u>no booking</u> required.

TEACHER Yes. That's an advantage, but I think that's a bit expensive for us, quite honestly. Is it possible to get a student concession? These people are all studying English here at the moment and they're on a bit of a budget, if you know what I mean.

RECEPTIONIST Yes. <u>Students</u> can get in for $19 a head.

TEACHER Oh, OK …That's about a 30% reduction, isn't it? I suppose that's not bad, when you think about it.

RECEPTIONIST To be eligible for that price they do need to show a <u>passport</u>.

TEACHER OK. I'll remember that. And do I need to book if I'm bringing a group?

RECEPTIONIST How many of you are there?

TEACHER Why? Are there group prices as well?

RECEPTIONIST Oh yes. If you have a minimum of ten people.

TEACHER So how much does that work out at?

RECEPTIONIST Well, there's a flat fee of $250 for a group of ten.

TEACHER Um … that's even more expensive!

RECEPTIONIST Yes, but you do get the added benefit of a <u>guided tour</u>.

TEACHER Yes. I'm sure it's very interesting but it does still seem to be quite pricey for our students.

RECEPTIONIST Um … Also, I should tell you that if you want to come as a group, you'll need to buy the tickets <u>in advance</u>.

TEACHER Right. Look … I think we'll just come down on our own.

Track 08

RECEPTIONIST Can I give you a word of advice?

TEACHER Yes. Sure!

RECEPTIONIST Well … for $4 you can buy a copy of the guidebook and that basically has all the information in it that you need. It has a full plan of the aquarium and information on all the <u>different fish</u>.

TEACHER Oh, what a good idea!

RECEPTIONIST Yes, you can get a copy at the gift shop here. Do you know where that is?

TEACHER Is it near the entrance to the building?

RECEPTIONIST No … not exactly at the entrance. It's actually beside the <u>café</u>.

TEACHER Oh, I think I know where you mean. Thanks. I might pop down this afternoon and pick one up and then I can give the students my own little tour. What time do you close tonight?

RECEPTIONIST We close at 6pm most evenings, but this evening we'll be open until 7.30.

TEACHER Thanks very much. I should be able to get down there after work.

RECEPTIONIST And one last thing.

TEACHER Yes?

RECEPTIONIST If you buy your tickets on the Internet you get a discount of 10%.

TEACHER Gee. That's worth knowing. Thanks a lot.

Track 09

WOMAN Good morning! *Golden Wheels* car rentals. How can I help you?

MAN Yes, good morning. I'd like to make a booking for a car, please.

WOMAN Can I just get your name, sir?

MAN Yes, Frank Moorcroft.

WOMAN Could you spell that please?

MAN Yes, Frank F–R–A–N–K Moorcroft M–double O –R–C–R–O–F–T.

WOMAN And the address?

MAN My home address?

WOMAN Yes, please. We need a home address.

MAN OK. It's number 26, Lake Road, Richmond.

WOMAN Right … and could I get your home telephone number there?

MAN Yes. Sure. Well … the area code is zero-two, and the number is … let me think … three–three, no, sorry, I haven't learned this number yet, um, it's three–six–eight–seven–four–five–double zero.

WOMAN Thank you. And do you have a current licence, sir?

MAN Yes, I do. But it's not an Australian licence. I haven't had time to get that organised since I arrived here.

WOMAN Oh … well, you do need an Australian one if you're living in this country.

MAN Oh, but I have an international licence. That should be OK, shouldn't it?

WOMAN Oh, that'll be fine. We'll just need to see it when you pick up the car. Right, now what kind of car were you looking for?

MAN Well … I've got my wife and our three children with me and quite a lot of luggage so …

WOMAN So you'll need a station wagon or a …

MAN I don't mind what make it is, but I'd like a four-door car … it's much easier with the kids, or maybe even something larger.

WOMAN Well, if you go up to a six-seater, you'll be into the next price bracket.

MAN No thanks.

WOMAN And when do you need the vehicle?

MAN Well, I'd like to pick it up in the morning, if that's possible.

WOMAN Not a problem. Let me just note that on the computer. Collect … car … on the … 23rd … of June.

MAN No. Tomorrow's the 24th of June, not the 23rd.

WOMAN Oh, of course, it is. I'm sorry.

MAN And what's the rental cost?

WOMAN Well, the rate is $70 a day if you have it for more than three days. Otherwise it's $90 a day.

MAN We'll need it for a week.

WOMAN Well, then it'll be $70 a day … That's $490 all up.

- -

WOMAN And where would you like to collect the car, sir? At our Melbourne city branch?

MAN No. We're arriving by plane so we'd like to pick it up from the airport.

WOMAN Yes, certainly. At approximately what time?

MAN The flight gets in at 11.00 in the morning, so by the time we've collected our bags, I'd say we'd need the car at around lunchtime.

WOMAN Right, I'll make sure it's available for you then. And do you require any other special equipment? Maps? GPS? That sort of thing?

MAN Yes, actually, we do. Thanks for reminding me. We have a two-year-old so she needs a child's seat. Can you organise that?

WOMAN Certainly can. I'll see that there's one in the car for you.

MAN And what about insurance? Is the car fully insured?

WOMAN You're partially covered, but we do recommend that you take out extra cover, in case you have an accident. Otherwise you'll have to pay the first $1,000 of any repairs. What do you think?

MAN Oh … I suppose I'd better have the extra insurance. Better to be safe than sorry!

WOMAN Good idea. I'll get that organised for you too.

Listening 3

Track 10

Every home and office should have a fire extinguisher. Although there's a good chance that it will sit on the wall for years collecting dust, it could end up saving your property, or even your life. So, what does a fire extinguisher consist of? The main part of the extinguisher is simply a large metal container that is cylindrical in shape rather like a bell jar. In the past these used to be red but nowadays they come in many different colours. The container is full of water or some other substance, such as foam, that can be used to smother a fire. At the top of the container is a lever and attached to the lever there is a thin, extended pin that goes down into a gas cartridge. This looks rather like a small bottle or flask and is right in the centre of the extinguisher. Below the lever there's a curved <u>handle</u>, which is used to hold the extinguisher and direct it at the fire. On the other side from the handle there is a horizontal nozzle that opens when the lever is pressed and emits a <u>jet</u> of water. At the neck of the container there is a small coiled spring that holds the pin in place and this is connected to a long <u>tube</u> which runs from the spring to the bottom of the container. This is called the discharge <u>tube</u> which is where the water comes out of the extinguisher into the air.

Track 11

A fire extinguisher can quickly put out a small fire before it spreads. First of all, take the extinguisher out of its case and pull out <u>the safety pin</u>. Nothing will happen when you do this, it just unlocks the extinguisher. Holding it by the handle, <u>point</u> the extinguisher at the fire or whatever is burning. Then all you have to do is to <u>press</u> the lever at the top of the container. This pressure causes the long pin to move down into the gas cartridge. As it does this, it <u>releases</u> gas into the upper part of the cylinder. The gas then forces the water in the main part of the container up the discharge tube and out of the nozzle, producing a jet of water which can put out <u>burning materials</u> such as paper and wood.

Track 12

1

YOUNG MAN So how did your first week of architecture go?

YOUNG WOMAN Not bad. But Monday is incredibly busy – I've got three two-hour lectures that day.

YOUNG MAN Really? What are they?

YOUNG WOMAN Well … we start with construction at ten o'clock. That's really just engineering theory. Then I have an hour off, to go to the library and catch up on some reading, <u>and at one o'clock we have a lecture on computer assisted drawing</u>. That's learning how to use computer programs to help you design buildings.

YOUNG MAN No time for lunch, then!

YOUNG WOMAN No, exactly! And we finish the day with a lecture on history.

YOUNG MAN Woah, that *is* a full day.

2

Now we recommend that you get yourself a small bag to carry your supplies in. But, please, not a heavy rucksack, the lighter the better. Make sure you wear a good pair of hiking boots with thick socks. You'll need a decent-sized plastic <u>water bottle</u> that can be easily refilled. Don't bring cans of soft drink as they don't quench your thirst! And we'll be stopping for a picnic lunch, so please bring <u>sandwiches or fruit</u>, that sort of thing. And we recommend a wide-brimmed hat to protect you from the flies which can be pretty irritating at this time of year. You may need sun tan lotion too, and of course, don't forget your binoculars, because the view from the top of the mountain is fantastic but you won't get the full benefit if you're just wearing sunglasses.

3

INTERVIEWER In what way are sharks different from other fish?

STUDENT Well, for one thing … they have to keep moving constantly.

INTERVIEWER And that's not the case with other fish?

STUDENT No. Bony fish can stay still because <u>they have a kind of bladder which keeps them afloat, but not sharks. Basically they're heavier than water</u>, you see, so if they don't keep moving, they sink.

INTERVIEWER Is that so?

STUDENT And another interesting thing is that they can't swim backwards, though they're not alone there actually. And we've recently discovered that even though they're big, they can still leap into the air from really deep water to catch their prey, things like seals, but they have that in common with other large fish.

INTERVIEWER Wow! They're pretty awesome creatures, aren't they?

4

<u>The Tjibaou Centre is a magnificent building that symbolises the existence of the Kanak people</u>, the original inhabitants of the islands of New Caledonia in the Pacific Ocean. It was designed by the world-famous Italian architect Renzo Piano, and was opened to the public in 1997. The Centre itself is based in every detail on the layout of a traditional Kanak village, <u>made up of three sections which contain exhibition spaces, a library, as well as conference and lecture rooms</u>. It's surrounded by beautiful gardens, and is naturally ventilated, with many spaces open to the elements.

5–7

I've always been interested in plane spotting, ever since I was a little kid growing up in Holland. I think <u>I just like the look of them</u>, you know … how each airline has a different tail to identify it, like a flag. I used to go to the international airport with my dad and we'd try to see every plane in an airline's fleet. They each have a serial number though it's quite a job to see them all. And I love seeing planes from unusual places, even though I don't really want to go there myself. I also like souvenirs from planes and I get my friends to bring me things whenever they fly anywhere. I've got tray tables and knives and forks. And I've even got a seatbelt. I take about 7,000 photos of planes a year, and I'm often down here at five in the morning to catch a shot of the planes landing. You're not actually supposed to get too near the airfield; you should be three metres away from the fence. Quite often the patrol cars come round and tell you to move away. But I love the sound of the jet planes, the louder the better for me! I've never flown in a plane, you know. I'm actually scared stiff of flying.

Track 13
Paddling around on a river in a small boat is not everyone's idea of fun and it can sometimes be a lot riskier than you think. But more and more people are getting involved in this new sport and taking their boats onto dangerous rivers to enjoy what is called *white-water canoeing*. Canoes, which are narrow boats to start with and usually hold only one or two people at the most, are particularly well known for being unstable and turning over in the water. Cynthia Barton, one of Britain's top canoeists, talks about what the sport is and how to get started if you're thinking of taking it up.

Track 14
A lot of people may be familiar with what I call recreational canoeing. That's where you take a canoe out onto a nice calm river … with a picnic and have a relaxing time. But if you're doing white-water canoeing, then you're doing something very different. White-water canoeing actually gets its name from the fact that when you do it you've got to be paddling very rapidly through the water and when you're doing that, you make a lot of froth and bubbles and the water looks white. First of all, you will need to think about equipment. You'll need to get yourself a good canoe and these can set you back anything from £500 to £1500 depending on the material they're made of. Personally, I wouldn't go for a cheap one, although obviously this depends on your budget. And to protect yourself against rocks when you fall out of the canoe, and believe me you *will* fall out, you'll need a good quality helmet. It needs to meet certain government standards, so make sure you go to a reputable supplier. And there's no point, particularly as a beginner, in wearing anything but a wetsuit. That's a must. I'd recommend one with short sleeves, rather than long sleeves. Then you'll have to get a life jacket too and I would also suggest that you get yourself a pair of river shoes. These are made out of the same material as the wetsuit. Some people think that ordinary rubber boots

will do, but they're much too loose and fill up with water. It is also essential to wear something to protect your hands from the paddles, and stop them from being rubbed.

Track 15
The popular rivers are, in fact, graded from one to six in the same way that ski runs are graded to tell people just how flat or steep they are. Once you're an expert, which can take some time, you can, of course, try anything … and really serious canoeists, who want a real challenge, go out a lot more in the winter when the water level is high and deliberately look for the most dangerous rivers. Whatever you say about this sport, it is never dull. Generally it's a fantastic sport for …

Listening 4

Track 16
Coming from Tudor Park, walk west along Marble Street past Cedar Square and a set of traffic lights. Turn left into Port Lane and the library is a circular building in the middle of Port Lane, opposite the dance centre.

....

Go east along Marble Street, past Saxon Road, and there's a statue in the middle of Cedar Square. Why don't we meet there?

....

The hospital is a square building on the corner of Moon Crescent and Marble Street.

....

To get to the tennis courts you go east along Beach Road, past the fish market, and they're on your right.

....

Go south down Box Lane and the café is on the corner of Tudor Park opposite the sea life centre.

Track 17
The airport has three terminals which are joined together to form one large building shaped rather like a crescent. If you're coming from the city by car, you'll see a big cargo building *on your left* as you approach the airport and then the car park is a rectangular building *beyond* this. You can park your car there and then make your way back into the terminals using the pedestrian walkway. For those who arrive from the city by bus, there are two bus stops at the airport. If you are flying to a city within Australia, you should get off at the first bus stop *opposite* the first building, *on your right. This is the Domestic Terminal* where all the flights to the major cities within Australia leave from. If you are going overseas, you will need to go to the International Terminal which is *in the centre* of the complex, so get off at the next bus stop. This terminal has a long, narrow concourse leading down to the departure gates. When you walk into the International Terminal through the main entrance

you'll find yourself in a large hall where you check in for your flight. The toilets are on the left side of the concourse and there are lifts leading up to the next floor *on the right*. You'll find a variety of restaurants and bars on the first floor and shops selling clothes and souvenirs, but remember, there are strict hand-luggage limitations, so don't buy more than you can carry in one bag. If you are flying to one of the small country towns, you will need to go to the Regional Terminal *at the north end* of the airport. Facilities are limited in this terminal but there is a small café where you can buy sandwiches and wait for your flight. To hear this information again, press …

Track 18

VISITOR Excuse me. Could you tell me how to get from the Jing'an Temple to the Peace Hotel?

LOCAL Um, yes. The best way to get from the temple to the hotel is to take the metro. It's really much faster than taking a taxi or a bus. You travel two stops and get off at the People's Square. When you come up to street level, you just walk along Nan Jing Road East.

VISITOR Oh yes, I've heard of Nan Jing Road. Is that the pedestrian mall?

LOCAL Yes, that's right. So there's no traffic there, which is good. The mall is packed with people and there are all sorts of shops to see there, new buildings, old buildings, you name it. Anyway, at the end of the mall is an area called the Bund, and the Peace Hotel is on the left-hand corner of this. There's a pedestrian tunnel which runs under the Huang Pu River, known as the Tourist Tunnel and the entrance is just outside the hotel. The tunnel comes up at the Oriental Pearl radio and TV tower which is one of the most famous landmarks in Shanghai.

VISITOR Oh, thank you so much!

Track 19

The Hillside Water Park is an ideal place for anyone who wants to have fun and cool down during the hot summer months. It is open seven days a week from 7am to 8.30pm and the enthusiastic staff are ready to help you enjoy your visit. So how do you get there? The park can be found in the northern part of Sunshine City and sits on a hill directly overlooking the tourist area and beach, which is how it gets its name. If you are staying in one of the local hotels, you can walk to the park but it will take about half an hour and, of course, it's all uphill. So you may prefer to go by public transport. The local buses will take you there for a small charge and these run every 15 minutes from the Grand Hotel. The number 45 takes you through the market and then up to the water park. This is a more scenic route and takes a little longer than the number 57 bus, which goes straight along Beach Road, turns left into Cricket Street and then arrives within ten minutes at the park entrance. Alternatively, you can take a taxi and if you are in a group or family this is probably the best option. However, don't expect your cab to be air-conditioned as very few have this luxury.

....

When you arrive, the entrance is at the south end of the park just to the right of the coach park. You have to go up quite a lot of steps to reach the pay kiosk and unfortunately there is no shade here, so do remember to bring a cap or hat with you. You can purchase drinks at the gift shop, which is near the stone arch. The main part of the park consists of a circular waterway and you can have great fun here floating round on a large inflatable ring. These are available everywhere but if it's so crowded that you can't find one, go to the lifeguard's hut at the north end of the park. It's easy to find as it's surrounded by trees. So back to the entrance. If you've already changed into your swimwear before you arrive at the park, you may want to head straight to one of our deckchairs in the sunbathing area. To get here, go through the arch and turn right. Walk alongside the circular waterway to the kids' pool, carry on past the shaded picnic ground on your right and, as the footpath bends left, the sunbathing chairs are in a large rectangular area on the right. There are other parts of the park where you can sunbathe, near the changing rooms and around the water slides, but this is the quietest spot. There are three pools in the park: the adult pool in the centre is the biggest. On one side of this is the kids' pool and on the other side is the fountain pool, which is suitable even for non-swimmers. However, don't dive in the pools. This is too dangerous with young children and for this reason there are no diving boards in the park. There is a first-aid centre on the site if you need it, just north of the water slides, but if you follow all the notices and rules that shouldn't be necessary. So have fun!

Listening 5

Track 20

1

Man Would you mind answering a few questions for a survey I'm doing?

WOMAN Not at all.

MAN How do you feel about the funding for university education? Do you think it should be free or should people have to pay?

WOMAN Well … in the past I used to believe that university education was a basic right and should be free but –

MAN But you don't now?

WOMAN Well … it's hard to say. I definitely believe everyone should have access to free <u>secondary schooling</u> but I'm not so sure about university. People sometimes don't value things when they're free.

MAN Oh! I don't know about that!

2

MAN As a medical student, how do you feel about the idea of private health care?

WOMAN I'm really against it. <u>I think it's everybody's basic right to receive free medical treatment.</u>

MAN Yes … but … look at the mess the National Health Service is in here! The hospitals are over-crowded, <u>the young doctors</u> are doing 16-hour shifts. It's exploitation!

WOMAN Yes, but at least we have a health service.

MAN Well, I think basic treatment should be available in public hospitals, but if people have the money, they should also be able to have private treatment.

WOMAN Ah, but then you have a dual system, one for the rich and one for the poor.

3

STUDENT A So, Jo, how are you going with your assignment on alternative energy sources since our discussion last week?

STUDENT B Well … one thing is certain. <u>The nuclear debate is back.</u> We've seen how much pollution oil and coal-fired power stations generate and the consequences of global warming are now really clear. So we have to find an alternative.

STUDENT A But it doesn't have to be nuclear, surely? What about wind or solar energy and …

STUDENT C Yes, we know about all that, but it isn't sustainable. It's not going to keep a city of 12 million people going through the winter. Whereas <u>nuclear energy</u> could.

4

MAN <u>Do you think it's a good policy to encourage young people to stay on at school after the age of 16?</u>

WOMAN A I don't believe in forcing teenagers to stay on at school if they really aren't enjoying it.

WOMAN B Oh, I'm not sure about that. They're not really old enough to know what's good for them, are they?

MAN Yes, but school can be very boring! I think a lot of kids are better off leaving school at 16 and learning a trade … you know, something like <u>hairdressing, or building or carpentry</u>. There's a desperate shortage of these people, you know.

WOMAN B Maybe … but … I really regret leaving school early, just because I wasn't encouraged to stay on.

5

STUDENT A I've been looking at the pros and cons of public versus <u>private funding for highways</u>, as part of my Economics assignment. Private funding is really the way to go.

STUDENT B Well … it may get the roads and tunnels built, but then we, the motorists, have to pay a fortune to use the roads. I mean, look at the cost of the City Tunnel here.

STUDENT A But that's OK. If you use the road, you should pay for it. They've been building toll roads like this for years in places like <u>France and Italy and America</u>.

STUDENT B Yes, I know. But I still think the state should fund this kind of thing.

STUDENT C Well, if you don't pay when you use it, you'll have to pay higher taxes. Either way, you're going to pay!

STUDENT B She's got a point, you know.

6

MAN OK, Marion, how did you go with your newspaper survey? <u>Are people still buying papers, or are they a thing of the past?</u>

WOMAN A Well … our survey has basically shown that older people still buy papers, but that most young people don't.

MAN Can you tell us a little more?

WOMAN A Yes, well … 80% of the people under 25 that I interviewed said they didn't buy a paper but read the news on <u>the Internet</u>.

MAN That's interesting. And what did you discover, Rosa?

WOMAN B Well, my group of over 25s nearly all bought a newspaper each day.

Track 21

1

STUDENT A Jamie, what did your tutor think about your essay on wildlife conservation?

STUDENT B Oh, I got quite a good grade but there was a long written comment at the end of it.

STUDENT A Yeah, I got one too. He said I could have spent more time on the background!

STUDENT B Yes, me too. I should have done a bit more reading.

STUDENT A I left out all that stuff about polar bears, which is pretty important, I guess.

STUDENT B He said <u>he liked the fact that I'd used lots of statistics</u> to support my argument.

2

TUTOR I'd like everyone to prepare a presentation for the tutorial sessions throughout the semester.

STUDENT A Are you going to give us a list of topics or can we choose our own?

Recording scripts

TUTOR   It's up to you to come up with a suitable topic, as long as it's related to the course.

STUDENT B   What if we all choose the same topic? Should we get together as a group to discuss this?

TUTOR   No … but I'd like you to make a time to <u>come and discuss it with me personally</u> so that I can see if you're on the right track.

STUDENT A   Wouldn't it be easier to just give us a list of topics?

TUTOR   I think you'll find my suggestion allows you more flexibility …

Track 22

STUDENT A   What are you hoping to study at university?

STUDENT B   I'd like to do medicine because, even though it's very competitive to get in, I feel it's a really worthwhile profession and I think you'd <u>always find yourself employed</u>, whereas I'm not so sure how useful a straight science degree is these days, unless you want to be a chemistry teacher.

STUDENT A   Yeah, that's possibly true perhaps, which is why I'm hoping to study law, because I feel with this degree <u>you can go in any direction. You don't have to be a lawyer as such, there are lots of different areas you could work in</u>. But … you know … if you're a dentist then that's what you are: you're a dentist. And what happens if you find out you don't like the work after all those years of study? What about you, Stan?

STUDENT C   I'm aiming to do languages at this stage. There's a lot <u>less pressure to get in</u> and I think an arts degree gives you a good broad education. I toyed with doing computing, but there are so many people out there studying IT that I thought I'd prefer to study something I'm really interested in.

STUDENT B   Fair enough.

Track 23

INTERVIEWER   Jim Torque is editor of the monthly automobile magazine *Steering Wheel* and he's here to tell us about a recent study they've done.

JIM   Hello.

INTERVIEWER   Now … let's start with how you went about your study.

JIM   Well, we picked four similar cars, in four different categories, and compared a number of features. To ensure objectivity, we refer to them here as Vehicles One, Two, Three and Four.

INTERVIEWER   OK … so tell us what you looked at.

JIM   Well, we tried to balance the good with the bad. For instance, the first car we tested had quite comfortable seats, was well finished, but the passengers complained that <u>it was cramped</u>, especially in the back seat. It proved very economical on fuel, so good for city driving.

INTERVIEWER   But not the car for tall people, eh? And the next one?

JIM   Well, by contrast, <u>when it came to petrol consumption Vehicle Two proved far from economical</u>, but did have the advantage that you could go from 0 to 100 in only 8.2 seconds. Good on the corners, so good road-holding, but definitely not cheap at $85,000.

INTERVIEWER   Bet I can guess what car that was!

JIM   Um … well, our findings on Vehicle Three were quite interesting. It appeared to be good value for money, and so looked attractive, but in fact we found that many standard <u>features are not included in the price, such as air-conditioning and remote locking</u>, so the buyer needs to be aware of this.

INTERVIEWER   Yes, I've noticed that many manufacturers now include a lot of things that you used to have to pay for.

JIM   Exactly. By contrast, Vehicle Four had a great many features included in the price, and so is good value for money, but our test drivers found that they were <u>not able to see well</u> through the rear window especially when reversing, so this is a potential danger and something we felt the manufacturers had overlooked.

Listening 6

Track 24

A

STUDENT A   Oh hi. I thought I might find you two here in the library! How are you going with this assignment on road transport?

STUDENT B   Not well! I just don't seem to be able to get hold of any of the textbooks that the lecturer put on the reading list.

STUDENT C   No. Neither can we. They're either out of print or out of the library.

B

WOMAN Dr Manfredi, welcome to *Radio Affairs*.

DR MANFREDI Thank you for having me on the programme, Julia.

WOMAN Now, there's been a lot of discussion in the media recently about the new tunnel which has been built to carry traffic under the city of Sydney. It's been open for 18 months but practically nobody, it seems, is using it. Is that because it's too expensive?

DR MANFREDI Well … it's a very complex issue …

C

SPEAKER A Oh hi, Murray. Hello, Jan. How's it going? Not too good by the look on your faces.

SPEAKER B Yeah! Well …

SPEAKER A What's the problem?

SPEAKER B Well … we're having a lot of trouble getting more funding for our research centre for next year.

SPEAKER C Basically, if the government doesn't come through with the five hundred thousand they'd initially promised us, we're going to have to close down the centre and lay off our two PhD students.

SPEAKER A Mmm, I see.

D

Speaker A OK … so let's have a look at the final marks for this group. Sandra, have you got the marks for the end of term exam?

SPEAKER B Well … there is a bit of a problem because several of the students were away for the exam, and so they've had to sit a supplementary, and we're still waiting for Mary to get back to us.

SPEAKER A But overall the standard was well above average for this group and I think we should feel quite happy with their performance.

Track 25

JOURNALIST Can you tell us, minister, what your government plans to do if they are returned to office after the next election? Particularly in the areas of health, research and education.

POLITICIAN We certainly plan to raise the level of funding for public hospitals, including providing funds to create more hospital beds.

JOURNALIST So that means building more hospitals?

POLITICIAN Yes. That is definitely on our agenda.

JOURNALIST And would your health package include an increase to the subsidy on prescription drugs? Many essential medicines are terribly expensive and some people can't afford them at all.

POLITICIAN We already have a very high level of subsidy for prescription medicines, and negotiations are currently taking place with the major drug companies to try to get them to improve efficiency and lower their prices. We see this as a more useful approach, which should result in less government money being spent on this.

JOURNALIST Oh. OK. Education is another very important area. Do you anticipate allocating more money to build schools, in particular primary schools, some of which are now very old?

POLITICIAN Yes, we do of course see education as important, but we feel that the current level of funding is appropriate and we hope that by closing some schools in areas where the population has dropped, that we'll be able to find the money to subsidise schools that are in need.

JOURNALIST And what about R and D, research and development? Compared to many other countries, the amount of money provided for scientific research in this country is extremely low. So much so that many of our best scientists are forced to go overseas.

POLITICIAN This is an area of serious concern, and we are planning to allocate over 3 billion dollars in university research grants over the next five years. We accept that this is an area that has been under-funded.

JOURNALIST Finally, minister, let's look at our road transport system. The current trend seems to be for the government to seek private funding for the construction of major roads … which the drivers then pay to use. Do you see this as fair?

POLITICIAN Basically, it makes sense. If a road or tunnel is built by a private company, then that company must be entitled to charge motorists to use it. This allows us to have a safe, modern road system at no additional cost to the state, which in turn means that we, as a government, don't have to set any additional funds aside for public works of this nature.

JOURNALIST I think there are many drivers who would disagree with you there, minister, but we'll have to leave it there for this evening, I'm afraid. Thank you for coming into the studio.

POLITICIAN Thank you.

Track 26

TUTOR OK, come on in … hi Ben, hello Mark, Sally. Let's get going shall we, because we've got a lot of ground to cover this afternoon. It's Ben's turn to give his tutorial paper today but, remember, we do encourage questions from the rest of you, so do try to join in and ask questions.

BEN OK.

TUTOR Now, I believe Ben's going to talk to us today about the exploration of the Red Planet.

BEN That's right. I'm going to be looking at the recent landing by the Americans of a spacecraft on the planet Mars and in particular focusing on the small rover robot.

MARK Is that the little robot that functions as a geologist?

BEN Yes, that's right. It's called a rover, like a land rover I suppose, and it can detect the geological composition of the ground it's standing on so, yes, it's a sort of geologist. It's actually quite amazing.

TUTOR I heard it described as being like a microwave oven on wheels.

BEN Yeah, well, from an appearance point of view, that's a fair description. I've photocopied a picture of it for you so you can keep this for reference and make some notes and I'll just hand that out now.

CLASS Thank you.

MARK Wow, you'd actually expect it to look more space age than this, wouldn't you? Like, more sophisticated.

BEN OK, well as you can see it's quite small. It actually only weighs 16 and a half kilos.

TUTOR Right, and what kind of speed is it capable of, Ben?

BEN Um, well I suppose that depends on the terrain, but I understand that it has a top speed of 2.4 kilometres, which isn't very fast, really.

TUTOR And can you tell us how it works … explain some of these things we can see here?

BEN Well … first of all on the top it's fitted with solar panels. It runs on solar energy, of course.

SALLY Does that mean it can't work at night?

BEN Yes, indeed it does. I guess it sleeps at night! So you have the solar panels on the top and underneath this is the part known as the 'warm box'.

MARK What's the purpose of that?

BEN Well, at night the temperatures on Mars can go below 100 degrees, so the warm box is designed to protect the electronics from the extreme cold. It is also fitted with two cameras on the front.

TUTOR OK. And what about its wheels?

BEN It's got aluminium wheels, each 13 centimetres in diameter. Each one has its own motor, so it's individually powered, which allows the vehicle to turn on the spot if necessary. And as you know, aluminium is very light.

···

Mark And how do they steer it?

BEN Good question! It's steered using virtual reality goggles worn by someone back on Earth, believe it or not.

SALLY What do you mean exactly?

BEN Well, you see, it takes 11 minutes for a radio signal to travel from command headquarters in California to Mars and the same amount of time for the answer to come back.

SALLY Oh of course … So there's a time delay.

BEN Yes, exactly. And, it's impossible to steer the rover in real time because of this. So they photograph the area around the rover and the scientists will decide where they want the rover to go.

TUTOR In other words, they plot a course for the rover.

BEN Exactly.

TUTOR OK, Ben, that's very interesting. Now can you tell us anything about this space mission itself? Why Mars?

BEN Well, people have been fascinated by Mars for a long time and it's generally believed that Mars is the only other planet in the solar system to have lots of water.

TUTOR Is it possible that people might one day be able to live on Mars?

BEN Well, of course, there's a lot of work to be done yet but, theoretically, I can't see why not.

TUTOR Thanks Ben, that was very interesting.

Listening 7

Tracks 27 and 28

1 Governments often make promises that they cannot keep. For instance, this government *says they will reduce unemployment, but the number of people out of work remains the same.*

2 This is how to approach writing an essay. First of all you should read the question very carefully. Then *you should make some notes.*

3 It is now extremely expensive to travel by train in many countries. Consequently *many people prefer to drive or even fly.*

4 Idioms are a colourful and fascinating aspect of English, but *you must use them carefully.*

5 On the one hand, it may be advisable to study hard the night before an exam. On the other hand, *it's wise to go to bed early and get a good night's sleep.*

6 <u>Firstly</u> I'm going to talk about the early life of Mahatma Gandhi. <u>Secondly</u> *we will look at his life in South Africa, and thirdly we'll cover the period when he became an activist in his homeland.*

Track 29

The McDonald brothers opened their first hamburger restaurant in California in 1940 *but* within eight years, they had closed it down and re-opened as a take-away restaurant. This was a place that offered food that was both cheap *and* <u>good quality</u>. They *also* offered practically no service. *For example*, you lined up for your food, paid at the counter and took it to your own table or car. *For this reason* the McDonald brothers were seen as restaurant pioneers *because* they were the first people to do this, to invent the idea of <u>fast food</u>. But that wasn't the only novel idea they came up with. They *also* brought in the entirely new concept of specialisation, where staff in the kitchen each had their own job. *In other words*, they had one person cooking the burgers, while another person was doing <u>the milkshakes</u>, and so on. They liked to advertise their sales success and *so* in 1950 they proudly put up a sign outside their restaurant telling the world that they had sold <u>one million</u> burgers. That doesn't seem so many nowadays, *but* in those early days it was quite an achievement. *Then* in 1961 the brothers decided they'd had enough of the hamburger business and *so* they sold the company for 2.7 million dollars *along with* <u>the name</u>. Today there is barely a country in the world where you cannot get a McDonald's hamburger.

Listening 8

Track 30

A Have you ever wondered why you can recognise people's handwriting? The many styles of handwriting which exist have attracted a wide range of scientific studies, each with its own aims. And, of course, each writing system, European, Semitic, East Asian, has its own complex history. Let's look at each of these in turn …

Track 31

B One of China's most famous plants is bamboo and you may be surprised to know that there are actually more than 300 species of bamboo plant covering about 3% of the total forest area in China. Bamboo is cultivated for use as a building material as well as a source of food so let's have a look at …

C The most common staple foods are bread, rice and pasta and most people are familiar with them all. Nevertheless, we each have our own idea of what a loaf of bread should look and taste like, or the best way to serve rice or to cook noodles, so let's consider some of the most common methods …

D Today, in our series of lectures on language, we are going to be looking at the way in which children acquire language. This area of study is characterised by three main features which may explain the interest in the topic …

Track 32

ANNOUNCER Jon Getnick is in with us in the studio tonight to talk about the origins of the game chess. Welcome Jon.

GETNICK Thank you. I'm sure you are all familiar with the wonderful game of chess. But have you ever stopped to think where it came from and when? Well, we believe the game dates back to before AD 600 and was first played in either Afghanistan or what is now <u>northern India</u>. The oldest written references that we have to chess date from then, but there are claims that chess existed earlier than this. We think the version played by Europeans and Americans today travelled through Iran to the main commercial centres of Europe by the <u>year 1000</u>. The game was then taken to Scandinavia by the sea-faring Vikings, so by the 1400s chess was played throughout Europe. There are quite a few variations to the game found in other parts of the world. For instance, one variation called Shogi is played in Japan. Another variation is played in <u>China</u>. One person whose name stands out in the history of chess is the chess master Howard Staunton. Staunton lived in England in the mid 1800s and gave his name to the <u>chess pieces</u> that are still used in competitions all over the world today and are, in fact, synonymous with the game. Other shapes and sizes exist, but these are by far the most common. Interestingly enough, however, the idea of chess competitions is relatively recent when we consider how long the game has been in existence. The first <u>championship</u> was played in 1866 in London and was won by a man from Bohemia called Steinitz. He was, in effect, the world's first official champion and he held the title until 1894 when he was beaten by a German called Emanuel Lasker, who in turn lost the title in 1921 to a Cuban called Capablanca. Many people today consider Capablanca as one of the top <u>three</u> players ever to live. His game influenced many who followed him and keen professional players today still study his game.

Recording scripts

Today, in our series of lectures on language, we are going to be looking at the way in which children acquire language. This area of study is characterised by three main features which may explain the interest in the topic. *Firstly*, people find it fascinating. This stems from the natural <u>interest</u> that people take in the developing abilities of young children. They are amazed by the way in which children learn, particularly their own children! *Secondly*, it's <u>important</u> to study how we acquire our first language, *because* the study of how children learn can lead us to a greater understanding of language as a whole. *The third point* is that it's a <u>complex</u> area of study. *This is because* of the enormous difficulties that are encountered by researchers as soon as they attempt to explain language development, especially in the very young child. In today's lecture we will cover a number of topics. *We will start* by talking about the <u>research methods</u> that are used. There are a number of ways that researchers can investigate children's language and these include the use of diaries, recordings and tests and later in the course we'll be looking at how researchers make use of these. We will *then go on to* examine the actual process of language learning, starting with the development of speech in young infants during their <u>first year</u>. This is the time associated with the emergence of the skills of speech perception, *in other words*, an emergence of the child's awareness of his or her own ability to speak. We will *then* move on to look at language learning in the older child, *that is*, in children <u>under 5</u>. As they mature, it is possible to begin analysis in conventional linguistic terms and so in our analysis we will look at phonological, grammatical and semantic development in preschool children.

....

In the *second part* of the talk I would like to review some broad educational approaches to how <u>linguistic skills</u> can be developed in school-age children. *Put another way*, how can we, as teachers, assist our young learners to develop <u>language</u> in the classroom? *First* we will look at some issues related to getting children to express themselves confidently when they talk, so we'll be looking at <u>spoken language</u>. We will *then* move on to that area which causes some children a lot more difficulty, and review a number of approaches in relation to <u>teaching children to read</u>. *For instance*, issues *such as* whether to teach them to recognise whole words or go back to the more traditional methods of spelling the words out to find their meaning. *And finally, we'll conclude* with an account of current thinking on perhaps the most neglected area of all, the child's developing awareness of <u>written language</u>, and how best to help them achieve in this area …

In today's lecture I want to look at one of Australia's least loved animals, *but* one that has an interesting history from which, I think, we can learn a fundamental lesson about problem solving. *While* Australia is famous for its many wonderful native animals, in particular the kangaroo and the koala, it *also* has some less attractive animals, many of which were actually brought to Australia in the 19th and 20th centuries. *First*, perhaps the most well known introduced animal is <u>the rabbit</u>, brought originally by the early settlers as a source of food. *Another* animal to be introduced by the settlers was the fox, and this was for the purpose of <u>sport</u> in the form of <u>fox hunting</u>. *But* perhaps the most unusual animal ever brought here was the cane toad. Here is a picture of one. It's a large and, some people would say, very ugly species of toad and was deliberately imported to this country by the <u>sugar cane farmers</u> in 1935 in an attempt to eradicate the beetle which destroys the sugar cane plant. *So* how does the beetle do this? Well, it lives in the cane and drops its eggs onto the ground around the base of the plant. The eggs develop into grubs and then they eat the <u>cane roots</u>. This, as you would expect, is far from good for the plant and the result is, of course, that within a short period of time the <u>plant dies</u>. The problems all happened because in the mid thirties there was a serious outbreak of cane beetle and the farmers became desperate to get rid of the pest which was ruining their livelihood. About this time, news was trickling in from overseas about a toad which supposedly ate the beetles which killed the cane. It was reported that this 'cane toad', which was native to <u>Central America,</u> had been taken to Hawaii, where cane is also grown, and introduced with apparent success. *So,* with the backing of the Queensland authorities, the farmers arranged to import one hundred toads from Hawaii. The toads were then released into the cane fields to undertake the eradication of the cane beetle. As predicted, the toads started to breed successfully and within a very short time their <u>numbers had swollen</u>. *But* there was one serious problem. It turned out that cane toads do not eat cane beetles. *And the reason for this* is that toads live on insects that are found on the ground and the cane beetles live at the top of the cane plant well out of reach of the toads; in fact they never come into contact with each other. Now you may well ask: how did this terrible mistake ever happen? *And the reason* is quite simply that the farmers were desperate to find a way of ridding their fields of the cane beetle and *so* <u>they accepted the reports that had been written without ever doing their own research</u>. Meanwhile, much of tropical northeast Australia is infested with the cane toad, which serves no purpose whatsoever, and experts claim that the toad is spreading south in plague proportions. The added irony is that in 1947, just 12 years later, an effective pesticide was developed which actually kills the beetle, thereby <u>ensuring the survival of the sugar cane industry to this day</u>. Now … as agricultural scientists, we have to ask ourselves: what lessons are to be learned from this tale? And I can think of three main points. *Firstly*, one should never rely on claims which are not backed up by evidence, i.e. in this case evidence that the cane toad actually eats the grub of the cane beetle and thereby kills the pest. *Secondly*, <u>we should look very carefully at possible effects of introducing any living species into a new environment</u>, and, *lastly*, one should not allow one's decision making to be influenced by a sense of desperation which may cloud the issue. *In other words*, one should always seek objective advice.

Speaking 4

Track 35
See answer key to Speaking 4, exercise 3, on page 187.

Track 36
I think that the person who is the most successful in my family would be my father. I think also that the answer to the question 'Who is the most successful person in your family?' basically depends on what you think 'success' means, so … my answer is in the context of working life, rather than personal life. And that's why I've chosen my dad. Um, he has a job that is rewarding, um, he feels like he's accomplishing something, that is obviously personally and professionally satisfying, but he also feels like he's contributing to society in a positive way, um, which is a quality that a lot of jobs these days seem to lack and is something that I gauge, um, success on. It's a bit hard to explain exactly what he does, but basically he works for a charitable organisation that runs retirement homes for old people, especially old people who haven't got much money. It's a management job, really, but working in a context which is really worthwhile. Um, he, um his success is due to a lot of different things basically … finding the right job for him, one that suited him and his personality as well as his qualifications, and the goals that he wants to reach in his working life. But he's also just worked hard over a lot of years, which means that, that … it's more likely that he'll be successful, I guess, if, if success comes from hard work, which it often does. I see my dad very regularly, about once a week. We often eat breakfast together before we go to our different, um … our uh respective workplaces, um, so, yes, I think that I'd have to say he was the most successful because he enjoys what he does, as well as making a decent living out of it and I admire that in him. I think that in a work context this is what success means.

Track 37
See answer key to Speaking 4, exercise 11, on page 188.

Speaking 5

Track 38
STUDENT 1   It's very important to enjoy your job. For one thing, we do it for many years, and another reason is that if we like what we're doing we'll probably be more motivated.

STUDENT 2   I believe the government ought to help people … low-income people … with their rent, but I don't really think they should actually provide cheap housing, because if you do it for some people then it isn't fair to those who don't get it. I mean, where do you draw the line?

STUDENT 3   Well … we often measure achievement by things like what type of job people do or how much they earn … or in other areas like sport, for example, we give awards and prizes.

STUDENT 4   Um … big cities offer lots of opportunities, such as work, shopping, cultural activities, but you have to balance this against the higher cost of living and the fact that big cities can be quite lonely places.

STUDENT 5   On the whole, it brings benefits because it brings foreign money … I mean … foreign exchange which is good for the economy, but on the other hand, it may disadvantage local people, especially if they don't work in the tourism industry themselves.

STUDENT 6   I think it's really important for people to get paid holidays … because they need a break and shouldn't have to fund their own time off. Also if you want people to work hard in a job, they need to have some rewards.

Answer key

Listening 1

1
  a at an accommodation office at university or college
  b at an airport
  c at the home of some young people/students
  d student/tourist waiting for a bus

2 *Other answers possible*
  a – I'm looking for somewhere to live. I need
     accommodation for the next three months.
    – How much can you afford? Which suburb do
     you want to live in?
  b – How long do you think we'll have to wait?
    – What do you think the problem is?
    – I hope the flight isn't delayed for too long.
  c – Can you put it on channel 9?
    – No, let's watch the news.
    – What's on at 8.30?
  d – So the next bus to the city is in 15 minutes.
    I'll be there in half an hour.

5

	Picture	Situation	Number of speakers
2	a	hotel reception / lobby	2
3	e	driver getting a parking ticket	2
4	b	university campus – asking for directions	2
5	d	making a service call washing machine broken	1 side of conversation
6	c	daughter and father at home	2

6

Key words	Do the speakers know each other?
check in have a reservation room 226	No
parking ticket meter has run out	No
find my way lost / wrong side go back / over there	Yes
customer service door doesn't close properly water pours out technician	No
parking ticket parked	Yes

7 description of a place

8 **2** a period of time
   3 a (living) thing
   4 a place

9 **1** 120   **3** the penguins
   2 2/two hours/hrs   **4** boats // a boat

10 **1** a number   **3** noun or adjective
    2 a time   **4** who is paying // how they are paying

11 **1** 226   **3** full
    2 7.30   **4** company

12 making an arrangement (to meet)

13 **2** a place
    3 an amount of money // a number

14 **1** 8.30 / eight thirty
    2 under the clock
    3 £13 / thirteen pounds

Listening 2

2 **3** something mechanical (being repaired)
   4 sum of money in $
   5 type of shop or person
   6 type of problem with book
   7 illness // disease
   8 date (appointment)
   9 event // arrangement
  10 telephone number

3 **1** Friday (night)
   2 (about) 7.30
   3 DVD // DVD player
   4 $45
   5 (university) bookshop
   6 out of print
   7 (the) flu
   8 Mon(day), 3.30 (pm)
   9 (farewell) party
  10 98184078

4

Words speaker used	Words in questions
B You'll need to pay	cost of repairs
C haven't been able to obtain	can't get
D could you come on	new appointment
E give us a call	please ring

6 **1** $27   **4** passport
   2 no booking **5** guided tour
   3 Student(s) **6** in advance

8 **7** (different) fish   **9** 7.30 (pm)
   8 café   **10** on the Internet

9 It's a number (for a time) not word(s).

10 **1** Lake Road
   2 36874500
   3 international
   4 four-door (car) / 4-door (car)
   5 24 (of) June / 24th June
   6 a week // one week
   7 (the) airport
   8 (around) lunchtime
   9 child('s) seat
  10 extra cover // extra insurance

11 That the rest of the address will follow – a road, street, etc. Make sure you can spell simple address words such as *Hill, Lane, Avenue*, etc.

12 The answer will be something like: station wagon, 2-door car, sports car, etc.

Listening 3

1 a It's oval-shaped, made of leather and has some stitching on one side.

  b It consists of a plastic sphere with small, coloured beads inside it and a long, thin handle.

  c It's a long stick with a curved end. It's made of wood and the handle is striped.

  d The outer case is plastic and there are glass lenses. There are two cylinders joined at both ends that you look through.

  e They're made of metal and very sharp with pointed ends. Some of them have a small, round head, while others have an eye at one end.

  f It's made of glass and starts as a cylinder then tapers towards the top to form a long, thin neck.

  g It's rectangular in shape and is wrapped in spotted paper. A pink ribbon is tied around it.

  h Part of it is made of metal and another part is made of rubber. It has a circular, flat bottom and then a small cylinder rises up from this and there is a flame at the end. A long thin rubber tube is used to attach the metal part to a tap.

4 1 container   **2** pin   **3** handle   **4** jet   **5** tube

5 & 6

Part	Description	Position
container	*large, metal, cylindrical, bell jar*	
lever		*at the top*
pin	*thin, extended*	*attached to / goes down*
gas cartridge	*small bottle/flask*	*right in the centre*
handle	*curved*	*at the top*
spring	*small, coiled*	*At the neck / holds pin / connected to*
discharge tube	*long, curved at the top*	*runs from / the bottom*
nozzle	*horizontal*	*on the other side*

7 6 (the) safety pin   **9** releases

  7 point   **10** burning materials

  8 press

8

	Which type of question it is	How many marks it is worth	What the topic is	Who the speakers might be
1	Type 1	1 mark	student timetable	students
2	Type 3	1 mark *	walking or hiking	walkers or tour leader
3	Type 2	1 mark	sharks	lecturer or someone giving a talk
4	Type 1	1 mark	architecture or building style	tour guide or radio programme
5–7	Type 3	3 marks	aeroplanes	passenger or airline worker or ordinary citizen

*This is only one question so you need both parts to get one mark.

9 1 B   **4** C

  2 B/D   **5–7** A D F *in any order*

  3 A

11 1 C   **2** B

12 1 more and more people are getting involved in this new sport

  2 well known for being unstable and turning over

14 3 B   **4–6** B D G *in any order*

15 A *a low-budget canoe* I wouldn't go for a cheap one

  C *a waterproof jacket* a life jacket

  E *a long-sleeved sweater* a wet suit … with short sleeves, rather than long sleeves

  F *rubber boots* get yourself a pair of river shoes

17 7 A

18 a deliberately look for the most dangerous rivers

  b B *winter* is mentioned but there is nothing about teaching

    C *high* is said but not *avoid*

Listening 4

1 a school // theme park   **c** Tudor Park // Neptune Avenue // sea life centre

  b Moon Crescent   **d** fish market // sea life centre

2 a Marble Street and Beach Road   **d** Diner Road

  b traffic lights   **e** dance centre

  c Neptune Avenue

3 A hospital   **D** cafe

  B library   **E** tennis courts

  C statue

4 A square building / on the corner

  B circular building / opposite the dance centre

  C in the middle of

  D on the corner / opposite the sea life centre

  E go east / past / on your right

6 1 E   **2** F   **3** D   **4** B

8 1 means of transport,

  2 place // number of stops,

  3 something (uncountable noun)

  4 a place/location

  5 a place/location

9 1 metro   **4** left(-)hand corner

  2 2/two stops   **5** just outside

  3 traffic

11 1 northern   **6** F

  2 half an hour //   **7** A

     30/thirty minutes   **8** D

  3 Grand Hotel   **9** H

  4 57   **10** C

  5 air(-)conditioned

Listening 5

2

Conversation	Topic	Number and type of speakers
2	D – Cost of health care	2 / one man, one woman
3	E – Nuclear energy	3 / two men, one woman
4	B – School leaving age	3 / two women, one man
5	F – Funding for highways	3 / two women, one man
6	C – Future of newspapers	3 / one man, two women

4 **1** secondary schooling // secondary education
2 (the) (young) doctors
3 nuclear (energy)
4 *ANY TWO:* hairdressing // building // carpentry
5 *ANY TWO:* France // Italy // America
6 (the) Internet

5 **1** C **2** B

9 **1** easy to find work
2 wide variety of job possibilities
3 easier to be accepted // lower exam mark required

10 **1** E **2** D **3** A

12 *Other answers possible*
A only a few colours
B additional expenses not revealed
C uses a lot of petrol
D not much space for your legs
E is not very stable on corners
F difficult to see out of the windows
G takes time to pick up speed

13 **1** D **2** C **3** B **4** F

14 For questions **1–3** in exercise **10**, you answer the questions by matching the three course advantages in the list to the correct course in the box (**A,B,C**, etc).

For questions **1–4** in exercise **13**, you answer the questions by matching the four similar things (Vehicles **1–4**) to the list of vehicle defects in the box (**A–G**).

15 *See recording script*

Listening 6

2 I thought the **assignment** was due in on Thursday.
*Is Thursday the day of the **exam**?*
I thought the assignment was due in on **Thursday**.
*Which **day** is the assignment due?*

4

Introduction	A	B	C	D
Where is the conversation taking place?	in a university library	radio interview	university or college	university office
What is the main topic of the conversation?	difficulty with assignment	traffic, new tunnel	(lack of) funding for research	exam marks
How many speakers are there?	3	2	3	2

5 surprise **B** concern **C**
satisfaction **D** annoyance **A**

6 *Other answers possible*
A Ensuring that people have work is more important than making money for shareholders.
B The health of a nation should come before comfort and leisure.
C Welfare and social services are essential whereas space research is not.
D Money spent on roads will reduce accidents.
E What children learn at primary school supports all their learning.

7 *Other answers possible*
A Everyone has the right to a job.
Companies should not only think of profits.
Companies need to make a profit to be able to employ people.

B Money should be spent on hospitals, not on building luxury hotels.
Hotels play an essential role in international business and leisure time.
C Money spent on space research is wasted.
Governments should spend money on social services.
Space research is essential to further our knowledge of the world and universe.
D The government should spend money on building good roads as these are safer.
Spending money on roads only encourages more cars.
E Early education is the most important because that's where we learn essential skills.
Secondary and further education are as important as primary education.

9 Discussion with a politician about plans

10 **1** A **2** C **3** B **4** A **5** B

12 **1** geologist **6** (two) cameras
2 microwave oven **7** aluminium
3 2.4 **8** 11/eleven minutes/mins
4 solar panels **9** a time delay
5 (the) warm box **10** (lots of) water

Listening 7

2 **1** **b** Options **a** and **c** do not provide an example of how car manufacturers can reduce our dependency on oil.
2 **c** Options **a** and **b** do not provide a further example of where Swahili is spoken

3 **1** Signalling a contrast or opposite – although / despite/ even though / whereas / However / but / unlike / while / On the one hand … but on the other / By contrast / even if
2 Introducing an example – For example / For instance
3 Giving a reason (cause and effect) – because
4 Providing extra information – In addition/also/as well as
5 Setting out the stages of a talk – First of all/Lastly/Then
6 Signalling an explanation or result – Consequently / so / in other words

4 *Other answers possible*
2 Studying abroad is worthwhile, <u>even though</u> *it can be challenging.* (contrast)
3 Working in the library is uncomfortable <u>as well</u> <u>as</u> *being quite boring.* (extra information)
4 The Internet has changed the way we all live <u>because</u> *it gives us access to the wider world.* (explanation)
5 I never learned to play a musical instrument, <u>so</u> *I don't know how to read music.* (explanation)
6 Learning a foreign language can be difficult and at times frustrating. <u>However,</u> *it can also be very rewarding.* (contrast)
7 The climate of South East Asia is tropical. <u>By contrast,</u> *the climate of Southern Europe is Mediterranean.* (contrast)
8 My brother never studied much at school <u>and consequently</u> *he failed his school leaving exams.* (result)
9 Rice is the staple diet in Asia, <u>whereas</u> *corn is the staple in Central America.* (contrast)
10 The effects of global warming are evident everywhere. <u>For example,</u> *the temperature of the sea is rising every year.* (example)

5

	Signpost word(s)	Direction
1	For instance …	Introducing an example
2	First of all … Then …	Signalling a sequence
3	Consequently …	Suggesting a result
4	but …	Signalling a contrast
5	On the one hand … On the other hand …	Signalling a contrast or opposite
6	Firstly … Secondly …	Setting out the stages of a talk

7 *See recording script*

10
1 good quality
2 fast food
3 (the) milkshakes
4 1/one million
5 (the) name

Listening 8

1 a handwriting
b *many possible answers*
c by looking at a number of scientific studies

1

Intro	Key words and phrases	Topic	Possible development
A	recognise handwriting / scientific studies	writing systems	how writing systems developed in different places

2

Intro	Key words and phrases	Topic	Possible development
B	bamboo, species, building materials, food	bamboo	how bamboo is used
C	bread, rice, pasta, taste, cook	staple foods	ways of preparing these staples
D	language, children, study	children's language	how children learn to speak

5 2 date // manner
3 country
4 noun – connected to the game
5 event
6 adjective // number

6 1 (northern) India
2 year 1000 // 1000 AD
3 China
4 chess pieces
5 championship // competition
6 three/3

8 & 9 *Signpost words signalling the answers are included in brackets*
1 interest (*firstly …*)
2 important (*secondly …*)
3 complex (*The third point …*)
4 research methods (*We will start by …*)
5 first year (*then go on to …*)
6 under five / under 5 (*that is …*)
7 A (*Put another way …*)
8 D (*First …*)
9 C (*then …*)
10 G (*And finally we'll conclude …*)

11 1 rabbit
2 (for) (fox) hunting // sport
3 (sugar) cane farmers
4 (cane) roots // (plant) roots
5 (plant) dies
6 A
7 B
8 C
9 A
10 C

Reading 1

1 a the IELTS Reading test module
b to provide information on the IELTS Reading test module
c students who intend to take the IELTS test

2 a How long flights affect pilots' ability to fly.
b People studying aviation / training to be pilots // airplane companies // people who travel by air
c Some more detailed information about how too much flying might affect pilots' decision-making.

3 a To provide a brief scientific explanation of the subheading and mention the possible implications
b The first sentence: *Globetrotting across several time zones on long-haul flights impairs memory and reaction times by shrinking part of the brain.*

4 a Pearls and an unpleasant part of what they are made of
b People who work in the jewel industry or ecology students
c Something about where pearls come from

5 a To explain the process by which pearls are formed
b With more information about pearls – perhaps some background to their production
c It is factual and descriptive.

6 a They separate the main ideas.
b The topic sentence(s) that carry the main idea(s).

8 A The vast oceans of the world … where eyesight counts for little
B … for whales and dolphins … What is crucial to them is sound.
C Sound … travels five times faster through water than through air
D Whales and dolphins use sound in two ways: for communication and for echolocation.
E … whales and dolphins also rely on echolocation to learn about their immediate environment, including prey …

9 *Other answers possible*
It is sound, not sight, that is important beneath the oceans. Sound travels much faster through water than through air and whales and dolphins use it to communicate and to find food.

10 A

11 1 C   2 E   3 A   4 D   5 B

12 prey

13 The influence of the Internet on consumerism or shopping

14 Para **A**   last sentence
Para **B**   first sentence
Para **C**   first sentence
Para **D**   second sentence
Para **E**   first sentence
Para **F**   first sentence and half of second sentence
Para **G**   first sentence

15 1 iv   2 viii   3 iii   4 i   5 ii   6 v   7 vii

Answer key

17		**Meaning**
a	in proportion to	in direct relation to
b	mulling over	taking some time to think about
c	turning up	arriving
d	peak periods	busiest times
e	influence	effect on
f	gain from	benefit from
g	take account of	take into consideration
h	try out	test (try using)

Reading 2

1 1 $18 billion, $34 billion
   2 The Department of Commerce in Washington DC
   3 22% and 2%
   4 stores run by *Sony* and *Apple*
   5 *eBay* and *Amazon*

2 The article is about what sand consists of.

3 2 part // measured
   3 TWO factors // size and shape
   4 Which event // beach // Kamoama
   5 Where // very ancient sand
   6 Who // efficient function // coastal technology

4 a The answer to **4** should be easy to find because you can scan for *Kamoama*.
   b The answer to **5** might be harder because you need to look for another way of saying 'very ancient sand'. Questions that require two answers can also be more challenging as you need to find both answers to get the mark.

5 1 concrete and glass
   2 (the/its) diameter
   3 age and origin
   4 (a) volcanic eruption
   5 (in) northern Scotland
   6 geologists

6 mis-spelled words // extra words // wrong words

7 The passage is about fish (salmon) losses in the Pacific Ocean and the impact this may have on different salmon species.

8 1 D   4 I   7 B
   2 H   5 A   8 C
   3 F   6 E   9 G

9

Para **1**	• this ritual • the decline	• the migration from and to rivers … • the fall in numbers of Pacific Northwest salmon more than a century ago
Para **2**	• there they spawn	• in the river where they were born …
Para **4**	• influences this	• affects their unique genetic signature (or code)
Para **5**	• other problems • these measures	• problems different from / in addition to hydropower on rivers that have disrupted salmon populations • using submersible screens to divert salmon away from turbines
Para **6**	• these devices • such impediments	• fish ladders • things like discharge from turbines
Para **7**	• these changes	• habitat being inaccessible and extreme water temperatures

10 1 nests // redds   4 smoltification
   2 gravel   5 river
   3 freshwater

11 6 turbines   10 habitat
   7 stream-type   11 water temperatures
   8 fish ladders   12 life cycle
   9 migration rates

Reading 3

1 It will discuss how blame can be used to improve the way people work. The sport of baseball will provide a model.

2 a *blame* (verb) – to identify the person (or sometimes thing) responsible for allowing a mistake to happen
   blame (noun) – the responsibility for a problem
   fault (noun) – the cause of a problem or mistake
   b The workplace (business management); sport (baseball)

4 *flops* — fails to succeed
   blunder — mistake/error (as a result of lack of care or thought)
   point fingers — accuse someone of a mistake
   give sb/sth a bad name — give sb/sth a bad reputation for (doing) something

5 a the main idea which is in two parts
   b examples of the main idea
   c new idea, again leading into the next paragraph
   d Suggestions and meanings as used in this text:
   constructive (useful/helpful)   *put forth their best*
   judiciously (wisely)   *efforts* (try hard)
   sparingly (not too often)   *maintaining*
   prod (encourage)   (keeping)
   ultimately (finally)
   e It should be possible to understand the main idea even if you don't know the meaning of every word or phrase.
   f Some exemplification of how to manage blame.

6 *Main idea* (2nd sentence): Thus, baseball provides an excellent microcosm in which to study blame because mistakes and failures are a routine part of every game.
   Supporting points (1st and 5th sentences): Baseball managers spend most of their time and energy managing things that go wrong.
   Thus, if managers and coaches got upset about every mistake, they would go mad by the end of the season.
   Examples (3rd and 4th sentences): In a typical game, managers, coaches and players can easily make more than 100 bad decisions – and still end up winning.
   Even very successful pitchers average more than two bad pitches per batter and if a batter bats well 40% of the time but badly the other 60% he is having a miraculous season.

7 1 B   2 D   3 C

8 a Libraries are making digital copies of books. // Technology is going to change the way libraries work.
   b The next three paragraphs of the text all develop the main idea expressed in the first sentence of paragraph 2.
   c *three* / *First* / *for example* / *similarly*
   d Very easy, because the text is organised around the three benefits.

9 1 T   2 F   3 NG   4 NG   5 T   6 F   7 NG

11 1 phone phreakers   5 *Wargames*
   2 musical tones   6 banks
   3 (the) 1980s   7 credit card
   4 hacking

178

Reading 4

1 a C **b** A, C and E focus on advertising and magazines.

2 1 A **2** B **3** A **4** A **5** C

3 C

4 1 ix **2** i **3** v **4** ii **5** vi **6** viii **7** iv

5 1 diesel power
2 12 per cent / 12%
3 size and efficiency
4 & 5 trees / buildings (*in either order*)
6 computer modelling

6 a 6 spelling error
b 4 & 5 plural required
c 2 *around* unnecessary because of *About* and it is a four-word answer
d 1 no article needed – grammatically incorrect
e 1 wrong answer
f 2 wrong answer – question is about amount of energy not money
g 6 scientists are already mentioned in the question
h 6 This is where they were built NOT what was used to help choose the location. Also the answer is four words long.

7

	Question phrasing	Passage
A	used to rely totally on	entire (electricity needs) were met by (lines 18–19)
B	energy needs	energy requirements (line 36)
C	its energy output	The power produced (line 38)
D	not be (built) near	away from (line 50)
E	barriers to the wind such as	obstructions like (line 50)
F	chose the best location	select the optimum site (lines 52–53)
G	with the aid of	was used (line 52)

8 B

Reading 5

1 household utility

2 1 a subscription pool **2** price and quality

3 *Words in paragraph* / *Words in questions*
1 Artists will be paid / fees to musicians
2 as never before / in future
in terms of / two issues
engage listeners / will be very important to consumers

5 1 subscription **4** online / interactive
2 18–24 **5** album (format)
3 fans **6** single-track purchases

6

Gap	Words in summary	Words in passage
2	young ones aged	18–24 age group
3	encourage large groups / take part in music-making	build online communities / feel engaged in the creative process
4	live concert downloads / activities	live concert downloads / forums
5	are losing their appreciation of / well produced and packaged	are increasingly unimpressed with / However cleverly the songs are arranged and attractively designed the cover art is
5	one expert / world of digital music sales	William Higham / digital music sales

8

Words	Meaning
antibiotic	a type of *drug* that destroys bacteria in the body
micro-organism	a very small organism that must be seen using a *microscope*
microbe	a micro-organism that can cause *disease*
bacteria	very similar to *microbes*
resistance	ability to *fight* against something, e.g. *disease*
toxin	something that is poisonous, e.g. *dangerous chemicals*
epidemic	outbreak of disease among a lot of people or animals, e.g. *flu*

9 1 E **2** B **3** A **4** C **5** E

10 1 K **2** O **3** D **4** G **5** M **6** H

Reading 6

1 Fact … *because of the way their dyes break down*

2 Main ideas
Paragraph **B** *Despite 119 years of refinement, the modern car remains astonishingly inefficient.*
Paragraph **C** *Go into a coffee bar, … so long as you are doing this in a foreign country, where you speak the language badly or not at all, you are probably acquiring a new language better than you ever could by formal study with a teacher and a textbook.*

a Paragraph **B** – the argument is well supported with many facts
Paragraph **C** – mainly opinion with little support for an argument
b Paragraph **B** – presents an argument
Paragraph **C** – is discursive

3 First underlining – *fact*
Second underlining – *argument*
a To discuss new research findings.
b There are different views and they conflict.
c There are no firm conclusions.
d 'New research suggests that humans are not a threat to penguins'.

4 *in any order* A / C / F

5 A … *a slow-moving human who does not approach the nest too closely is not perceived as a threat by penguins.*

Answer key

C *… the decline in penguin numbers is caused by other factors.*

F *He points out that species behave differently*

B numbers are declining but there is nothing about them becoming endangered

D there is mention of 'young' but nothing about them being harder to research

E they may 'flee the nest'

G there is nothing about this in the passage

6 1 C   2 A   3 C   4 D   5 B

7 a The degradation of Australian land and what is being and should be done about it.

   b Eight people are referred to – they don't all agree.

   c according to / does not deny that / says / disagrees

8 1 D   3 B   5 E   7 F
    2 E   4 A   6 C   8 C

9

1	more diverse	5	getting solutions into place
2	they just don't have the spare funds	6	pristine … natural
3	"illogical"	7	Meteorologists …
4	trading	8	co-operation

Reading 7

1 Informative or argumentative text in a popular magazine – the language in the subheading is conversational so it is not a factual report. It may inform readers of new research or it may persuade readers to try a new or different approach.

4 1 D   2 H   3 B   4 F   5 A

5 a A media studies student would be most likely to read it. This is a typical textbook passage.

   b a mix of the two

6 C

7 1 Likely answer yes but children read books with parents
   2 Yes – the sentences above provide plenty of support.
   3 The following sentence explains that more than one person works on a play or film.
   4 It is about how much a writer's work may be changed and for what reason.
   5 *Answers may vary*

8 1 Y   3 NG   5 NG   7 N
    2 N   4 N   6 Y   8 Y

Reading 8

1 A The title and headings tell us what is in the museum. Also, the hours, fees and additional attraction.

   B The title and headings give the name of the museum and highlight a new attraction and opening hours.

2

Key word(s) in question	**Type of words needed**
2 What process	an action or 'ing' word
3 How many	a number
4 What … prize	an object // a sum of money // something of value
5 When	a time
6 Which part	a place // an area

Answers

1 1 (during) Carnival week   4 a helicopter ride
    2 chocolate making   5 Wednesday evenings
    3 15 (or more)   6 (the) Reading Room

3 C

   a Say which type of company issued the card
   b They are all companies of some sort.
   c safe and sound // cover // lost luggage, medical expenses
   d A, mentions travel but not holidays
      B, mentions reverse charge calls only
      D, mentions medical expenses but not medical care

4 1 T   2 F   3 F   4 NG   5 T   6 T

5 1 shop around for the best price (same meaning)
    2 additional daytime services (opposite meaning)
    3 prices vary seasonally (opposite meaning)
    4 cars and motorbikes (=vehicles) (charge not mentioned)
    5 services can be limited in the low season (same meaning)
    6 car rental … best choice to go further (same meaning)

7 1 a place   4 a type of performance
    2 a period of time   5 an item or action
    3 a way of buying tickets   6 something in a museum

8 1 Belmore park   4 outdoor concerts
    2 2/two days   5 booking
    3 online   6 birds

Reading 9

1 student accommodation / one – Sturtin Hostel

2 2 on-the-spot reservations (H)
    3 offer assistance in finding a suitable person to share a room with (G)
    4 code of conduct (C)
    5 for students run by students (D)

3 1 B   2 E   3 F   4 G   5 B   6 D   7 C

4 a ii
   b They do not describe the main idea that this is a course for new-comers to computers. They focus on parts of the course only.

5 a iii
   b They focus on details within the text rather than on the main idea of enrolment conditions.

6 1 v   2 ii   3 iv   4 i   5 ix

7 Para **B**   *initially aimed at … more recently*
   Para **C**   *where to purchase the best herbs*
   Para **D**   *classes commence with a demonstration / observed a good chef*
   Para **E**   *roll up their sleeves, put on an apron … recreate the dishes*
   Para **F**   *all degrees of competency*

8 a a course outline for a design course
   b prospective students

9 B / E

10 3 20 years   5 real world
     4 teachers   6 product design

11 a The heading is a question – anticipating that the reader may not be familiar with the term.
  b It's about a new form of broadcasting.
  c On the Internet.

Reading 10

1 a The text is about a new way of milking cows that is being introduced into Australia.

  b Part **1** Paragraphs **1 & 2**: introduces the idea and talks about where it is happening
  Part **2** Paragraphs **3 & 4**: explains how the system works (relates to the diagram)
  Part **3** Paragraph **5**: outlines the challenges/difficulties in using it in Australia

  c The different parts of the text relate to the three different task types.

2 1 computer technology
  2 human input
  3 Netherlands (and) Britain
  4 (a) microchip (implant)
  5 (a) robotic arm
  6 brushes and rollers / rollers and brushes (must have all three words)
  7 D

3 a cattle / beast / animals
  b 1 revolutionise   **6** soothe
    2 emerged   **7** notify
    3 take off   **8** encourage
    4 identify   **9** graze
    5 sterilise   **10** trial

4 The article describes the growing interest in hotels made of ice and how they are constructed.

6 1 original ice hotel … display artworks
  2 most people … spend the night
  3 inside … walls … fragile appearance
  4 sculptures … difficult … carve
  5 walls … moveable frames
  6 river adjacent … hotel … unpolluted
  7 fibre-optic cables … specially produced

7 1 Y   **2** N   **3** N   **4** NG   **5** Y   **6** Y   **7** NG

8 1 D   **2** E   **3** A   **4** E   **5** F   **6** A   **7** B   **8** D

Writing Task 1 Assessment criteria

1

Assessment criteria	Skills and strategies
Content	E, H, N, Q
Organisation	A, G, K, R
Vocabulary	B, D, M, P
Grammar	C, F, I, J, L, O

2 *Answers may vary*

Writing Task 2 Assessment criteria

3

Assessment criteria	Skills and strategies
Organisation	A, G, K, R
Vocabulary	B, D, M, P
Grammar	C, F, I, J, D

4 For content in **Task 2**, you must show that you can answer the question in the task clearly and effectively using your own ideas. For content in **Task 1**, you must show that you can write a summary of a diagram, table, chart or graph which has been made by someone else.

Writing 1

5

Number of students

6 1 60 per cent/the highest percentage   **3** 20 per cent … percentage
  2 percentage   **4** lowest/smallest percentage

9 Yes, this could be a bar chart. The percentages would form the vertical axis and the methods of transport the horizontal axis. The three countries would be presented as the coloured bars for each transport type.

10 1 most common/popular; 65 per cent/%
  2 10 per cent/%; least common/popular
  3 figures
  4 percentage
  5 16 per cent/% (and) 20 per cent/%
  6 20 per cent/%
  7 most common/popular; on foot

12 a people (car owners)
  b years
  c car owners in millions

13 Car ownership in Britain has risen dramatically.

14 a Car ownership has risen dramatically since 1960.
  b Car ownership rose dramatically over a forty-five-year period between 1960 and 2005.

15 a Since 1960, the number of car owners in Britain has risen dramatically from below 2 million to over 30 million.
  b The number of car owners in Britain rose dramatically from under 2 million in 1960 to over 30 million in 2005.

16 a How industrial pollution caused by fossil fuels increases the acidity of the world's oceans and how this acidity is harmful to coral and plankton
  b They indicate the stages in a process of causes and effects.
  c It shows how acidic the water is expected to be by 2100 // how much acid there is expected to be in the water by 2100.

17 1 is polluting   **5** attacks
  2 are released   **6** will rise
  3 are burnt/burned   **7** become
  4 pass   **8** be destroyed

Writing 2

1 The bar chart shows the rise/increase in the number of tourists visiting Brazil over the six-year period between 1995 and 2000.

2 The number of tourists visiting Brazil rose considerably. The chart shows a considerable increase in the number of tourists visiting Brazil.
Adding *considerably/considerable* not only describes the information shown in the chart, but also interprets it by telling the reader what the overall trend is.

3 Between 1995 and 2000 the number of tourists visiting Brazil rose considerably from just under two million to over five million.

4 The table gives information on how many Japanese tourists are travelling outside Japan over an 11-month period. Generally, the numbers fluctuate, although more people seemed to be travelling in the latter half of 2005 than in the first part of 2006.

6 2 a steady rise // a gradual increase
3 a stable/constant pattern
4 a peak
5 a dramatic increase // a sharp rise
6 a gradual decrease/fall

7 2 it rises steadily // it increases gradually
3 it remains constant / stable
4 it reaches a peak
5 it increases dramatically // it rises sharply
6 it falls/declines gradually

8 *Other answers possible*
A Graph A provides information on the changing percentage of new recruits in a company over a 10-year period. According to the figures, recruitment fell significantly during this period. Between 1997 and 2000 there was only a slight drop from 15 to 11 per cent but after that, the figures fell more markedly to a low of 5 per cent.
B Chart B shows the average number of working hours per week at the company between 2000 and the present. These figures show a steady increase. In 2000, employees were generally doing a 40-hour week but this figure has now risen to a high of 50 hours per week.
C Information relating to the estimated cost of days taken off sick by employees is provided in graph C. Over the same period, these figures have also risen but most significantly in the last three years. From 2000 to 2003, the pattern was stable, with costs being approximately $200,000 but since then the figure has risen dramatically, hitting a peak of $1 million in the present year.

9 a The number of hamburgers sold at Harry's over a one-year period.
b The graph shows fluctuation / a fluctuating trend.
c The simple past tense.

10 *Other answers possible*
- The sale of hamburgers was *stable* throughout January, February and most of March.
- *Fewer* hamburgers were sold in April than in March according to this graph.
- There was a dramatic *rise* in the sale of hamburgers between June and August, when numbers increased from 1900 to 3000.
- Hamburger *sales peaked* in August when 3000 were sold.
- In October *sales dropped* to their lowest point at 1250.

11 Hamburgers were more popular in summer than in winter, according to the graph.

12 The graph shows the fluctuation in the number of passengers at a London underground station. It illustrates peaks, troughs and plateaux, as well as increasing and decreasing trends. You should have circled the two peaks at 08.00 and 18.00 and the drop at 16.00.

14
- The writer does not state the purpose of the graph.
- There is no overview.
- The key trends have not been highlighted.
- There are some figures but they have been rather randomly selected and do not help the reader identify the key trends.
- There is no rounding-off point to the answer.

15 *Model answer*
The graph shows the fluctuation in the number of people at an underground station over a one-day period (1). According to this data, there is a sharp increase in use between 6am and 8am, with 400 people using the station at 8 o'clock. After this, the numbers fall dramatically to less than 200 at 10 o'clock (2). However, between 11am and 3pm, the number of people rises and falls evenly, and this pattern includes a plateau around lunchtime of just under 300 people using the station. Numbers then decline and the smallest number of users, just 100, is recorded at four in the afternoon (3). Between 4pm and 6pm, during the evening rush hour, numbers rise rapidly again, reaching a peak of 380 people at 6pm but from (4) 7pm numbers fall significantly. There is only a slight increase again just after 8pm, which tails off after 9pm.

The graph shows that the station is most crowded in the early morning and evening rush-hour periods and least crowded mid-afternoon (5).

16 a 1   **b** 2, 3 and 4   **c** 5

17 You should have circled: *this data / with / After this / However / this pattern / then / and / again / but / which / and*

Writing 3

1 The number of landline telephones per thousand people

2 The chart compares telephone ownership in a number of different countries in three different years: 2000, 2002 and 2004.

3 The past simple tense.

4 & 5
1 The graph shows the number of telephones owned per thousand of the population in different countries over a five-year period.
2 Overall, the number of phone owners per thousand of the population varied considerably. However, numbers tended to fall in countries with the highest level of phone ownership, whereas numbers generally rose in countries which had fewer phone owners in 2000.
3 By far the highest level of phone ownership was in Singapore, where just under 430 people per thousand were owners in 2004. This figure is slightly lower than the 2000 figure of around 460 per thousand.
4 In Brunei Darussalam the second highest levels of phone ownership were recorded, and the numbers fluctuated around the 250 per thousand level across the five years.
5 Countries like Cambodia and Vietnam had much lower levels of phone ownership and these increased up to 2004, rather than decreasing.
6 In the remaining countries, the number of landline phone owners remained below the 100 per thousand level between 2000 and 2004.

7 *… figures have doubled since research began reaching a current high of around 30 per cent for both male and female adults*

8 1 5 per cent   **2** two-year   **3** 24 per cent

10 The trend for men has been similar during this period, although levels were quite a bit lower in the mid to late nineties. However, between 1998 and 2000 a surge took place when the male figure hit 21 per cent. Since then, the percentage of obese men has risen considerably to reach 30 per cent. Generally, the rate of increase in obesity has been higher in men than in women. (*73 words*)

11 *Model answer*

The graph shows how the hours children aged 10–11 spend on computers and watching television have changed over the past few years. In the past, children spent more time watching television and less time on computers but now this trend seems to have reversed.

Between 2000 and 2003, the time children spent watching television remained the same, at an average of 21 hours per week. Then this figure fell, reaching a low of 15 hours per week by 2004. Since then, apart from a slight fluctuation, the figures have stabilised at this level.

Computer use, on the other hand, shows a different trend, starting in 2000 at three hours per week and rising to a weekly figure of 10 hours in 2003. This was then followed by a surge which reached 15 hours per week by 2004 and currently this trend seems to be on the increase.

Clearly computer use is becoming more popular than TV viewing. (*160 words*)

12 a The diagram illustrates the stages in the production of plastic items.

   b *plastic / oven / molecules / mould / quality*

   c *forces* – pushes / *releases* – comes out

   d *equipment/machinery and words to describe it:*
     plant / tanker / drum / rectangular / narrow / belt / forklift truck / box
     process verbs: *fed into / heat / discard / observe / check*
     words to describe the plastic: *molten / material / harden / flawed*

   e *first / initially / then / after that / as a result / also / eventually / when / once*

13 & 14

Para 1	Introduction and overview of diagram	complex process number of steps / equipment / people
Para 2	How process begins up to production of long molecules	transported to plant / pass to oven / heated at high pressure
Para 3	From molecules to mould	passes into moulder / narrow end pushes into mould / hardens / comes out of mould
Para 4	What happens to finished product	checked for flaws / put in boxes / taken to warehouse / stored

Model answer

The diagram illustrates the various stages in the production of plastic items. Clearly this is a complex process that requires a range of equipment and machinery and, at some stages, skilled workers.

Initially, the raw materials have to be transported from the oil refinery to the plant. On arrival, they are poured into a large drum and from there they pass into a special oven, which heats the material at high pressure so that long molecules of plastic form.

The granules are then funnelled into a rectangular moulder with a narrow end. The moulder melts the plastic in order to push it out into a mould. When the plastic has hardened in the mould, the items can be removed and any waste material discarded.

Before they can be packaged, the finished products have to be checked for any problems, so next they are placed on a belt and observed by an expert. If they pass the inspection, they can be packed into boxes and taken to a warehouse for storage. (*170 words*)

Writing 4

1 1 most
   2 twice
   3 second highest
   4 470 million
   5 third largest
   6 the same
   7 as
   8 least
   9 less/lower

2

1	frequency of grammatical errors	the most frequent grammatical error	the second most frequent grammatical error	the least frequent grammatical error
2	height of smog levels	the highest smog level	the second highest smog level	the lowest smog level
3	density of populated areas	the most densely populated area	the second most densely populated area	the least densely populated area
4	significance of reason for disease	the most significant reason for disease	the second most significant reason for disease	the least significant reason for disease
5	length of study periods	the longest study period	the second longest study period	the shortest study period

3 1 better
   2 equally
   3 the highest; (the) furthest
   4 Unlike; lower
   5 the same; different
   6 the best; fewer

7 *Model answer*

The charts provide data on average male and female incomes. From this comparison it can be seen that men earn more than women at most stages in life.

Male graduates find that their earnings increase rapidly over the years to £700 per week at around the age of 40. The highest earning males are aged between 40 and 60, when their income stabilises. Non-graduate males experience a similar trend in their earnings, though the levels of pay are slightly lower.

Women, on the other hand, do not see a constant increase in their earnings. After the age of 24, weekly graduate earnings rise to about £425. Then they hit a plateau which does not change until retirement. The same pattern occurs for non-graduate females, whose highest earnings amount to less than £350 per week between the ages of 25 and 29 and continue at that level.

Clearly women never achieve the high income levels of their male counterparts. (*158 words*)

- **comparisons** men earn more than women / income levels are almost the same / the highest earning males / the levels of pay are slightly lower / highest earnings amount to less than £350
- **linkers** from this comparison / similar trend / on the other hand / the same pattern

10 *Model answer*

The diagram and table provide information on different types of dredger that are used to clean up dirty water. Canal and coastal dredgers perform a similar function but they differ considerably in terms of their size and power.

183

A canal dredger carries a suction pump with rotating blades, which are lowered into the canal by two hydraulic arms. These stir up the mud, called slurry, on the bottom of the canal, and this is then sucked up by the centrifugal pump. From the pump, the mud is discharged through a large tube into a shuttle boat located behind the dredging boat. When the shuttle boat is full of mud, it is towed away and the mud is dumped.

Compared to a coastal dredger, a canal dredger is a lot smaller. It is only 22 metres long, rather than 85 metres and is also less broad. Coastal dredgers are made to be used in the sea and can suck up sand and mud from a depth of 35 metres, while canal dredgers are made for much shallower waters.

Clearly dredgers have to be specially designed to suit the environment in which they will operate. (*193 words*)

Writing 5

1 The letter is to the local Council. Its purpose is to ask the Council to remove an old car from the street.

2 Dear Sirs, … Yours faithfully,

3 To ask your old teacher to write a good reference for you.

4 1 name
2 what you've done
3 job
4 wanting this job
5 good points about yourself

8 1 Formal
2 Formal
3 Informal
4 Formal
5 Informal
6 Formal
7 Informal
8 Informal

9 *Model answer (opening paragraph)*
Dear Mr Hill,

It's been a long time since we saw each other, so I hope you can remember me. I've been working in Canada as a nanny since leaving school three years ago and I'm now back home. I have recently applied for a job as a nursing assistant at a hospital in London and I wonder whether you would be able to write a reference for me. (*69 words*)

10 d / e / f *in any order*
2 amazing bird life
7 crocodiles in river
8 cabins with bunk beds
g / h / i *in any order*
3 prices going up next season
5 wilderness may change
9 great fun

14 *Model answer (first three paragraphs)*
Dear Sirs,

I am writing in the hope that you can help me with a problem regarding a camera that I recently bought.

On 24 April, I purchased a Tycoon digital SLR camera from the 'Golden Duty Free' store at Bangkok Airport on my way from Auckland to London. The camera cost $599 and I paid for it on my Visa credit card.

When I arrived at my hotel in London almost 24 hours later I discovered, to my horror, that the box which contained the camera did not include the battery or the battery charger. The space in the box for the charger was empty. (*106 words*)

15 1 Formal
2 Informal
3 Formal
4 Informal
5 Informal
6 Informal
7 Informal
8 Formal

16 *model answer (last paragraph)* I am now in London and I am not returning to Bangkok, so I need to get the missing parts here. As you are the representative of the company in this country, I would be grateful if you could arrange for the parts to be sent to me. I attach a copy of the receipt with this letter for your information.

I look forward to hearing from you.
Yours faithfully,
(*70 words*)

Writing 6

1 The tone is very direct and rude.

2 Readers might be offended and react in an uncooperative way, i.e. these requests and suggestions will convey the wrong message.

3 *Other answers possible*
I would be grateful if you would *send me a brochure*
I would like to buy *a ticket for tonight's show.*
Perhaps it would be better if you *employed more staff?*
I would recommend that you *give up smoking.*
I am interested in *study*ing *at your school.*
I would appreciate it if you would *park your car further away from mine.*
I was wondering if I could *use you as a referee?*

4 & 5 1 F (n)
2 B (n)
3 A (i)
4 B (f)
5 C (n/f)
6 D (f)
7 E (n/f)
8 E (n/f)
9 A (n)
10 D (n)
11 A (f)
12 C (n)
13 D (n/f)
14 A (f)
15 G (n)

6 *Other answers possible* disappointment / surprise / anger / shock / good wishes

7 A too formal
B too informal
C too informal
D too formal – inappropriate ending to an informal letter

8 A I'd love to keep in touch more often and I forgot to ask you for your cell phone number. Can you let me have your address so that I can send you the photos?
B I hope you are well and are still working at Kingston High because I would like to ask a favour of you. I wonder whether you would mind being a referee for me?
C I think there must have been a mistake, as this account has been paid in full.
D Many thanks for organising everything so well. Best wishes,

10 A informal – sympathy and good wishes
B formal – request for action
C formal – complaint
D informal –apology

Writing 7

1 a The topic is consumerism and its influence on our behaviour.
b Have we become less concerned about other people because of our desire for material possessions?
c The information in brackets gives us examples of *more and more possessions.*
d They introduce examples and also suggest that you may add other qualities to these options.
e No – it is important to present arguments and justify them.

2 a The topic is mobile phones and their influence on society.
b The two questions form the two main parts.
c You can do any one of these options.
d It is best to aim for 50–50 but sometimes a different ratio is acceptable because there are more obvious arguments on one side of the task than the other.

3 a There are two main parts but remember that you also need to add your personal opinion.

b The two views are equally strong so you should try for 50–50. However, your own opinion will add to whichever view you support and may mean that you write more on that part.

c You can agree with the first view or agree with the second view or see both sides of the argument, i.e. agree with both views.

4 There are two parts but they are closely linked and may be discussed together. Both the roles of parents and teachers should be referred to when dealing with the first part.

7 There are two parts.

8

Disadvantages
• Extra cost
• Learner drivers might have to wait longer for a test.
• It may not be possible to include a written test every time.
• Difficult to organise

9 Makes driving safer

12 *Main idea:*   children need protection
Supporting ideas: work and family responsibility
not appropriate at this age
adults may let children work
children might lose education
and care

14 *Model answer*

There are certain groups of people who would certainly benefit from taking a driving test at regular intervals. These include elderly people, who are often more forgetful than younger drivers and so need to be reminded of the road rules. Also, some people use their cars quite infrequently. People who live near the town and don't need to drive to work might only use their cars for longer trips and so refresher courses would help them. Thirdly, some young drivers simply drive too fast and this tendency would be reduced if they were reminded more often of the dangers of speeding.

Note that this paragraph contains about 100 words and so would be enough to cover one part of the answer.

Writing 8

1 *Suggested answer*

Obesity rates among young children are growing. Parents are to blame for this because they have the strongest influence over their children's eating habits. Do you agree or disagree?

2 A *I agree with the statement in the task … many societies already have systems to help poor people but perhaps they do not run these well enough.*

B *I think it may be their own fault … I think the problem cannot be solved by giving them more state benefits.*

C *the problem has many different root causes … People have to take some responsibility for their own welfare but … some people cannot work for good reasons*

3 A suggestions as to how societies' welfare systems could be better run

B reasons why people may be to blame and suggestions as to how they could be encouraged to help themselves

C ways people can be responsible for themselves and examples of people who cannot do this / situations that make this difficult plus the type of support they need

4 Nine words will not be counted as part of the student's answer – *members are poor and struggle each day to survive* is copied from the task.

5 There is no position – only a repetition of the task.

7

Position	1st Main idea	2nd Main idea
• No vaccines – diseases return • Laws needed	• Preventative medicine most effective	• Immunisation part of human progress
	Supporting points • Lives saved • Diseases, e.g. polio, reduced	**Supporting points** • Have better hygiene – why not also better medical programmes? • Don't want to go backwards

8 *Model answer*

Now that diseases like polio have been eradicated in many societies, it is true that children are at far less risk these days. However, parents who choose not to immunise their children are relying on the fact that other parents do still immunise their children. If the number of parents choosing not to immunise increases, there is a risk of the diseases returning.

9 *Alternative answer*

The question of whether we should oblige parents to immunise their children against common diseases is a social rather than a medical one. Since we are free to choose what we eat or drink or how much exercise we take, why should the medical treatment we decide to undergo be any different? *Introduction poses a new question to introduce the topic*

Medical researchers and governments are primarily interested in overall statistics and trends and in money-saving schemes, which fail to take into consideration the individual's concerns and rights. While immunisation against diseases such as tetanus and whooping cough may be effective, little information is released about the harmful effects of vaccinations, which can sometimes result in growth problems in children or even death.
Concessional argument

The body is designed to resist disease and to create its own natural immunity through contact with that disease. When children are given artificial immunity, we create a vulnerable society, which is entirely dependant on immunisation. In the event that mass immunisation programmes were to cease, the society as a whole would be more at risk than ever before. *Writer's opinion stated plainly and forcefully – as fact*

In addition there is the issue of the rights of the individual. As members of a society, why should we be obliged to subject our children to this potentially harmful practice? Some people may also be against immunisation on religious grounds and their needs must be considered when any decisions are made. *Main idea with supporting arguments*

For these reasons I feel strongly that immunisation programmes should not be obligatory and that the individual should have the right to choose whether or not to participate. *Personal opinion to sum up. Re-statement of original question in own words.*

(*Band 9 answer 254 words*)

Answer key

10 *this view* refers back to the idea that it is more satisfying to stick to one career path from an early age.

12 **1** enjoyable   **2** experiences

13 *Model answer*
Having said that, there are some people who know from a very early age what they want to do in life and who never change their mind. Many famous people, such as actors and sports personalities, often say this in interviews and perhaps it is this dedication that enables them to achieve their goals.

14 *Model answer*
Job satisfaction is related to things like enjoying what you do or doing useful, rewarding work. Of course you must also earn enough money and be physically capable of doing the job, so there are many things to consider when we choose a career and the right outcome does not depend on being faithful to one choice that was made as a youngster.

15 *Model answer*
Clearly, the age at which we decide on a career can vary. As we get older, we develop a more mature understanding of ourselves and what we want from life. In terms of future job satisfaction, the possibility of making career decisions later in life can only be a good thing.

Writing 9

1 *Other answers possible*
 A These days *it seems that* people prefer to have smaller families.
 B *It is generally accepted that* football is now the most popular sport in the world.
 C *In my view*, it is important to travel and find out about other cultures.
 D *Some people argue that* mobile phones should be banned in public places.

4 *Other answers possible*
 B Many people feel that too much cardboard and plastic is used to package goods in supermarkets. <u>Admittedly</u>, it may be true that some shoppers want this. <u>However</u>, all it does eventually is to create a lot of waste that takes a long time to break down.
 C The problems caused by the increasing number of vehicles in cities are never-ending. <u>Although</u> one answer is to build more roads on the outskirts, this only results in more cars and lorries on the roads and so the problem continues.

5 *Other answers possible*
 B *I am unconvinced that* the Internet is a useful resource for children, *when* it contains so much uncensored material.
 C *It is doubtful whether* running is good for you, *when* people get so many physical injuries as a result.
 D *Some people find it hard to accept that* gambling is legal, *when* it causes so much misery and poverty.

7 *By this I mean that they seem to spend all their free time downloading Internet material or looking up websites*

8 *Other answers possible*
 1 *That is to say*, extended families tend to provide more support for family members.
 2 *By 'tolerant' I mean* that they accept different ideas and values.
 3 *To be more precise*, I think all students should be able to decide for themselves what they study.
 4 *In fact*, successful people have sometimes had many different jobs and learnt something from each of them.

10 The opening paragraph includes
 I would argue that …   presenting a personal idea
 by this I mean   explaining a term more precisely
 While I admit that   making a concession
 I am convinced that   presenting a personal idea
 Overall   signalling a conclusion

12 *Model answer*
It is probably true to say that most schools have students who are noisier than others and take some time to settle down in class. *Some people argue that* if they go on to affect the way other children in the class behave, something *should be done* about it. However, I am not sure that teaching them separately is the answer.

 Most people prefer to learn in calm surroundings. *Clearly*, it is much better to be able to hear the teacher than to have to struggle to follow instructions because someone else is talking all the time. *In my view*, school is a place where children *should work* hard and behave well. *That is not to say that* they *shouldn't enjoy* themselves too, *but overall* their attitude to school *should be* a serious one.

 Students who ignore school codes of conduct are, to a certain extent, being quite selfish. *Also, I'm not convinced that* ignoring their bad behaviour is helpful to them. Studies have shown that naughty children respond better to a strict approach in school.

 I tend to think that it is the school's' responsibility to control disruptive children. *I do not mean by this that* they *should administer* physical punishment *but I do think* teachers *should be trained* to deal with difficult pupils. *In addition*, head teachers should establish rules and ensure that everyone follows them.

 While I accept that there may be children who are so badly behaved that they cannot be taught in a 'normal' school, I feel that most children can and *should be taught* together.
 (*261 words*)

Writing 10

1 **a** No
 b There are too many disjointed ideas without support. There are few linkers. The style is too conversational for a written essay.

2 **a** Para 1 – Cities were designed before cars.
 Para 2 – Charging motorists to enter the city is a solution.
 b so, naturally / For instance / in fact / Understandably / A good example of this is / Indeed / In my experience

3 **1a** for example   **b** If this were the case
 2a In fact   **b** Of course
 3 In my experience
 4a For one thing   **b** A good example of this is

4 **1a** This reduction   **b** where
 2a These figures   **b** These/Such attitudes
 3a these/such qualities   **b** One
 4a This rise   **b** this trend
 5a Those   **b** those/others

5 **1** Generally speaking   **4** such as; Unfortunately
 2 when; however   **5** while
 3 However

6 *Reference words are underlined, other linking words and expressions are in italics.*

There is always controversy over whether it is important to spend large sums of money on medical research *or* whether more of <u>this money</u> should be directed towards treating patients.

Obviously some medical research is essential. <u>Without it</u>, we would have no vaccinations against diseases *such as* polio, no drugs *such as* antibiotics and no treatments *like* x-rays and radiotherapy. *Nevertheless*, the field of medical research is very competitive and <u>this</u> has financial disadvantages. Take, *for example*, the current research being conducted on the HIV virus. <u>In this field</u> it is arguable that money is being wasted *in that* scientists throughout the world are working independently towards the same ultimate goal, to find a cure for AIDS, *and with* the same hope of becoming famous in the process. *Surely* it would be more productive and less costly if <u>these scientists</u> joined forces and an international research team was set up *with* joint international funding.

7 *Other answers possible*

1 Mobile phones used to be so expensive that only the wealthy owned them, but today they are extremely common.
2 Many young people who are overweight watch television between 5.00pm and 8.00pm, when the advertisements for unhealthy food are shown.
3 These days 'hard copy' mail is used mainly in formal situations, while emails have become the most common form of written communication.
4 Although some people believe human beings are responsible for global warming, others think it is caused by climatic factors which cannot be altered by lowering pollution levels.

Speaking test Assessment criteria

1

Assessment criteria	Skills and strategies
Fluency	A, C, H, J
Vocabulary	B, I, L, P, Q
Grammar & Accuracy	D, E, K, M, R
Pronunciation	F, G, N, O

Speaking 2

2 *Other answers possible*

1 It is very important for me to learn English *because* I want to get an interesting job in the tourist industry *and* it'll be much easier *if* I have good English.
2 I work in a bank, *which* can be quite interesting, *although* the nature of the job is changing, *as* many people do their banking on the Internet now.
3 My favourite sport is tennis *because* it's a lot of fun to play, *but* I *also* enjoy watching it.
4 *At the moment* I live in a very small apartment, *but* I hope to live in a larger *one* next year.
5 *Even though* fast food is very popular in many countries these days, it is bad for our health *and* expensive, *so* I think cooking at home is more sensible.
6 It was impossible to know everyone at my school *because* it was very large, *with* hundreds of children.
7 I love movies *and* I like watching TV, *but* I don't like live theatre, *or* opera *either*.

3 *Other answers possible*

2 What kind of work do you do?
3 What is your favourite sport?
4 Where do you live?
5 What do you think of fast food?
6 What was your school like?
7 What kind of entertainment do you like?

8 1 c 2 b 3 f 4 h 5 d 6 a 7 e 8 g

9 & 10 *Content words which link back to the question are underlined, other linking words and expressions are in italics.*

1/c I think <u>walking</u> is <u>good for you</u>, as well as <u>watching what you eat</u>. *So* I try to <u>take</u> some <u>exercise</u> every day *and* <u>eat</u> lots of <u>fruit and vegetables</u>.
2/b Both, in fact. I have a <u>part-time job</u>. *But* it's not the <u>job</u> I want to do when I finish my <u>course</u>. It's just a way of <u>earning</u> some <u>extra money</u> while I'm <u>studying</u>.
3/f Well … I really enjoy <u>listening to songs</u>, particularly <u>songs</u> from my country. *And* I like to have <u>music playing</u> when I'm studying. In fact, I can't study without <u>music</u>.
4/h Um … that's hard to answer. I suppose <u>I like summer best</u> of all *because* I love the <u>warm weather</u>, and I have lots of good memories of <u>summer holidays</u> with my family.
5/d At first I didn't like <u>being in London</u>, *because of* the <u>crowds</u>, *but* now I'm used to it and I think it will be quite hard to go back to my <u>quiet little village</u>.
6/a I prefer <u>staying at home</u>. I'm not very keen on <u>crowds</u> and *also*, it's much cheaper than <u>going to the movies</u>.
7/e By <u>public transport</u> normally. We still have <u>trams</u> in <u>my city</u> and *as* they're really <u>efficient</u>, a lot of <u>people</u> use them.
8/g New Year is a very important <u>celebration</u>. *For instance*, in our family we all <u>get together to enjoy</u> each other's company. It's a very <u>special occasion</u>.

Speaking 4

1 Topic **D** (page 148)

2 1 She begins by mentioning the time of year.
2 Past simple, present simple and present perfect.
3 *Inca trail / trekking / archaeological sites*
4 *incredibly challenging / an experience … unlike any … I've ever had / absolutely spectacular / amazing / the sense of absolute relief / the satisfaction of having accomplished something amazing*
5 Yes – two minutes.
6 Yes, very well.
7 She uses the expression *What I really enjoyed was …*

3

In September, I went on a trip to Machu Picchu in Peru and did the Inca trail. <u>Peru was a country that I'd always wanted to visit, mainly because</u> South America's a different continent I had never visited before, even though I've done quite a bit of travel. I guess Peru was <u>high on my list of priorities</u>. Umm … so I did the Inca Trail, which was four days of camping and trekking, and it was <u>incredibly challenging</u>. <u>It was an experience unlike any I've ever had before</u>.	E, K A B K, P

Answer key

I've done some camping and I've also done some bush walking in the past, but … really <u>trekking at altitudes of</u> sort of four and a half thousand metres was, um, was really unlike anything else … It was absolutely <u>expactu-spectacular … the, um…</u> and there were many interesting and intricate stone <u>archaeological sites</u> to see along the way. I probably remember <u>the friends that I trekked with the most</u>, 'cos you really are going through something together … it's … it's an amazing thing to do, <u>even though</u> you have all the luxuries really … when you … when you organise it through a tour company. Ah! You have, um, you know … beds to sleep on in your tent and <u>sleeping bags and things like</u> that, but it really is <u>quite harsh living</u>. Um … so the friends <u>that I made when I trekked</u>, were, um, ones that I hope to have for life …The views were absolutely breathtaking as well. I think <u>what I really enjoyed was the sense of absolute relief at the end, and the satisfaction of having accomplished something amazing. I'd willingly do</u> it all over again.

B
C, H
G, O
D
A
I, L
J
K, L
R

7 Topic **B** (page 147)

8 1 Not strictly, but this is not important.
   2 To show that success can be interpreted in different ways.
   3 To add something personal to her answer.
   4 Present simple (to describe habitual actions).
   5 *working life / rewarding / accomplishing / personally and professionally satisfying / admire / management job / worthwhile / personality / qualifications / goals*
   6 With a rounding off sentence about her father and 'success' generally.

10 2 ●
He feels like / he's accomplishing something / that is
● obviously / personally and professionally satisfying … /
   3 It's a bit hard / to explain / exactly what he does.
   4 It's a management job really, / but working / in a context /
which is really worthwhile.
   5 I see my dad / very regularly, / about once a week.
   6 He enjoys / what he does, / as well as making / a decent
living out of it.

Speaking 5

1 & 2

Question	Topic	Key words in question
1	C	work
2	A	to live / cheap housing
3	B	personal achievement
4	E (A possible)	living in a large city
5	D (E possible)	tourism
6	C	workers / paid holidays

3 1 Is it important to like what you do for a living?
   2 Is it the responsibility of the government to provide homes for poor people?
   3 What type of things indicate that a person is successful?
   4 What are some of the good things about living in a large city?
   5 Is tourism generally good or bad for a country?
   6 Why is it a good idea for employers to pay people to take holidays?

4 & 5

	Answer given	Linkers used
2	ought to help (but no) cheap housing / if you do it for some … then it isn't fair to (others)	but / because if / then / I mean
3	type of job / how much they earn / awards and prizes	things like / or / for example
4	opportunities / work, shopping, cultural activities	such as / but
5	(mainly positive) benefits /brings foreign money / foreign exchange / good for the economy / may disadvantage local people	On the whole / but on the other hand / especially
6	important / (people) need a break / need to have some rewards	because / and / Also

8 • in my view / So … for instance
   • in countries where / so that / and / But in warm climates

10 *Other answers possible*
   • Personally, I've never lived in a cold climate but I think some of the advantages might be …
   • I've always lived in a warm climate, so …

13 *Other answers possible (Linking words or expressions are underlined)*
   <u>I agree</u> it's important for all countries to reduce their dependency on fossil fuels such as coal, <u>because this is affecting our climate</u>. But our politicians must work together at a global level <u>to encourage the development of cleaner industries</u>.

14 *Possible areas:* global warming / climate and lifestyle / climate and tourism / climate and health

15 1 C   **2** D   **3** B   **4** A

Speaking 6

1 1 c compare two things
   2 b make a suggestion
   3 a give an explanation
   4 e agree or disagree with something
   5 d make a prediction about the future

6 *Other answers possible*
   <u>While I agree that everyone</u> should be free to choose to go to university and have the opportunity of studying at a high level, <u>I also think that</u> not everyone wants to do this. <u>Certainly</u>, some people are much happier doing a trade or joining a business, and they often earn more money doing this.

The IELTS test format

There are two versions of the IELTS test.

Academic module	General Training module
For students seeking entry to a university or institution of higher education offering degree and diploma courses	For students seeking entry to a secondary school, to a vocational training course or for people taking the IELTS test for the purposes of immigration or employment

Note: *All candidates must take a test for each of the four skills: listening, reading, writing and speaking. All candidates take the same Listening and Speaking modules but may choose between the Academic or General Training versions of the Reading and Writing modules of the test. You should seek advice from a teacher or a student adviser if you are in any doubt about whether to sit for the Academic module or the General Training module.* **The two do not carry the same weight and are not interchangeable.**

The test modules are taken in the following order:

Listening 4 sections, 40 questions 30 minutes + 10 minutes transfer time		
Academic Reading 3 sections, 40 questions 60 minutes	OR	**General Training Reading** 3 sections, 40 questions 60 minutes
Academic Writing 2 tasks 60 minutes	OR	**General Training Writing** 2 tasks 60 minutes
Speaking 11 to 14 minutes		
Total test time 2 hours 55 minutes		

SAMPLE ANSWER SHEET: Listening

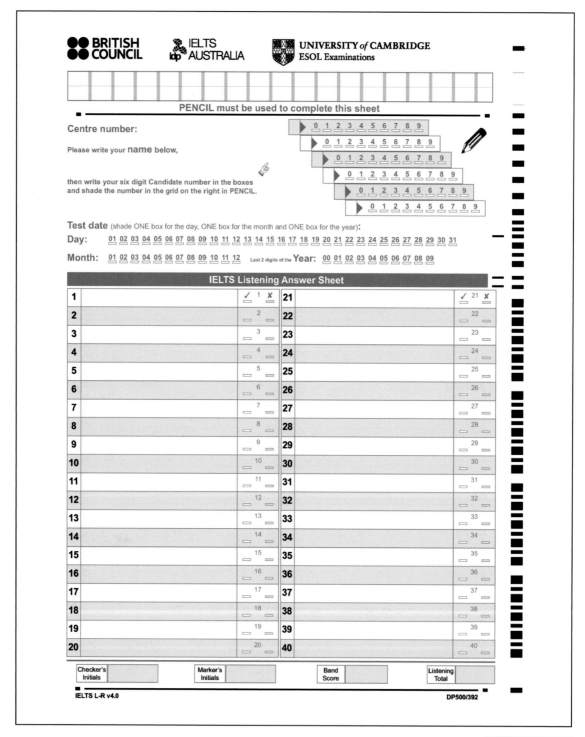